Social and Cognitive Development in the Context of Individual, Social, and Cultural Processes

In recent years a proliferation of theoretical and empirical scholarship has emerged on how social and cultural factors shape development. This work has provided important information about the multiple goals and pathways of development throughout the world, yet many issues still remain open for continued analysis and refinement.

This book addresses how individual, social, and cultural factors intersect during development by bringing together contributions from an international group of scholars with diverse theoretical perspectives who conduct research in varied cultural contexts.

The book is divided into three sections: *Contexts of Development, Developing through Culturally Shaped Social Interactions*, and *Some Final Thoughts: Infancy as the Foundation for Intersecting Individual, Social and Cultural Processes*. The first section focuses on how wider contexts of development are structured through interactions among individual, social and cultural processes. Specific chapters in this section consider how the wider cultural context is constituted and enacted by individuals, including children and their caregivers, as they engage in social interactions. The second section focuses on how social interactions and cultural values shape specific aspects of development, including the development of object manipulation, future orientations and self-conceptions. The book ends with an integrative analysis of how infant experiences form the foundation of adult relational self-conceptions.

Catherine Raeff completed her Ph.D. at Clark University and is currently an Associate Professor in the psychology department at Indiana University of Pennsylvania. Her work on parent–child interactions and self-development now focuses on how cultural values shape developing modes of independence and connectedness. **Janette B. Benson** is an Associate Professor of psychology at the University of Denver, where she is a Sturm Professor of Excellence in Education. She has co-edited with Marshall Haith, Rob Roberts and Bruce Pennington, *The Development of Future-Oriented Processes*, and co-authored with Marshall Haith, the infant cognition chapter in the last edition of the *Handbook of Child Psychology*.

Routledge International Library of Psychology
Series editor: Peter K. Smith

Social and Cognitive Development in the Context of Individual, Social, and Cultural Processes

Edited by Catherine Raeff and
Janette B. Benson

Routledge
Taylor & Francis Group

LONDON AND NEW YORK

First published in 2003 by Routledge
11 New Fetter Lane, London EC4P 4EE

Simultaneously published in the USA and Canada
by Routledge
29 West 35th Street, New York, NY 10001

Transferred to Digital Printing 2004

Routledge is an imprint of the Taylor & Francis Group

Typeset in Baskerville by LaserScript Ltd, Mitcham, Surrey
Printed and bound in Great Britain by
TJI Digital, Padstow, Cornwall

British Library Cataloguing in Publication Data
A catalogue record for this book is available from the British Library

Library of Congress Cataloging in Publication Data
Social and cognitive development in the context of individual, social, and cultural
    processes / edited by Catherine Raeff and Janette B. Benson
        p. cm.
    Includes bibliographical references and index.
    1. Child development. 2. Child psychology. 3. Infants–Development. 4. Cognition in
    children. 5. Social interaction in children. 6. Cognition and culture. I. Raeff, Catherine,
    1964- II. Benson, Janette B., 1956-
    HQ772.S58 2003
    305.231–dc21
                                                                            2003041583

ISBN 0-415-22447-0

Contents

Figures

Tables

Contributors

Janette B. Benson is an Associate Professor of Psychology at the University of Denver, where she is a Sturm Professor of Excellence in Education. She has co-edited with Marshall M. Haith, Rob Roberts and Bruce Pennington, *The Development of Future-Oriented Processes*, and co-authored with Marshall M. Haith the infant cognition chapter in the last edition of the *Handbook of Child Psychology*.

Nancy Budwig is Professor of Psychology at Clark University. Her interests include children's language development and the role of language in social-cognitive development. Budwig's work appears in articles in *Journal of Child Language*, *Human Development*, *Theory and Psychology*, and other journals and full-length monographs.

Michael J. Chandler is Professor of Developmental Psychology at the University of British Columbia. His research generally centers on the study of social-cognitive development, and, most recently, has come to focus on cross-cultural comparisons of epistemic and identity development as these differently unfold in Canada's aboriginal and culturally mainstream youth.

Feyza Çorapçi, a graduate student in the Department of Psychological Sciences at Purdue University, has made numerous conference presentations, and is senior author of a publication on parenting and home chaos. Her research addresses low-income children's social competence and parent–child transactions in relation to the home environment, and culturally driven parental norms and coping strategies.

Alan Fogel is Professor of Psychology at the University of Utah. The author of several books, his research focuses on the developmental emotions and self-awareness in preverbal infants, and on the development of interpersonal relationships as a link between culture and person.

Marshall M. Haith is Professor Emeritus at the University of Denver, where he has conducted research on perceptual and cognitive development for three decades. His current research focuses on the acquisition of future-oriented processes in infants and young children.

Jeffrey J. Lockman is Professor of Psychology at Tulane University. Dr. Lockman's research interests center on perception–action development, cognitive development and spatial understanding. His current work focuses on the development of tool use in young children.

Catherine Raeff completed her Ph.D. at Clark University, and is currently an Associate Professor of Psychology at Indiana University of Pennsylvania. Her work on parent–child interactions and self-development focuses on how cultural values shape developing modes of independence and connectedness.

M. Cristina Ramirez Ph.D. is a trauma psychologist at Detroit Receiving Hospital and Adjunct Assistant Professor at Wayne State University. Her current research focuses on the relation between coping with trauma and degree of physical injury, and patients' perceptions of the helpfulness of psychological debriefing.

Bryan W. Sokol is an Assistant Professor in the Department of Psychology at Simon Fraser University. In addition to his interests in epistemic development, Bryan's research includes the study of children's developing identities and moral reasoning.

Ayelet Talmi Ph.D. is a postdoctoral fellow with the Developmental Psychobiology Research Group, the University of Colorado. Her current research examines preterm and fragile infants' interactions with their parents in the neonatal intensive care unit.

Chikako Toma is a researcher at the National Institute for Japanese Language in Tokyo, Japan. Within a sociocultural–historical approach to development, one of her current research projects focuses on how learning and meaning are organized in American schools, and how Japanese sojourn children participate in everyday school activities.

Jaan Valsiner is the founding editor of the journal, *Culture & Psychology*, and has published many books, including *Culture and Human Development*. He is currently the chair of Clark University's Psychology Department, where he edits the journal *From Past to Future: Clark Papers in the History of Psychology*.

Theodore D. Wachs is Professor of Psychological Sciences at Purdue University and is a Fellow of the American Psychological Association. The author of numerous books and articles, his current research investigates how environmental characteristics and nutritional status influence young children's individual development.

James V. Wertsch is the Marshall S. Snow Professor of Arts and Sciences at Washington University in St. Louis. He received his Ph.D. from the University of Chicago and has held positions at Northwestern University, the University of California, San Diego, and Clark University. His most recent book is *Voices of Collective Remembering* (Cambridge University Press 2002).

Preface

Amidst the fragmentation that currently characterizes the field of developmental psychology, the life work of Ina Č. Užgiris is a model of integration filled with innumerable theoretical insights yet to be explored. This book was originally intended to honor Ina on the occasion of her sixtieth birthday, but sadly she died before it was completed. Its chapters were written by Ina's students and colleagues, and they are all meant to honor and extend her contributions to developmental psychology. In honoring Ina Užgiris it is fitting that the chapters cover a wide range of theoretical and empirical issues. At the same time, the concept of interaction, which she emphasized in her own work, provides an integrative framework for understanding the complexities of developmental processes and trajectories. We were fortunate to have interacted directly with Ina, and to us she remains an enduring example of integrity and intellectual dedication. It is our hope that the ideas presented in this book will challenge others to take up where she left off. And so it is with respect, gratitude, and affection that we dedicate this book to the memory of Ina Č. Užgiris.

Acknowledgements

We are extremely grateful to Joe Whiting at Routledge and his editorial assistants, Annabel Watson and Amrit Bangard, for their patience and ongoing support of this project. We also thank Marilyn Pelot for helping with the arduous task of coordinating and formatting the chapters into the final manuscript.

Introduction

An interactive approach to development

Catherine Raeff and Janette B. Benson

In recent years there has been a proliferation of theoretical and empirical scholarship on how social and cultural factors shape developmental processes. This work has provided important information about the multiple goals and pathways that development may take throughout the world. Despite this progress, many issues remain unresolved. The contributions to this volume begin to address these issues by building on the theoretical and empirical work conducted by Ina Č. Užgiris, starting with the publication of her dissertation research in 1964 and ending with a posthumous publication in 2000. Ina Užgiris consistently inspired and challenged those whom she met professionally to think in new and integrative ways about the complexities of human behavior and development. As students and colleagues the contributors to this volume were all so inspired and challenged, and our collective efforts here are meant to honor Ina Užgiris and her efforts to advance our understanding of human development.

The breadth of Užgiris' professional work defies simplistic categorization; however, one theme throughout her work involves the notion of interaction. Užgiris was concerned with the importance of social interactions as an arena for development, and also with the complex ways in which individual, social and cultural factors interact during development. She was a staunch Piagetian throughout her distinguished career, and from this framework she began to consider how individual constructive processes interact with social and cultural factors well before the contemporary field of developmental psychology adopted its current mantra of social interactions and cultural processes (e.g. Užgiris 1970). She also once noted specifically that

> My starting point is similar to that of others who have argued against treating the individual and society as independent entities that are brought together only gradually in the course of development. The central term for me is *interaction*, and a foregrounding of interaction requires that both the individual and society be viewed as mutually constructed.
>
> (Užgiris 1996: 17–18)

In the following overview, we will present some of Užgiris' insights into the concept of interaction. In particular, we outline some of the historical trends in developmental psychology that have led contemporary scholars to recognize the inseparability and interactive nature of individuals, social interactions, cultural value systems and developmental processes.

Individuals and social interactions

It is almost a cliché to note that the enterprise of scientific psychology in general, as well as developmental psychology in particular, began with a focus on the individual in isolation from social and cultural phenomena. In some social science circles, the individual and society were even pitted against one another and viewed in terms of a virtually unending conflict. However, given the fact that human newborns are so obviously dependent on others, it became increasingly untenable for developmental scholars to ignore the role of social factors in development.

The importance of social interactions for development, particularly with caregivers, has been recognized for centuries (Aries 1962, Sommerville 1990), but contemporary systematic investigations of children's social contexts were not undertaken by developmental psychologists until the 1950s. These early investigations focused on how parents implement different parenting strategies in different kinds of situations with their children (e.g. Sears, Maccoby and Levin 1957). However, studies based on these approaches failed to link particular child-rearing practices to child outcomes. With the rediscovery of Piaget in the early 1960s, child development researchers become increasingly sensitive to the child's contributions to parent–child interactions. Accordingly, studies focused on discerning how children may affect their parents' behavior, as well as on understanding individual differences among children raised by the same parents (Bell 1968, Bell and Harper 1977, Wenar and Wenar 1963). Research on attachment and on the variety of capabilities that predispose human newborns to active participation in social interactions further solidified the position that parent–child interactions partake of both partners' active and bidirectional contributions (Bowlby 1969, Schaffer 1977, 1984, Stern 1977, 1985, Trevarthen 1980, Tronick 1982, Fafouti-Milenković and Užgiris 1979, Užgiris 1989).

An interactive approach to child development began to emerge which highlights the importance of social interactions as an arena that provides children with various opportunities to practice their incipient competencies. In addition, this interactive approach underscores the importance of understanding both the child's and the adult's active contribution to the structuring of their interactions. As a pioneering figure in elaborating this interactive approach for infant development, Užgiris (1989, Fafouti-Milenković and Užgiris 1979) further pointed to the importance of understanding how interactions are structured in terms of the partners' bidirectional, reciprocal, and joint activities. She explains:

> An interactive approach to infant development, by emphasizing the activities while constructed in relation to a partner, subordinates an analysis of the contributions of each partner to an analysis of the forms of activity carried out jointly. The joint activities are taken not as the outcome of the efforts of

one or the other partner but as the products of their joint efforts while engaged with each other.

(1989: 293)

Užgiris built upon her research on infant cognition that advanced our early understanding of sensorimotor development (e.g. Užgiris 1964, 1976, 1977, 1989, Užgiris and Hunt 1975/1989) to focus her theoretical and empirical work on understanding infant imitation from an interactive perspective (e.g. Killen and Užgiris 1981, Užgiris 1972, 1981, 1984, 1990, 1996, 1999, Užgiris, Benson, Kruper and Vasek 1989). For the most part, imitation had traditionally been understood in terms of the individual child's cognitive development. Traditional imitation research characterized the child as somewhat of a "passive" mimic, and in 1984 Užgiris pointed out:

> In only a few studies has there been consideration of the process of imitating a model and the possibility of changes in this process with development. Furthermore, there is relatively little information about the overall prevalence of imitation during infancy or the preferential imitation of different types of acts in different contexts. The emphasis on imitation as a mirror of the infant's abilities has deterred the study of imitation as an activity that is a part of the infant's interactions with the world.

(p. 2)

So much of infant imitation takes place during the course of social interactions, and by shifting her focus to imitation Užgiris began to consider how individual constructive processes interact with social processes to shape development. This adoption of an interactive approach to infant imitation permitted Užgiris to emphasize that imitation between an infant and caregiver is a form of social interaction that conveys mutuality and reciprocity between the partners. She explained that:

> in the context of interpersonal interaction, imitation is a means of communication with the partner. The basic message that imitation conveys is mutuality or sharing of a feeling, understanding, or a goal. It serves to affirm the act of the initiator in the context of the ongoing interpersonal engagement and thereby promotes continuation of the interaction.

(Užgiris 1984: 25)

This interactive perspective which emphasizes both partners' contributions to social interactions further allowed Užgiris to elucidate how infants' imitative acts depend in part on how they construct the meaning of their social partners' acts, as well as the interpersonal situation in general. That is,

> with changing cognitive abilities, an infant's understanding of the inter-personal situation is likely to change as much as his or her understanding of a

specific modeled act. The infant's interpretation of the interpersonal situation deserves consideration in relation to progressive changes in imitation.

(Užgiris 1984: 3)

Thus the role of the individual is embedded in, but not obscured by, the social interactions of everyday life.

Individuals and their participation in culturally shaped interactions

As investigators moved beyond focusing just on individuals to also considering the bidirectionality of social interaction, studies revealed that aspects of parent–child interactions differ throughout the world and also in relation to family variables (such as socioeconomic status and ethnic background). Thus scholars began to appreciate the developmental role of the wider cultural and societal context as an important component of development that had been previously overlooked. Initially, attempts to understand how context shapes children's social interactions and development focused on directly measurable factors such as socioeconomic status or social support. Studies also attempted to discern how different contexts, in the form of different physical locations – for instance, home, day care and school – might affect children's development. Contexts and settings were essentially viewed as static variables that could be correlated with child outcomes. This elaboration on the role of context further emphasized a need to link children's activities in concrete social settings to wider cultural practices and meaning systems.

We have already noted that Užgiris' work on imitation emphasized how individual and social processes interact during infancy. In addition, she further explained that imitative activity, carried out during the course of social interactions, is also inherently cultural. That is, one function of imitation is "to bring the culturally constituted world known to the adult into the infant's experience" (Užgiris 1999: 192). Moreover, cultural dimensions of human functioning are viewed as inseparable from individual and social dimensions of experience. With her focus on infancy, Užgiris emphasized how when infants interact and communicate with others during the course of a wide range of daily activities

> cultural practices permeate communication patterns, interests, and schemes of action. However, they permeate them as a dimension of activity, and therefore, can become part of the knowledge structures in their own right. Yet they do not exist as a body of knowledge, a separate layer of context for everyday human activities, but only as a dimension of those activities embodied in communication and the manner of doing things.
>
> (Užgiris 1996: 35–36)

This approach to culture is consistent with other approaches that conceptualize culture as a system of symbolic action patterns (e.g. Goodnow, Miller and Kessel

1995, LeVine 1984, D'Andrade 1984) which is both constituted by and constitutive of individuals as they engage in social interactions in social and institutional settings. This view of culture brings to light the importance of the symbolic or cultural meaning of different modes of human functioning and how they reflect cultural values. Within this perspective, individual, social and cultural processes interact in many ways. First, interaction among these processes exists insofar as individuals contribute to the social interactions that reflect cultural meanings according to their own developing competencies and interpretations. Second, individuals develop through participation in such culturally meaningful interactions. Third, culture is constructed and transformed as individuals interact across varied settings. A key implication of this interactive position is that the wider context of development, including social relationships and cultural meanings, is no longer conceptualized as a separate, static and quantifiable variable that can be tacked onto developmental analyses. In contrast, a true interactive perspective suggests that the wider context of development emerges out of, and is enacted through, interactions among individual, social and cultural processes as developing individuals actively participate in culturally shaped social exchanges.

Given the theoretical recognition that individual, social and cultural factors are inseparable and interactive aspects of human behavior and development, it is important to further our understanding of how they operate. Indeed, an exploration of the different facets of the interaction among individual, social and cultural dimensions of children's developmental experiences represents a major challenge for contemporary developmental psychology. As such, a main objective of the current volume is to explore some of the ways in which individual, social and cultural factors are linked and influence each other during development. Given the enormity of this challenge, one book can only address a limited set of issues. The focus of this volume is on how individual, social and cultural factors intersect to shape wider contexts of development that provide children with opportunities to engage in culturally valued modes of behavior. Single chapters focus on one or another aspect of these interactions.

The first section of the book examines how the wider social and cultural context of development is structured through interactions among individual, social and cultural processes. Rather than viewing this wider context of development as external to or impacting on developing individuals, the different contributors grapple with how the wider context emerges and is constituted as individuals engage in culturally shaped social interactions. The first section begins with a chapter by Valsiner, who offers a theoretical perspective on how social interactions constitute the wider context in which development occurs, and how social interactions involve exchanges between an individual's personal world and the collective culture. In turn, personal worlds and collective cultures are also taken to be mutually constitutive as they are dynamically constructed through social interaction. Valsiner further emphasizes the point that the ongoing dynamics of social interaction are indeterminate, thus requiring individuals to adjust to and anticipate the ongoing co-construction of sociocultural contexts. He concludes by suggesting that imitation provides an initial means that infants can use to cope with the future indeterminacy of the interactions in which they participate.

Building on the theme that culture is constituted through social interactions among active individuals, Raeff's chapter analyzes how the wider cultural context of child development can be understood in terms of patterns of cultural activity that are partly composed of interactions between parental ideas about child-rearing and parent–child interaction patterns. Rather than viewing parental ideas as static individual cognitions that influence parent–child interactions, Raeff argues that parents' ideas reflect their active individual constructions of cultural representations of parenting and children. Thus the construction of parents' ideas and parent–child interaction patterns are two forms of activity that reflect cultural values and together constitute wider patterns of cultural activity. In this way, cultural representations and values are enacted and constructed as individuals engage in social interactions. This approach further raises questions about the utility of trying to predict interaction patterns from parental ideas. Another theoretical discussion is a consideration by Wachs and Çorapçi of how environmental chaos, conceptualized as a physical aspect of the environment, operates in conjunction with social and cultural factors to produce varied contexts of development. In particular, they discuss evidence that points to how social and cultural factors may buffer some of the negative effects of chaos. In addition, this chapter points to the importance of extending our notions of the physical environment to include components that are manufactured by humans.

Subsequent chapters describe cross-cultural studies that further elucidate the interactions among individual, social, and cultural factors in constituting the context of development. A study of parent–child play in the United States and Colombia is the setting for Ramirez (Chapter 4), who focuses on how cultural values about interpersonal relationships are enacted through social interactions. In this work, culture is not separated from children's ongoing activities but is taken to be constituted through and reflected in the very activities in which children participate. Next, Budwig demonstrates how children in the United States and Germany use language to contribute to the ongoing dynamic construction of social contexts as they participate in social interactions with others. Budwig argues that the wider context of development is constituted through individual participation in culturally shaped interactions. She suggests the need to move beyond a static, representational view of language to considering how language can be used by children to structure social contexts. These analyses show that children and caregivers do not step into pre-existing contexts but instead jointly negotiate their social contexts through linguistic communication.

The last chapter of this first section is by Toma and Wertsch, who describe extensive analyses of Japanese fourth-graders working on a joint project and show how individual children actively contribute to the ongoing dynamics of intersubjectivity. These analyses also demonstrate how the children maintain intersubjectivity as they work to balance the conflicting social goals of solving a cognitive problem, and maintaining group harmony. They discuss how social interactions and intersubjectivity are constructed by individuals as they work to maintain varied social goals that can come into conflict.

The second section of the book examines some of the ways in which social and cultural processes can affect specific aspects of social and cognitive development during infancy, childhood and adolescence. This section begins with considerations of how social interactions may shape the development of behavior that has traditionally been viewed from an individual maturational perspective. First, Lockman discusses how infant object manipulation may be shaped through social interactions with social partners, including parents and siblings. Then Benson, Talmi, and Haith consider how children's conceptions of time – in particular their acquisition of future orientation – initially builds on individual biological rhythms but is then further developed through culturally shaped social interactions. This section concludes with Chandler's and Sokol's discussion of self-development in relation to varied cultural values. The final chapter is by Fogel, who integrates themes from the book into a discussion of how infancy provides a foundation for the embodiment of various aspects of the self. He focuses on how infants' participation in relational systems lays the groundwork for how people experience themselves in relation to their bodies and emotions; how people experience themselves in relation to others; and how the self is experienced in relation to the natural world. He concludes by suggesting ways in which an enhanced recognition of human embodiment, that begins in infancy, can enhance scientific inquiry as well as societal functioning.

In many ways, the diversity of empirical issues and specific conceptual concerns represented in this book mirrors the diversity that represents contemporary developmental psychology. The theoretical insights offered in Ina Užgiris' interactive approach to development provide us with an overarching and integrative conceptual framework that enables us to more systematically consider the complex and varied ways in which individual, social and cultural factors intersect during social and cognitive development. In addition, these considerations will no doubt contribute to new and fruitful empirical questions and theoretical discussions that will help to shape the future of developmental psychology.

References

Aries, P. (1962) *Centuries of Childhood: A Social History of Family Life*. New York: Vintage Books.
Bell, R. Q. (1968) "A Reinterpretation of the Direction of Effects in Studies of Socialization", *Psychological Review 75*: 81–95.
Bell, R. Q. and Harper, L. V. (1977) *Child Effects on Adults*. Hillsdale, NJ: Lawrence Erlbaum Associates.
Bowlby, J. (1969) *Attachment*. New York: Basic Books Inc.
D'Andrade, R. G. (1984) "Cultural Meaning Systems" in Shweder, R. A. and LeVine, R. A. (eds.) *Culture Theory*. Cambridge: Cambridge University Press.

Fafouti-Milenković, M. and Užgiris, I. Č. (1979) "The Mother–Infant Communication System," *New Directions for Child Development no. 4.*

Goodnow, J. J., Miller, P. J. and Kessel, F. (eds.) (1995) "Cultural Practices as Contexts for Development," *New Directions for Child Development no. 67.*

Killen, M. and Užgiris, I. Č. (1981) "Imitation of Actions with Objects: The Role of Social Meaning," *Journal of Genetic Psychology 138*: 219–229.

LeVine, R. A. (1984) "Properties of Culture: An Ethnographic View" in Shweder, R. A. and LeVine, R. A. (eds.) *Culture Theory.* Cambridge: Cambridge University Press.

Schaffer, H. R. (1977) *Studies in Mother–Infant Interaction.* London: Academic Press.

— (1984) *The Child's Entry into a Social World.* London: Academic Press.

Sears, R. R., Maccoby, E. E. and Levin, H. (1957) *Patterns of Child Rearing.* Evanston, IL: Row, Peterson & Co.

Sommerville, C. J. (1990) *The Rise and Fall of Childhood.* New York: Vintage Books.

Stern, D. (1977) *The First Relationship.* Cambridge, MA: Harvard University Press.

— (1985) *The Interpersonal World of the Infant.* New York: Basic Books.

Trevarthen, C. (1980) "The Foundation of Intersubjectivity" in Olson, D. R. (ed.) *The Social Foundations of Language and Thought.* New York: W. W. Norton & Co.

Tronick, E. (1982) *Social Interchange in Infancy: Affect, Cognition and Communication.* Baltimore, MD: University Park Press.

Užgiris, I. Č. (1964) "Situational Generality of Conservation," *Child Development 35:* 831–841.

— (1970) "Sociocultural Factors in Cognitive Development" in Haywood, H. C. (ed.) *Social–Cultural Aspects of Mental Retardation.* New York: Meredith Corporation.

— (1972) "Patterns of Vocal and Gestural Imitation in Infants," *Determinants of Behavioral Development*: 467–471.

— (1976) "Organization of Sensorimotor Intelligence" in Lewis, M., (ed.) *Origins of Intelligence: Infancy and Early Childhood.* New York: Plenum Press.

— (1977) "Plasticity and Structure: The Role of Experience in Infancy" in Užgiris, I. Č. and Weizmann, F. (eds.) *The Structuring of Experience.* New York: Plenum Press.

— (1981) "Two Functions of Imitation in Infancy," *International Journal of Behavioral Development 4*: 1–12.

— (1984) "Imitation in Infancy: Its Interpersonal Aspects" in Perlmutter, M. (ed.) *The Minnesota Symposia on Child Psychology vol. 17*: 1–32. Hillsdale, NJ: Lawrence Erlbaum Associates.

— (1989) "Infants in Relation: Performers, Pupils, and Partners" in Damon, W. (ed.) *Child Development Today and Tomorrow* (288–310). San Francisco: Jossey-Bass.

— (1989) "Transformations and Continuities: Intellectual Functioning in Infancy and Beyond" in Bornstein, M. and Krasnegor, N. (eds.) *Stability and Continuity in Mental Development: Behavioral and Biological Perspectives.* Hillsdale, NJ: Lawrence Erlbaum Associates.

— (1990) "The Social Context of Infant Imitation" in Lewis, M. and Feinman, S. (eds.) *Social Influences and Socialization in Infancy.* New York: Plenum Press.

— (1996) "Together and Apart: The Enactment of Values in Infancy" in Reed, E. S., Turiel, E. and Brown, T. (eds.) *Values and Knowledge.* Mahwah, NJ: Lawrence Erlbaum Associates.

— (1999) "Imitation as Activity: Its Developmental Aspects" in Nadel, J. and Butterworth, G. (eds.) *Imitation in Infancy.* Cambridge: Cambridge University Press.

— (2000) "Words Don't Tell All: Some Thoughts on Early Communication" in Budwig, N., Užgiris, I. Č. and Wertsch, J. V. (eds.) *Communication: An Arena of Development.* Stamford, CT: Ablex Publishing Corporation.

Užgiris, I. Č., Benson, J. B., Kruper, J. C. and Vasek, M. E. (1989) "Contextual Influences on Imitative Interactions Between Mothers and Infants" in Lockman, J. J. and Hazen, N. L. (eds.) *Action in Social Context: Perspectives on Early Development.* New York: Plenum Press.

Užgiris, I. Č. and Hunt, J. McV. (1975/1989) *Assessment in Infancy: Ordinal Scales of Psychological Development.* Urbana, IL: University of Illinois Press.

Wenar, C. and Wenar, S. C. (1963) "The Short Term Prospective Model, the Illusion of Time, and the Tabula Rasa Child," *Child Development 34*: 697–708.

Part I

Contexts of development

1 Interaction and development

Accounting for emergence

Jaan Valsiner

Human interaction entails subjective experience, an orientation towards future goals, and constant innovation. Each moment of interaction is situation-specific, yet its consequences transcend the here-and-now of any situation and lead to new, relatively stable states. Such states, known as "steady states" (in open systems terminology) or "stages" (a term often used to describe child development), are but the next launching pads for further development. It is the unity of being in a state, and moving out of that state into another one, that constitutes the general theoretical problem of understanding how interaction is a vehicle for development. Discerning how interaction can make a difference for human life-worlds and development was central to the work of Ina Užgiris for at least two decades (e.g. Užgiris 1979: vii).

Yet how is it possible to show the ways in which such interaction works? Psychology is still a very young science, and has yet to establish a logic of inference of its own. It is particularly in need of making sense of complex phenomena that entail past-to-future directionality and that are open to modification by subjective volition. Interaction is a phenomenon of high complexity, and in order to investigate phenomena of such complexity, the metatheoretical web of science needs explication.

Methodology in its confines: rules and (mis)representations

It seems that the core of any science – and psychology is no exception – is one's metaphysical assumptions about human nature, which drive one's choice of methods. There are two perspectives on methodology in psychology: first, the view that reduces it to a collection ("toolbox") of methods and, second, the view that treats methodology as a multilevel process of knowledge construction, known as the "methodology cycle" (Branco and Valsiner 1997). In the former case, social consensus can lead researchers astray in their derivation of evidence from phenomena.

For instance, the socially mediated acceptance of conceptually inappropriate practices in a given discipline, such as the obligatory quantification of data that has come to haunt psychology, can lead it into a state of stagnation, if not regression, in our understanding of complex psychological phenomena. It can be proven that quantification is but one operation in guaranteeing the objectivity of the data. Quantitative methods are a sub-class of qualitative ones (Valsiner 2000a), as they are based on assumptions about the data that proceed beyond a nominal scale (towards ordinal, interval and ratio scales).

Consider a second example, i.e., the mixing of population and individual levels of analysis, which has been rampant in psychology (Valsiner 1986). Data obtained on the basis of inter-individual variability (such as correlation coefficients) become interpreted by the researchers as if these applied to the individual cases, or within each case. The result has been a loss of focus upon variability or, more precisely, treating inter-individual variability ("individual differences", as it is often called) as if it were equivalent to intra-individual changes. This assumption has been proven wrong (Nesselroade and Molenaar 2003), indicating that inter-individual and intra-individual variabilities are non-isomorphic.

These are only two examples from psychology during the twentieth century that may be claimed to have been progressively regressing in its knowledge base. This kind of regression has occurred as a result of two historic changes in psychology during that period. First, the discipline has moved from a focus on general theories (in connection with critically relevant data) to the notion of inductively driven accumulation of evidence and the tendency to make decisions about scientific matters by way of consensus ("democracy of literature" – see Valsiner 2000b). This move has been intertwined with the prevalence of empiricism in the practices of psychology and also with the postmodern assumption of the partial nature of knowledge. Fragmented and context-specific knowing has become glorified as the highest possible state of knowing by adherents of the postmodernist credo in the social sciences. As a result, questions about the universality and generality of scientific knowledge have become overlooked.

The second historical change entails psychology's increasing tendency to find for itself a societal niche in the realm of applications for its know-how. This tendency has set the demands from a given society's "social orders" to psychology's usefulness ahead of the basic theoretical questions of the discipline. These "social orders" within Western democracies superimpose on psychology the assumption that the average (or majority) depiction of some psychological evidence is applicable to individual cases within a population, despite clear evidence for huge inter-individual variability within that population.

Indeterministic phenomena *versus* deterministic methods in psychology

A search for general models of interaction begins with the following basic issue: whether the processes involved are deterministic or entail indeterminism in some form (Fogel, Lyra and Valsiner 1997). All developmental phenomena are necessarily unpredictable, and thus models that are aimed at making sense of developmental phenomena require that an indeterministic component exists in them. In different versions, indeterminism has been taken into account under labels such as "probabilistic epigenesis" (Gottlieb 1999) or "bounded indeterminacy" (Valsiner 1987). Yet it is the translation of these general notions into empirical research practices that leads us to knowledge (or artifact) in our research. The conceptual vehicle that is usually in action for such translation is some notion of probability.

Probability as a stabilizer of thought

Probability terminology helps to capture the indeterminacy of phenomena in ways that leave us with a nuance of certainty. Thus, in comparing the statements "Tomorrow it will either rain, or will not rain" and "The probability of rain tomorrow is 0.50" one is able to capture the moment of stability projected into the uncertainty. Probability expression allows the speaker to come to grips with the inevitable uncertainty of life in his/her mind at a given time. Hence, the use of probability terms in lay thinking is a semiotic means that stabilizes our thought processes.

There are different ways in which the notion of probability can be construed. Despite the indeterministic connotation that the use of probability terminology brings into developmental psychology, the varied uses of probability have added theoretical confusion about uncertainties in phenomena rather than contributing to clarity.

Let us continue with the example used above, i.e. a statement that "The probability of *x* is 0.5". This statement indicates, in *precise* numerical terms, the maximum uncertainty of the outcome (*x*). This numerical precision provides the statement with a "halo effect" of certainty; namely, *we feel certain* about the outcome (*x*), that *is in itself uncertain* (random), by way of using of numbers. We accept uncertainty when it becomes translated into a presentation that feels certain. For a contrast to the numerical statement, consider "Maybe *x* will happen, or maybe not".[1] The uncertainty implicit in that non-numerical statement is an undesirable state from which human beings try to escape, and they use signs to accomplish that.

Three kinds of probability: How indeterminacy is described and encoded

I assume here that each depiction of uncertainty, in terms of some probability notion, is a construction of the human mind. Probability notions are simultaneously assumed to be a semiotic means that help people stabilize their encounters with uncertainty and also help them to engage in interpersonal communication about such encounters with uncertainty. There are three kinds of probability notions – frequentistic, subjective and propensity – each of which may use the same terms, yet their ways of construing the probability notions are cardinally different. Thus, the very same probability presentation (e.g. $p\,(x) = 0.5$) can represent three different ways of knowing.

The frequentistic probability construction

First, there is knowing about the *accumulated actual history* of a particular event. This leads to treating accumulated past frequencies of an event (x) as if these can provide us with an estimate for future occurrences of a single case. Thus if x has happened in 50% of cases in the past n occurrences of events (i.e. an account of the past, accumulated over time), the notion of "Probability of x = 0.5" is accumulated. All the occurrences of the past are treated as mutually independent. So far, the probability statement, based on observed frequency, is a *post factum* description of the accumulated history up to the present moment.

However, the construal of frequentistic probability does not end with such accumulated description. The notion "probability of x = 0.5" creates in its user the belief that *the single* next x that *might* occur "has" the probability of 0.5. The user of the probability notion here translates population knowledge about the past to the individual case that is expected to occur in the immediate future. Furthermore, evidence of past occurrences of x *becomes translated into the essence of x* that is applicable to each and every x that occurred or that will occur. Note that no novelty can come into being in this account because the relative proportions of the distribution of events (x, not-x) are assumed to continue into the future.

It is thus obvious that the notion of frequentist probability – and all of its applications in psychological methodology – are "conceptually blind" for use in developmental science. The basic assumption of frequentist probability is that of stability, from past (observed and accumulated) to the future (expected). In contrast, any theoretically consistent developmental perspective begins from the assumption of non-stability.

Probability as subjective belief

The second way of knowing using the probability notion is that of *subjective belief* (Bayesian probability). This is an established, already automatic, explication of one's quantified "degree of belief" in the future occurrence of an event. I may *believe* that x might occur at the next moment or not and estimate its probability to be 0.5. As a projection of an estimator's belief into the object, the belief has the same limitations for developmental science as the frequentist probability notion has. It is the accumulated history of the past, and it is not open to the emergence of novelties (unless there is a belief established that is oriented to what has not yet been experienced). The actual ways of establishing the "degree of belief" remain more unclear in this case than in the case of frequentist probability, because its roots are in the introspective processes of making relative certainty in one's subjective realm. Actually, the frequentist perspective can be seen as a special case of the subjective probability notion, one in which a person's degree of belief in the future occurrence of x coincides fully with the past history of occurrences of x.

Probability as propensity

The third way of knowing is that of knowing the environment within which a given event (x) can exist. For example, if I know that the environment allows only two events, x and one other (y) to exist, then my *propensity probability* estimate $p(x)$=0.5 is based on such knowledge. This probability notion is ahistorical because as long as the structure of the environment is known, there is no need to know about any past occurrences of x, nor is it necessary to have an invented belief about x. This propensity probability is static because the structure of the environment is given, not emergent. Propensity probability becomes unusable unless the environment (and/or x) is known to change by some specifiable function (see below, the discussion of hypergame).

All in all, it becomes clear that the notion of probability is a conceptual way of treating uncertainty in terms of certainty. Two of the three ways of probabilistic knowing (frequentist and subjective probability) encompass the past history of events, albeit by either breaking up historical interdependencies (the case of frequentist probability) or by not explicating historical inter-dependencies (subjective probability). The third notion of probability, that is, propensity probability, is ahistorical when the issue of the past is considered. *In addition, all three ways of probabilistic knowing are non-developmental, since they do not recognize the emergence of novelty* as the central feature of the phenomena under consideration.

Practical fusions in the use of probability notions

The use of a probability notion often fuses the notions of subjective and frequentist probabilities, as if the observed frequencies of past events, accumulated in a time-independent fashion, become indicators of our belief in expected occurrences in the future. This is a necessary feature of the use of signs, because semiotic mediation in general works on the basis of past experience (representation) in order to cope with the indeterminate future (presentation).

Interaction researchers face this problem of fusing subjective and frequentist probabilities in the form of using probabilistic methods in practice. For example, it is often assumed that interaction is Markovian in its nature, i.e. that the maximum "time span" of functional connections is that of immediate antecedent/consequent relation (t and $t+1$). Linear Markovian models reduce the complexity of future-oriented strategic action to determinacy by the behavioral events that have occurred in the immediate past. This reduction is exemplified by the use of frequentist conditional probability notions, namely, looking at relative frequencies of events at time $t+1$, given their previous state t. This practice is inductive, arriving at the determination of conditional probabilities on the basis of conditional frequencies. An *aggregated frequency* of similar-looking behavioral events that occurred after some other event (frequency. A/after B) is treated *as if* it were the probability of a next event occurring in the series ($p\{A/B\}$).

An accumulated frequencies mental frame is changed by introducing the label of probability such that a summary description of the past becomes treated as an "epistemic token" for the prediction of the future. The probability estimate *becomes inserted into* the *next singular* antecedent (a new specimen of *b*) and it *is assumed* that it represents the propensity of that *b*, to turn into a next concrete *a*. The reality of the aggregated past occurrences is turned into a mystical inherent power estimate for the move to the next singular future event. The future is assumed to follow as a result of inherent causal (probabilistic) "forces" of the (accumulated) past. A similar situation is the case in different methods of time-lag and sequential analyses. That is, past events, in a form of some quantitative accumulation, are expected to predict the future. It is more than mildly ironic that psychology's efforts to take time into account arrive at results that *de facto* eliminate time from theoretical focus. Developmental perspectives require a different orientation, namely moving from the past to an anticipated future.

Development in general: theoretical problems

In the history of the discipline of psychology, development seems to have had a history of a focus often claimed, then lost, and further regained (Cairns 1998). In the most general terms, it is the notion of differentiation, first emphasized by Johann Wolfgang von Goethe in the eighteenth century and later recaptured in Heinz Werner's and Bernard Kaplan's "orthogenetic principle", that represents development in general:

> Developmental psychology postulates one regulative principle of development; it is an orthogenetic principle which states that wherever development occurs it proceeds from a state of relative globality and lack of differentiation to a state of increasing differentiation, articulation, and hierarchical integration.
>
> (Werner 1957: 126)

A basic conceptual issue is how this general model is translated into empirical research practices.

The notion of differentiation in development entails hierarchization and subordination. The *rigid/flexible* opposition applies to this process; that is, hierarchical organization is the basis for flexible (rather than rigid) behavior. Flexibility guarantees plasticity, and it also leads to stability (rather than to a labile state). Hierarchization leads to the establishment of the semiotically mediated affective "tones" of a setting that govern the whole setting while being imbued with human cultural value.

The *syncretic* nature of psychological phenomena refers to their contents (or functional) state without differentiation. For example, a dream image can contain several meanings that are maintained as separate in our waking lives. The fused meanings in the dream are an example of syncretic phenomena, while the waking-time distinction of the meanings refers to a differentiated (*discrete*) picture. The unstructured fields of phenomena, such as in dreams, are syncretic.

Direction towards a future state

In addition, development is a process oriented between two anchor points: the point of origin and the point of future orientation. In contemporary uses of dynamic systems notions for modeling development, this Wernerian feature is encoded into the notion of *attractor point* (Van Geert 1994) which is a reference point towards which some current formal model assumes that the developmental process to be striving.

The personal world in constant interaction with external world

Heinz Werner was a close colleague of William Stern at Hamburg University through the 1920s and early 1930s. For Stern, the *dialectic of the concrete* (in contrast with Hegel's "dialectic of the abstract") constituted the core issue for the psychological analysis of person–environment relations. It is that "dialectic of the concrete" which one can observe in the processes of interaction.

Stern's personalism starts from the premise that each person has his/her own person-relevant or "personal world", that is, a world of the person's own construction (Stern 1938). The interdependent nature of that world is beyond doubt:

> However great the power exerted by the world to make the individual fall in with its trend, he nevertheless continues to be a "person" and can react to its influence only as a person, thereby modifying and deflecting its very tendency. And vice versa, however strikingly novel and penetrating the effect of the impress by which the genius of an artist, the founder of a religion, a statesman, puts a new face upon the world; since this modified world has no creative genius, it can absorb novelty only in a diluted, simplified form; and since it meanwhile follows its own laws and is subject to other influences, it perforce modifies all acquisitions.
>
> (Stern 1938: 90)

The personal world affords both continuity and change within the person. The person's assimilative/accommodative processes transform the encoded information from/about the world into internalized personal knowledge. These processes were summarized by Stern in a general scheme (Fig. 1.1).

The person–world relationship exists between two infinities, the inner infinity (intrapersonal) and the outer infinity (extrapersonal). The locus of constructing new psychological phenomena is at the surface of contact between the person and the external world.

To summarize, *psychological phenomena are proximal phenomena* because they emerge at the *boundary* where the person and the external world meet. In terms of time, that is the boundary of the future and the past, or the infinitely small moment that constitutes the present. There is always some indeterminacy operating at this time-based boundary. Human interaction guides coping with that uncertainty.

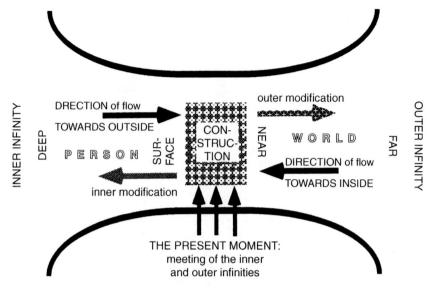

Figure 1.1 A schematic representation of person ↔ world relations (after William Stern's general model)

Duality of processes that relate person and the world

The personal world is constructed by two parallel processes in relations between the person and the external world. First, personal world construction happens through *participation in the world*, which constitutes the centrifugal direction, or the process of spontaneous actions guided by the material character of the person (Stern 1938). Secondly, there is the world "feeding into" the person which constitutes the centripetal direction, or the process of reacting to the demand characteristics of the world.

However, Stern's scheme has two limitations. First, it lacks a conceptualization of how the person and the world are structured. Second, it lacks clarity regarding how the development of new forms of deep structures of the person takes place, as well as how the development of structures of the distant regions of the world takes place. Although Stern specified the unity of centripetal and centrifugal processes, he did not clarify how these processes feed into each other over time. In other terms, his scheme does not include explicit coverage of the systemic developmental continuity of either the person, or of the world.

Mutually linked processes

One of the insufficiencies of Stern's scheme is easily eliminated if the processes linking the results of the centripetal processes as a starting point for further centrifugal processes (and the results of centrifugal processes in the world, feeding into the centripetal ones) are added to the scheme (see Fig. 1.2).

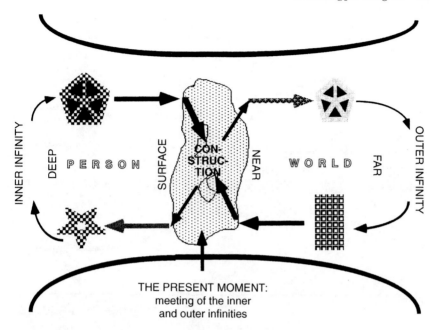

Figure 1.2 Person ↔ world relations in the process of creating internal and external structures

The posited constructed structures in the scheme need to move through the "deep" domains of both person and world, i.e. the inner infinity and the outer infinity, where their fate is not determinable. Perhaps the major strength in Stern's scheme (Fig. 1.1) was the recognition that both the inside and the outside of the person entail such infinity.

At this point it is necessary to make explicit how *proximal construction* takes place. In short, proximal construction represents the main problem that remained unsolved by Stern, and also remains unsolved by our contemporary psychology (see Fig. 1.3).

In Fig. 1.3 there are two conditional inputs into the domain of proximal construction, emanating from the centripetal and centrifugal processes, respectively. Each of them is conditional upon the expectations for the nearest future (denoted *Expected Inform* and *Expected Outform*) that are posited to exist within the person ↔ world system due to its developmental continuity. These are expected (or desired) immediate futures that the person acts to construct in the internal and external worlds, respectively.

Thus, the basic problem for science is clear: how to discover the ways in which the centripetal and centrifugal processes "meet" in the proximal construction zone. As a result of that "meeting" (which may be labeled variously as interaction, transaction or interpenetration), new actual forms of the internal personal and external world structures emerge. The rules of subjective synthesis

CENTRIFUGAL PROCESS

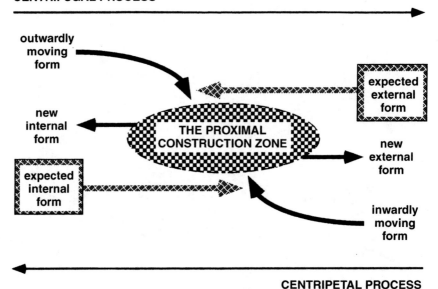

Figure 1.3 Person ↔ world relations in the construction zone

are as far from psychologists' knowledge in the year 2002 as they were at the times when the focus on synthesis emerged as a task in early twentieth century (Vygotsky 1925/1971). Other theoretical schemes of a developmental kind, i.e. the "zone of proximal development" (Valsiner and Van der Veer 1993) or the development of skills (Fischer and Bidell 1998) have attempted to make sense of similar phenomena in different terms.

Psychological development as distancing

Any sign-mediated psychological process entails distancing by the Subject from the Object context in which the Subject operates. The feeling and thinking person is simultaneously within the given context and not within it. S/he is within the context by the inevitability of existence (its open systemic nature). Yet the construction of signs allows her or him to create and quickly modulate the distance between him/herself and the very context within which the person is so inevitably intertwined.

In developmental psychology, a distancing model has been worked out over three decades by Irving Sigel (1970, 1993, 2002), following the theoretical traditions of Karl Bühler and Heinz Werner. Distancing is indicated when the person (actor) establishes a SUBJECT ↔ OBJECT relationship with the immediate setting. Thus, any goal-oriented action in a here-and-now setting (with objectives oriented towards an outcome in the future) entails distancing.

It is precisely the capacity and propensity to make and use semiotic devices that allows human beings to become distanced in relation to their immediate life contexts. The person becomes simultaneously an actor who is immersed in the given "situated activity context" and a reflexive agent who is distanced from the very setting in which he/she is immersed. Thus, every "situated activity context" is simultaneously a "*non*-situated distancing context", as the person acts in the "activity context" on the basis of his or her distanced perspective in relation to the context.

This *duality of situatedness and distancing* is relevant for transcending the adaptation demands of any momentary here-and-now context. It guides development towards increasing autonomy (see the discussion of persistent imitation, below). Yet any autonomy is a result of the immediate dependence upon the here-and-now context, as the open-systemic nature of any developing system – be it biological, psychological or social – entails. Without distancing, no considerations by a person of contexts other than the given here and now would be possible. With distancing, cultural phenomena, i.e. sign-mediated psychological processes, become differentiated into a duality of the personal and collective cultures.

Personal culture and collective culture: mutuality of difference

The notion of culture has been used (and abused) in the social sciences on a grand scale. The duality of personal and collective cultures is a conceptual device for maintaining the centrality of the person in the theoretical construction of sociocultural kind.

The notion of "personal culture" refers to internalized subjective phenomena (intra-mental processes), and the immediate (person-centered) externalizations of those processes. The latter make personal culture publicly visible, as every aspect of personal reconstruction of one's immediate life-world reflects that externaliza- tion. Thus the personal system of created meanings becomes projected to the world through the personal arrangement of things that are important for the given person. This kind of projection is reflected in the personal construction of publicly visible symbolic domains such as body decorations, clothing and the social display of personal objects. It is also visible publicly in personally relevant interpersonal interaction rituals.

The counterpart of the personal culture in the interpersonal field is the collective culture. The collective culture *is composed of* externalizations of personal meaning systems of always limited groups of people. The results of externalizing personal cultures into an interpersonal field creates a collective culture. The resulting collective culture is a relatively stable entity of collective origin. It is a social phenomenon that is anchored in the person's world of experiences.

A collective culture may consist of all of one's experience field of other people, including friends, acquaintances, passers-by, beggars at church steps, policemen in the street, TV personalities, old paintings created long ago, and so on. These other people have externalized their personal–cultural systems in specific ways.

I, living my own life, encounter the results of these externalizations and use those as input into my own construction of my personal culture. I externalize the results of that construction, and thus begin as one of the participants in the collective culture of somebody else.

Dynamics of relations between the collective and personal cultures

The developing person is constantly surrounded by social suggestions from the collective culture. Such social suggestions may surround the developing person directly, by way of externalized cultural messages from specific "social others." Alternatively, such social suggestions may surround the developing person indirectly, by way of the collective cultural encoding of activity settings. The forms into which these messages are encoded are highly heterogeneous, ranging from the usual "airwave" transmission of acoustic and visual information to external forms and colors of objects. They may also include the haptic, tactile or olfactory experiences of the child, as well as specific emotiogenic episodes in which the child is a participant observer (Rogoff 1990).

The emergence of collective cultures has been demonstrated by classic studies of social norm construction (Sherif 1936). Human beings, when jointly experiencing a situation, create a joint understanding of that situation that becomes consensually validated and begins to function as a social norm. The social construction of group norms, and the resiliency of these norms, is constantly evidenced by various kinds of religious sect that establish their own standards by which to live and methods of evaluating others' ways of life.

Collective culture as dynamic process

In addition, collective culture is constantly constructed and reconstructed by various persons who are organized into a hierarchical structure in a given society, with constant migration within the hierarchy. *Collective culture is created through communicative interchanges between the people who construct it.* In this way, the collective culture is always present in a variety of parallel forms that are constructed, in parallel, by different persons participating in different social groups. Thus interaction is the process within which the dynamic relation between personal and collective cultures takes place.

Interaction and human development

Even if development is a probabilistic process, it cannot be theoretically modeled through existing notions of probabilities (see above). Analyses of interaction processes need to focus on the constant construction of a future state out of a *range of* possibilities, through a bidirectional constraining process (Lawrence and Valsiner in press; Valsiner and Lawrence 1997). Any theoretical model of such processes needs to consider the future, rather than assume the non-inventive recurrence of the past.

Infants' interaction with other human beings can be seen as the foundation of all human ontogeny. This view is merely a repetition of the basic theoretical notion that development is possible in the case of open systems which are organized wholes that depend upon their exchange relations with the environment. If the notion of a system is superimposed upon the organismic unity of a human infant, then the "social other", be it an adult or older sibling caregiver, becomes in this theoretical system depicted as part of the necessary and unpredictable environment. Or, as James Mark Baldwin claimed:

> the child begins to learn in addition the fact that persons are in a measure individual in their treatment of him, and hence that individuality has elements of uncertainty or *irregularity* about it. This growing sense is very clear to one who watches an infant in its second half-year. Sometimes the mother gives a biscuit, but sometimes she does not. Sometimes the father smiles and tosses the child; sometimes he does not. And the child looks for signs of these varying moods and methods of treatment. Its new pains of disappointment arise directly on the basis of that former sense of regular personal presence upon which its expectancy went forth.
>
> (1894: 277)

The environment of the developing child is filled with events that are unexpected, and many of those unexpected evens are the results of the goal-oriented actions of other human beings. Thus interaction is in principle indeterminate because it entails different partners creating constantly unexpected new forms of action among previously known ones. The changes introduced by any of the partners lead to a disequilibration of the current ongoing process, evoking tendencies towards progressing equilibration (*equilibration majorante*, in Piaget's terms). That process gives rise to new syntheses, and thus are the cornerstone of all development.

The crucial feature of interaction is the loose coupling (Valsiner 1981) of the interacting partners. They have the freedom of entering into, and exiting from, the interaction process. Furthermore, while interaction partners are involved in that mutual process of interacting, they can change their goal orientations, modes of participation, and the complementarity of their conduct with that of the partner(s) at any instant. Contrary to the original fascination of adult–infant interaction researchers (Condon and Sander 1974) with the temporary moments of "harmony" in the behavioral interchanges of mother–infant dyads, the full picture of interaction includes the field of possibilities ranging from full complementarity ("harmony") to full non-complementarity (breakdown of any coordination) in the interaction process. The interacting persons can bring their task-accomplishment-oriented strategic actions into the interaction process (see, for example, Kindermann and Valsiner 1989). Although different persons interacting with an infant would bring their individual peculiarities to a specific instance of the interaction process (e.g. Fafouti-Milenkovic and Užgiris 1979), the basic structure of the interaction process develops according to robust general laws (Lyra 1999, Lyra and De Souza Silva 2003). This fluid, and simultaneously non-fluid, nature of interaction leads to the theoretical issue of what kind of general formal systems can be used for theoretical models of making sense of that social reality.

The basic illusion of "sharing" and the relevance of metacommunication

In any interaction situation, *environments are "shared" between persons only in terms of a generalized abstraction* (e.g. all human beings "share" the environment of the earth). Yet in terms of the *exact positioning* of the self, each individual occupies a unique position. For example, my present geographically specifiable "spot" or location is uniquely mine, and no other person exists in that same spot. The same is true for communicative positioning because people involved in communication are necessarily based in different perspectives.

It is only through the use of metacommunicative devices that human beings can believe that they are "sharing" a perspective. Metacommunication is communication about communication, and it is a process that creates the context for interpreting the immediate message. The act of interaction itself (or its absence) can be a metacommunicative message. For example, when two people are in a room, one of them expects the other to say something, i.e. enter into interaction. If that does not happen, s/he may interpret the other's failure to do so as "dislike", "arrogance" or the like, while the actual person may just be a proverbial traditional or formal individual who is unable to begin interaction without somebody else having made an introduction!

Under usual circumstances, though, a partner in interaction assumes that there "exists understanding" between her and the other(s). That assumption can become a metacommunicative signal in the interaction process. All claims by mothers that "My baby understands me" (or "My baby is *the only one* who understands me") can be seen as metacommunicative tools in the mother's "autodialogue" with herself (Josephs, Valsiner and Surgan 1999), aside from the obvious possibility that it has the function of showing off to the investigator her motherly qualities.

Basic inequality in interaction: the field of positions

The social world creates further differentiation between communicating individuals, even beyond the "geographically located uniqueness" described above. Human development entails social relations and interaction between individuals whose relations are unequal in social power, and also in the semiotically constructed notion of "responsibility". Thus, parent–child or teacher–student relations are set up by the social roles of the relating individuals *as unequal*. That is, parents and teachers are in control over the life-worlds of their children and students, even if the latter are active co-constructors of their life spaces. Social power is constantly being created semiotically, thus amplifying a difference of positions of the individuals who are involved in communication. Communication is always between people who are unequal in terms of their positions, and the issue for a theory of communication is how a particular version of inequality of positions becomes transformed as the process of communication takes place.

The issue of the positioning of the person in various communicative contexts has been of serious concern to people who conceptualize communication. Ragnar Rommetveit's example of "Mrs. and Mr. Smith" may provide a good illustration here. Mr. Smith is a husband who has started to mow the lawn in his front yard, on a Saturday morning. This ordinary act can lead to a variety of *positions* that people may assume in interaction:

> What is going on in Mr. Smith's garden ... may under different dialogically established background conditions be made sense of in a variety of different ways and brought into language by expressions such as MOW THE LAWN, BEAUTIFY THE GARDEN, ENGAGE IN PHYSICAL EXERCISE, WORK, ENGAGE IN LEISURE-TIME ACTIVITY, and NOT WORK. A neighbour prying into the miserable relations of the Smiths may even tell us that he "sees" Mr. Smith AVOID THE COMPANY OF HIS WIFE. And this may indeed also be the way in which Mrs. Smith, left alone in the kitchen with the morning coffee in front of her, makes sense of what is going on... We hear her say *"He is once more avoiding a confronta..."* At that moment her bitter voice is drowned by the sound of telephone, and she picks up the receiver. It is her friend Betty who is calling, and Betty initiates their chat by asking: *"That lazy husband of yours, is he still in bed?"* To which Mrs. Smith answers: "No, *Mr. Smith is WORKING this morning, he is mowing the lawn.*"
>
> A short time afterwards Mrs. Smith receives another call, this time from Mr. Jones, who, she tacitly takes for granted ... wants to find out whether Mr. Smith is free to go fishing with him. He asks: "Is your husband working this morning? And Mrs. Smith answers: "No, *Mr. Smith is NOT WORKING this morning, he is mowing the lawn.*"
>
> (1992: 25–26)

This example provides for a rather realistic account of how quickly the position of the same person in communicative relations can change. The process of coordinating the positions of the communication partners is considered *attunement* (Rommetveit 1992: 26), which involves the reflexive stance of A relative to uncertain hints from B. The coordination process also consists of counter-attunement which is the reflexive stance of B relative to A.

Let us extend the realm of different attunement patterns between communication partners. Let us assume that Betty could have mentioned any of the following to Mrs. Smith:

(a) "That *lazy* husband of yours, is he *still* in bed?"
(b) "That husband of yours, is he *still* in bed?"

(c) "That husband of yours, *is he in bed?*"
(d) "That husband of yours, *what is he up to?*"
(e) "That husband of yours, *is he working?*"
(f) "That husband of yours, *is he mowing the lawn?*"
(g) "That husband of yours, *how is he today?*"

An analysis of (a) and (b) from the above list of Betty's possible statements leads to different possible constructions on behalf of Mrs. Smith, each of which is dependent upon Mrs. Smith's assumed position relative to Betty's. This position can be *convergent, divergent, oppositional,* or *neutralizing.* Let us extend the example to see how Mrs. Smith could interpret Betty's messages (a) (b), and answer accordingly, from each position:

Position	*Interpretation*	*Possible answer*
CONVERGENT:	"Betty understands my problems."	"It *took me much effort to get him out of bed,* now he is working. . ."
DIVERGENT:	"Betty has weird ideas about my husband."	"No, Mr. Smith is working. . ."
OPPOSITIONAL:	"Stupid cow, it is none of your business what happens in my life."	"No, Mr. Smith is working. . ." "You are mean!"
NEUTRALIZING:	"I know you are envious, but I make no issue out of your little bites."	"Oh, he is fine. . . but what about you and me having coffee together later today?"

It is clear from this extension that mere attunement to the other as well as counter-attunement by the other is insufficient to characterize the ongoing communication process. The positioning by Mrs. Smith is co-constructed with Betty's implied message, and can take a number (in our example, four, but the number is not a given) of directions. Note that some of the directions (divergent, oppositional) may lead to a similar response ("No, Mr. Smith is working. . ."), or may result in direct confrontation ("You are mean") if the oppositional stance is carried out into the direct communication process.

However, the communication process entails the renegotiation of positions. As Rommetveit suggested,

> Consider. . . the following plausible continuation of Mrs. Smith's chat with Betty. Betty, having been told that Mr. Smith is working (mowing the lawn), says:
>
> *Is he really? Is he WORKING HARD?*

The sustained topic... is in this case determined by the interrogator's concern about Mr. Smith's alleged laziness. Betty was the one who set the perspective at the very beginning of their conversation... It is nevertheless Mrs. Smith who has brought her husband's activity in the garden into language of WORK.

(1992: 32–33)

Human communication thus entails the quick assumption of positions and their maintenance. The positions assumed by different communicating partners are *necessarily different*, even if these can converge at times. Furthermore, the particular positions can be presented in different disguises, some of which entail emphasis on their difference and others which entail creating an image of similarity in perspective. This positioning can be constructed in an instant, surely based on previous experience yet organized by the present situation. Its function is to create the bridge to the future. Any formal model of interaction that is an adequate representation of the fluidity, dynamic and constructive nature of the process needs to consider the range of possibilities that exist in the present. It is the formal model of hypergames that provides some new possibilities for the study of interaction and its development.

Interaction as hypergame

As is clear from the discussion above, theoretical models of interaction cannot be limited to mechanistic assumptions that the accumulation of past events mirrors the future of the developing system. The *fluidity* of the ongoing interaction, at any moment in time, is in principle indeterministic as it constitutes the ground for the construction of developmental novelties.

Interaction is a dynamic process. Such dynamic processes can be modeled through the formal system of hypergames (Harsanyi and Selten 1988). Hypergames

> are games where one or more players are not fully aware of the nature of the game situation. This unawareness may include *lack of knowledge of the consequences* of their own and other players' different choices. The players may have an *inaccurate understanding of the preferences* of others, or they do not possess full and correct information on the range of options available to other players. Furthermore, they may be *unaware of the identities of all the players involved in the game*.
>
> (Fraser and Hipel 1979: 805, added emphases)

The following characteristics of hypergame are directly applicable to any interaction situation:

1 *Lack of knowledge of consequences*. Partners in interaction do not have full knowledge about the consequences of their own actions. In cases where any action by one partner is capable of leading to *at least* the indeterminate

choice situation of responding or not responding by the other, the consequences of one's actions are unknown. If the possibility is entertained that the second partner responds in ways that are novel, and hence unexpected, the hypergame nature of interaction is proven.

2 *Partners have inaccurate understandings of one another's "preferences".* Here the non-developmental orientation of the contexts in which hypergame theory emerged shows its terminological limits. In the case of interaction, the set of "preferences" is never fixed, and does not exist on its own. Rather, during interaction partners create their actions on the basis of their current set goal orientations. Since the direction of these goal orientations can change at any moment, and the *orientation* entails a *range* of possible actions (i.e. is directionally indeterministic), interaction fits the basic notions of hypergame theory.

3 *The set of functional participants in the interaction is in principle unknown.* Even if interaction in its observable forms takes place between n partners (the number of actual participants), there can be a larger number of functional participants involved (FP > n). This larger number of functional participants is made possible by the actual interacting partners using different intra-psychological "social others" (e.g. in the sense of Bakhtinian "voices") in setting up goal orientations, and action directions, within the interaction. Because that kind of importation of "invisible others", or of socially shared representations, is a fully intra-psychological event, it is never completely clear who is interacting in the contexts of interaction.

These features of hypergame theory as applied to interaction lead to the need for concurrent coverage of immediate goal orientations and actions by the interaction partners. Mere observation, by outside observers, of the ongoing interaction would fail to reveal the future-oriented nature of the emerging interaction episodes.

Persistent imitation as the mechanism of development

The interaction process is the location – or field – within which the processes of development take place. Yet interaction cannot explain development, and analyses of interaction need to entail explanatory schemes that show how development takes place in the field of interaction.

At every encounter with the world, the developing person faces novel, or emergent, demands for a constant pre-adaptation to facing further indeterminate challenges. Thus, the developing person *does not follow* the existing demands of the world but *anticipates future possible challenges*. Interaction therefore is a process that is possible through conduct directed towards some future objectives, even if the latter are ill-defined. Development is directional, and that directionality is behind all kinds of interactional encounters that the developing person has with others and with the world at large.

How is such anticipation of the future worked out in interaction? A simple solution to that question is provided by James Mark Baldwin's notion of *persistent imitation*, which involves an organism acting upon the world on the basis of an externally given model but *not following* the model as it occurs. Instead, the organism *experiments with selected features of the model*, and in that kind of imitative process transcends the model. This notion of a creative kind of imitation allows the developing organism to distance him/herself from the here and now in favor of some immediate expected future state of affairs. Imitation produces a wealth of constructed versions of novel phenomena, some of which may be preserved while others may disappear after not finding a need for their use.

The issue of imitation was a central topic in the work of Ina Užgiris during the course of her entire productive life (see Užgiris 1984, 1990, 1999). In her last publication, she expressed her hope that imitation will lead us to discovering the basic mechanisms for the emergence of consciousness. She writes:

> Drawing upon a consideration of imitation activity within a framework of cultural situatedness, I suggested that the few scattered reports in the literature suggest that it is indeed possible that *imitation activities contribute to consciousness by indexing cultural values of independence and collaboration.* It is my hope that researchers in the future will systematically examine nonverbal systems across cultures much as language socialization researchers have begun examining verbal routines as powerful sites of socialization.
>
> (2000: 139, added emphases)

The ways in which Ina Užgiris' conception of imitation, and particularly the persistent imitation, or innovative experimentation discussed by James M. Baldwin, contribute to consciousness is the crucial challenge for developmental science. What particular forms of understanding that contribution we invent in our theories remain – so far – an open question.

General conclusions

The crucial change in understanding human development through interaction is the move from viewing interaction as if it reflected the demands of the here-and-now context, to that of viewing interaction processes as constant efforts to *pre-cope* with the *anticipated immediate future*. The internalization of meaningful reflection, verbal and nonverbal, upon the world is the basis for further interaction with the world. Thus it might be important to point out that interaction is very important for development as it guides internalization. At the same time, interaction is not important for development in the sense that it consists of irrelevant tiny details during the life course of interactants.

Ina Užgiris always looked for relevant psychological phenomena, and searched for their explanations. Her focus on interaction and imitation was a productive choice. Yet our understanding of the processes of development is still only in its infancy. The concept of imitation has usually been presented in psychology in its common language sense rather than in terms of the Baldwinian notion of "persistent imitation." Developmental science's struggle has been to bring together general notions of development with concrete empirical research practices. Some of the latter (e.g. Markovian conditional probability analyses) may be dead-end streets for developmental science. Others, such as hypergame theory, may potentially become usable, yet probably within some limits. Developmental scientists continue to struggle within their own minds for developing their perspectives, and no social consensus needs to curb that process.

Note

1 This verbal depiction of the uncertainty, through covering all possible outcomes, finds its role in an art that is parallel to psychologists' self-declared role of "prediction", i.e. in fortune-telling. Such coverage constitutes the *omniscopus* use of language (Aphek and Tobin 1990, p. 46). Again, the illusion of certainty is created, albeit through a psychological effect (*pars pro toto* – or at least one part of the prediction will happen, therefore the prediction is certain).

Acknowledgements

I thank the editors of this volume for helpful critical feedback on a previous version of this chapter. The writing of the chapter benefited from my stay in Brazil and joint work with my colleagues at the University of Brasilia and the Federal University of Pernambuco, which has been supported by the US–Brazil Collaborative Program on Development of Human Communicative Processes in Different Socio-Cultural Contexts (NSF INT–9813720).

References

Aphek, E. and Tobin, Y. (1990) *The Semiotics of Fortune-Telling.* Amsterdam: John Benjamins.
Baldwin, J. M. (1894) "Personality-Suggestion", *Psychological Review 1*: 274–279.
Branco, A. U. and Valsiner, J. (1997) "Changing Methodologies: A Co-constructivist Study of Goal Orientations in Social Interactions", *Psychology and Developing Societies 9, 1*: 35–64.
Condon, W. S. and Sander, L. W. (1974) "Synchrony Demonstrated Between Movements of the Neonate and Adult Speech", *Child Development 45*: 456–462.
Fafouti-Milenkovic, M. and Užgiris, I. Č. (1979) "The Mother-Infant Communication System" in Užgiris, I. Č. (ed.) "Social Interaction and Communication During Infancy" (pp. 41–56). *New Directions for Child Development no. 4.* San Francisco: Jossey-Bass.
Fischer, K. and Bidell, T. R. (1998) "Dynamic Development of Psychological Structures in Action and Thought" in Damon, W. and Lerner, R. (eds.) *Handbook of Child Psychology*, Fifth ed vol. 1. *Theoretical Models of Human Development* (pp. 467–561). New York: Wiley.
Fogel, A., Lyra, M. C. D. P. and Valsiner, J. (eds.) (1997) *Dynamics and Indeterminism in Developmental and Social Processes.* Hillsdale, N.J.: Erlbaum.
Fraser, N. M. and Hipel, K. W. (1979) "Solving Complex Conflicts", *IEEE Transactions on Systems, Man, and Cybernetics*, smc–9, 12: 805–810.
Gottlieb, G. (1999) *Probabilistic Epigenesis and Evolution.* The Heinz Werner Lectures, vol. 23. Worcester, MA.: Clark University Press.
Harsanyi, J. C. and Selten, R. (1988) *A General Theory of Equilibrium Selection Between Games.* Cambridge, MA.: MIT Press.

Josephs, I. E., Valsiner, J. and Surgan, S. E. (1999) "The Process of Meaning Construction" in Brandtstätdter, J. and Lerner, R. M. (eds.) *Action and Self-Development* (pp. 257–282). Thousand Oaks, CA.: Sage.

Kindermann, T. and Valsiner, J. (1989) "Strategies for Empirical Research in Context-Inclusive Developmental Psychology" in Valsiner, J. (ed.) *Cultural Context and Child Development* (pp. 13–50). Toronto-Göttingen-Bern: C. J. Hogrefe and H. Huber.

Lawrence, J. A. and Valsiner, J. (in press) "Making Personal Sense: An Account of Basic Internalization and Externalization Processes" in *Theory and Psychology.*

Lyra, M. C. (1999) "Desenvolvimento de um sistema de relacoes historicamente construido: contribucoes da comunicacao no inicio da vida" in *Psicologia: Reflexao e critica* 13: 2, 257–268.

Lyra, M. C. and Souza, M. (2003) "Dynamics of Dialogue and Emergence of Self in Early Communication" in Josephs, I. E. (ed.) "Dialogicality in Development", vol. 6 of *Advances in Child Development Within Culturally Structured Environments*. Stamford, CT.: Greenwood.

MacMurray, J. (1957) *The Self as Agent*. London: Faber & Faber.

MacMurray, J. (1961) *Persons in Relation*. London: Faber & Faber.

Nesselroade, J. R. and Molenaar, P. C. M. (2003) "Quantitative Models for Developmental Processes" in Valsiner. J. and Connolly, K. (eds.) *Handbook of Developmental Psychology.* London: Sage.

Rogoff, B. (1990) *Apprenticeship in Thinking*. New York: Oxford University Press.

Rommetveit, R. (1992) "Outlines of a Dialogically Based Social-Cognitive Approach to Human Cognition and Communication" in Wold, A. H. (ed.) *The Dialogical Alternative: Towards a Theory of Language and Mind* (pp. 19–44). Oslo: Scandinavian University Press.

Sherif, M. (1936) *The Psychology of Social Norms*. New York: Harper & Brothers.

Sigel, I. (1970) "The Distancing Hypothesis" in Jones, M. (ed.) *Effects of Early Experience* (pp. 99–118). Coral Gables, Fla.: University of Miami Press.

— (1993) "The Centrality of a Distancing Model for the Development of Representational Competence" in Cocking, R. R. and Renninger, K. A. (eds.) *The Development and Meaning of Psychological Distance* (pp. 141–158). Hillsdale, NJ: Erlbaum.

— (2002) "The Psychological Distancing Model: A Study of the Socialization of Cognition", *Culture & Psychology* 8, 2: xxx–yyy.

Stern, W. (1938) *General Psychology From the Personalist Standpoint*. New York: Macmillan.

Užgiris, I. Č. (1979) Editor's notes in Užgiris, I. Č. (ed.) "Social Interaction and Communication During Infancy" (pp. vii–ix), *New Directions for Child Development*, no. 4. San Francisco: Jossey-Bass.

— (1984) "Imitation in Infancy: Its Interpersonal Aspects" in Perlmutter, M. (ed.) *Minnesota Symposia on Child Psychology*, vol. 17. *Parent–Child Interactions* (pp. 1–32). Hillsdale, NJ: Erlbaum.

— (1990) "The Social Context of Infant Imitation" in Lewis, M. and Feinman, S. (eds.) *Social Influences and Socialization in Infancy* (pp. 215–251). New York: Plenum.

— (1999) "Imitation as Activity" in Nadel, J. and Butterworth, G. (eds.) *Imitation in Infancy* (pp. 186–206). Cambridge: Cambridge University Press.

— (2000) "Words Don't Tell All: Some Thoughts on Early Communication Development" in Budwig, N., Užgiris, I. Č. and Wertsch, J. V. (eds.) *Communication: An Arena of Development* (pp. 131–141). Stamford, CT.: Ablex.

Valsiner, J. (1981) "Loose-Coupling Model of Adult-Infant Interaction", paper presented at the Annual Meeting of the Southeastern Psychological Association, Atlanta, GA, March 26.

— (ed.) (1986) *The Individual Subject in Scientific Psychology.* New York: Plenum.
— (1987) *Culture and the Development of Children's Action.* Chichester: Wiley.
— (2000a) "Data as Representations: Contextualizing Qualitative and Quantitative Research Strategies." *Social Science Information 39, 1:* 99–113.
— (2000b) "Entre a 'Democracia da Literatura' e a paixao pela compreensão: Entendendo a dinâmica do desenvolvimento", *Psicologia: Reflexão e critica 13, 2:* 319–325.
Valsiner, J. and Lawrence, J. A. (1997) "Human Development in Culture Across the Life Span" in Berry, J. W., Dasen, P. R. and Saraswathi, T. S. (eds.) *Handbook of Cross-Cultural Psychology,* second edition, vol. 2. *Basic Processes and Human Development* (pp. 69–106). Boston: Allyn & Bacon.
Valsiner, J. and Van der Veer, R. (1993) "The Encoding of Distance: The Concept of the Zone of Proximal Development and Its Interpretations" in Cocking, R. R. and Renninger, K. A. (eds.) *The Development and Meaning of Psychological Distance* (pp. 35–62). Hillsdale, NJ: Lawrence Erlbaum Associates.
Van Geert, P. (1994) *Dynamic Systems of Development.* Hemel Hempstead: Harvester/ Wheatsheaf.
Van der Veer, R. and Valsiner, J. (1991) *Understanding Vygotsky: A Quest for Synthesis.* Oxford: Blackwell.
Vygotsky, L. S. (1925/1971) *The Psychology of Art.* Cambridge, MA.: MIT Press.
Werner, H. (1957) "The Concept of Development from a Comparative and Organismic Point of View" in Harris, D. B. (ed.) *The Concept of Development* (pp. 125–147). Minneapolis: University of Minnesota Press.

2 Patterns of culturally meaningful activity

Linking parents' ideas and parent–child interactions

Catherine Raeff

For some time now, analyzing the interrelations between parents' ideas and parent–child interactions has represented a simultaneously problematic and promising theoretical and empirical developmental issue. It is readily recognized that both parents' ideas and parent–child interactions are important aspects of a developing child's social and cultural context, making it important to understand the content of parents' ideas in relation to the structuring of parent–child interactions. In addition, analyses of parents' ideas and parent–child interactions can further our understanding of some of the ways that individual, social, and cultural factors intersect as they shape children's developmental experiences. That is, analyzing parents' ideas and parent–child interactions in relation to each other can provide information about: first, how individual, social and cultural processes shape the construction of parents' ideas; second, how individual, social and cultural processes shape the structuring of parent–child interactions; third, how the construction of parents' ideas and parent–child interactions are linked to form wider patterns of culturally meaningful activity; and fourth, how individual, social and cultural processes intersect as children actively participate in modes of parent–child interactions that are linked to particular parental ideas.

While many of these varied issues will be touched upon, it is certainly beyond the scope of this one chapter to delve into all of these issues in detail. The central goal of this chapter is to offer a theoretical perspective that focuses on understanding how parents' ideas and parent–child interactions gain significance in relation to each other. This chapter also focuses on how parents' ideas and parent–child interactions gain significance in relation to wider cultural representations and expectations of parenting and parent–child relationships, thus constituting culturally meaningful patterns of activity. This approach is part of the cultural psychology tradition that seeks to describe and understand within cultural complexities, and that is geared towards understanding the multi-faceted ways in which culture shapes human behavior and development (Shweder, 1990). We begin with a selective overview of some theoretical issues pertaining to parents' ideas in relation to parent–child interactions, followed by an explication of the current perspective. The chapter will then end with an empirical illustration of the current perspective, using data from a study of adolescent mothers and older mothers.

Before turning to some of the literature on parents' ideas and parent–child interactions, a word regarding terminology is required. Increasing interest in varied aspects of parental cognitive and evaluative activities during the last ten to twenty years has led to many theoretical and empirical considerations of how they may be related to parent–child interactions. However, there is little consistency in the definition and usage of terms, and different investigators have discussed this topic in terms of parental values, attitudes, goals, beliefs, ideas, and knowledge (e.g. Goodnow 1988, Holden 1995, Holden and Edwards 1989, Kohn 1963, McGillicuddy-DeLisi 1982, McGillicuddy-DeLisi and Sigel 1995, Miller 1988, Murphey 1992, Sigel 1985). In this chapter, I use the term "idea", following Goodnow (1988) to serve as a relatively broad construct that represents varied kinds of parental constructions of parenting and parent–child relationships. As Goodnow (1988) writes, the term "ideas"

> has a better fit with the range of material covered in studies of the way parents think about parenting and development. That material ranges from views about desirable outcomes to judgments about the nature of the raw material, attributions of causality, knowledgeability about development, opinions about conditions that influence development, judgments about ways to assess a child's progress, and estimates of children's competence at various ages.
>
> (p. 288)

Some theoretical issues

A great deal of research has been conducted to discern whether parents' ideas and parent–child interactions are correlated, and whether they are predictive of one another. Some studies indicate that parental ideas and the structuring of parent–child interactions are indeed correlated, but many studies have also failed to show consistent relations between parents' ideas and parent–child interactions. Despite such conflicting findings, there is continued interest in trying to discern how parents' ideas and parent–child interactions are interrelated, and a number of theoretical issues have arisen revealing the complexities of this area of inquiry.

Although most studies typically acknowledge bidirectional relations between parents' ideas and parent–child interactions, there has been a tendency to focus on how the ideas determine and predict varied aspects of parent–child interactions (e.g. Holden 1995). One problem with this approach is that it is difficult to specify what constitutes consistency between ideas and interactions because there may be many ways for certain ideas to be represented and enacted during the course of actual interactions with a child (McGillicuddy-DeLisi and Sigel 1995, Sigel 1985). Furthermore, within a single cultural context, the enactments of certain ideas may change across different activity settings, and certainly the enactment of parental ideas in varied activity settings may differ across cultures. Similarly, one mode of interaction may represent the enactment of varied ideas, depending on a given parent–child pair and a given social and cultural setting. Although the ways in which ideas can be enacted in parent–child interactions may not be infinite, trying to discern the myriad possibilities to support predictions from parents' ideas to modes of parent–child interactions remains an arduous task.

Thus, studies that have pointed to correlations between parents' ideas and parents' behavior during parent–child interactions have typically focused on relatively specific ideas and concomitantly specific aspects of parental behavior (e.g. Holden 1995). These findings are in keeping with the principle that strong correlations between attitudes and "overt" behavior are most likely to occur when they are both analyzed at the same level of specificity (Ajzen 1996). For example, mothers who believe that children construct their own knowledge of the world are likely to encourage their children to reflect and think in abstract terms specifically during teaching interactions (McGillicuddy-DeLisi 1982). Similarly, in other studies of parents' beliefs about children's cognitive development and parents' teaching strategies in teaching situations, the following correlations have been found: first, parents who believe that children learn through negative or positive feedback are likely to use punishment and rewards, or to explicitly tell their children what to do; second, parents who believe that children need logical explanations to facilitate successful learning are likely to make varied suggestions about how to proceed with a learning task; third, parents who believe that children learn through direct instruction are likely to tell their children what to do; and four, parents who believe that children learn better through observation and imitation are likely to model or demonstrate (Elias and Ubriaco 1986). These studies have elucidated important links between specific parental ideas about children's cognitive development and specific aspects of parental behavior during parent–child teaching interactions. However, an alternative approach is required to understand the links between other aspects of parents' ideas and the overall structuring of parent–child interactions.

It may be difficult to discern one-to-one correspondences between less specific kinds of ideas and the structuring of parent–child interactions because parental ideas are multidimensional, and do not exist in isolation from other ideas that parents have about a variety of issues (e.g. Goodnow and Collins 1990, Holden 1995; McGillicuddy-DeLisi and Sigel 1995). Moreover, parents may be more strongly committed to some ideas than to others, and parents may even express seemingly inconsistent or contradictory ideas about children and child development (Goodnow 1995). It is rather unlikely that any single measure of parental ideas, be it a pencil and paper questionnaire or an interview, can probe such varied aspects of a parent's ideas. It is also unlikely that the varied dimensions, strengths of commitment and links to ideas in other domains of functioning would be fully elucidated.

For example, some parents may claim that children should basically be as free as possible to explore the world in their own ways in order to ultimately become self-reliant. However, during an observation of parent–child interactions one might find that some of these same parents limit the extent to which they permit their children to run around, express themselves and explore the environment.

In this case, the parents may also think that children should not disturb others, indicating how the idea that children should be free to do as they please exists in relation to other ideas involving consideration for other people. Thus any assessment of parental ideas will leave some missing dimensions, making it difficult to correlate stated ideas with parent–child interactions, or to predict parent–child interactions from measures of parents' ideas.

Linking parents' ideas and parent–child interactions is further complicated by the fact that many studies tend to reify parental ideas as virtually static entities that parents hold or have access to in various interpersonal contexts with their children (Holden 1995). Alternatively, parents' ideas may be conceptualized in terms of ongoing constructive activities (e.g. Lightfoot and Valsiner 1992), whereby parents actively construct ideas as they participate in varied sociocultural settings, including developmental psychology studies. As parents' lives change, and as their children's competencies and characteristics change, parents continue to engage in actively constructing ideas about child development, parenting, and parent–child relationships. (Goodnow 1985, Mills and Rubin 1992). Thus parents' ideas are under ongoing construction, particularly in relation to changing modes of parent–child interactions, suggesting that parent–child interactions may affect the construction of parents' ideas.

The traditional view which tends to reify parents' ideas, and treats ideas as static and unidimensional determinants of behavior during parent–child interactions, is also problematic because it implies that parents first engage in conscious reflection about their varied ideas and then proceed to interact with their children in certain ways. This view seems to be based on the assumption that ideas serve as a kind of separable motivational or intentional component that is prior to action. However, not all modes of overt or physically observable action follow from separate, deliberate moments of prior intention (e.g. Hampshire 1959/1983, Searle 1983). Indeed, in many interpersonal situations, including those with children, there may be little opportunity to step back and reflect upon how to act. It may also be difficult to consider what one's ideas are and how they would be best realized in a particular situation. When parents are asked to interact with their children in a teaching situation, or when they are in a situation that requires some kind of discipline, it is possible that they may have a chance to briefly reflect and assess their goals for the situation before using a particular teaching or discipline strategy. However, not all parent–child interactions consist of teaching or discipline. Instead, parents and children interact with each other as people in a relationship that requires ongoing negotiation, suggesting that much of parental behavior during parent–child interactions is unlikely to be subject to prior, deliberate reflection.

Trying to predict the organization of parent–child interactions from measures of parental ideas may also ultimately prove futile because the dynamics of parent–child interactions are multiply determined and multifaceted, and thus cannot easily be traced back to a single causal idea or even set of ideas. As such, it may be impossible to specify all the relevant behavioral determinants of parent–child interactions, but a few are worth mentioning. First, the immediate setting of a particular interaction episode may provide some situational constraints that can affect the structuring of parent–child interactions. For example, parents may have different behavioral expectations of their children at home, in a laboratory, at the beach or in the supermarket. Second, a parent's behavior during parent–child interactions may be shaped in complex ways by varied aspects of his/her childhood experiences with his/her own parents. Third, a parent's emotions may affect the course of parent–child interactions (Goodnow 1995, McGillicuddy-DeLisi and Sigel 1995). Fourth, parents may espouse certain ideas about parenting and parent–child relationships, but these ideas may not mesh effectively with a particular child's individual characteristics, thus pointing to the importance of the child's contributions to parent–child interactions. Furthermore, parental behavior towards children changes as children's competencies develop, suggesting that parents' behavior during parent–child interactions is dynamic and subject to ongoing reorganization. In addition to these varied individual and social factors, cultural values and meanings about parenting, parent–child relationships, and child development also shape how parents interact with their children (Goodnow and Collins 1990, Harkness and Super 1996, Lightfoot and Valsiner 1992, McGillicuddy-DeLisi and Sigel 1995, Valsiner and Litvinovic 1996).

An interpretive approach

This brief overview indicates that correlative and predictive models of the interrelations between parents' ideas and parent–child interactions alone may prove of limited value in the long run. Instead, an interpretive approach to the co-occurrence of parental ideas and modes of parent–child interactions can enhance our understanding of their significance in relation to each other, and in relation to cultural representations of parenting and parent–child relationships. The current interpretive approach is based on the position that human functioning consists of dynamic modes of activity that are symbolic, i.e. that human activity has meaning beyond the face value of its physical and observable behavioral components. The meaning of human activity is culturally constituted, and reflects or enacts cultural representations of appropriate behavior and being. Within this view, culture as a whole is defined as a system of symbolic action patterns that is constructed by a group of people through social interactions. As symbolic action patterns, cultural activities are enactments of values and meanings through which people organize experience and create their under-standings of the world (e.g. D'Andrade 1984, Geertz 1973, LeVine 1984, Shweder, Jensen and Goldstein 1995). As people engage with one another in different modes of activity and cultural institutional settings, culture is also constantly being constructed and transformed in relation to the competencies, frameworks, and interpretations of the individuals involved. Thus not only do cultural factors shape the ongoing dynamics and symbolic significance of human activities, but cultural representations are also continuously shaped by individuals as they engage in varied modes of activity.

The current interpretive approach also holds that modes of culturally symbolic activity are constituted by interactions among individual, social, and cultural processes. This approach is in keeping with what is fast becoming a tradition in developmental psychology: that psychological functioning and development occur at the crossroads of inseparable individual, social and cultural processes (e.g. Fogel 1993, Rogoff 1995, Užgiris 1989, 1996, Wertsch 1991, 1995). As constituents of symbolic activities, individual, social and cultural processes are taken to be analytically distinct, but because they are reciprocally interrelated no single process is taken to be prior to any other process. Moreover, the varied modes of activity that people engage in during the course of their days, weeks, months, and years do not exist in isolation from one another. Instead, the co-occurrence or combination of different modes of activity form wider patterns of culturally meaningful activity whose significance is derived from cultural representations of appropriate behavior and being (see also Chandler and Sokol, Chapter 9). Thus, understanding the meaning of a mode of activity involves explicating how individual, social and cultural processes interact. In addition, understanding how the co-occurrence of different modes of activity within a domain of functioning constitute wider patterns of culturally meaningful activity involves interpreting the modes of activity in relation to each other and in relation to cultural representations.

In this chapter, the structuring of parent–child interactions and the active construction of parental ideas are viewed as two distinct modes of activity that are constituted through reciprocal interactions among individual, social and cultural processes. Taken together, these modes of activity constitute wider patterns of culturally meaningful symbolic activity whose significance and coherence are based on how they reflect cultural representations of parenting and parent–child relationships. Patterns of culturally meaningful activity may be constituted by several identifiable modes of activity, and thus it is likely that the construction of parents' ideas and the structuring of parent–child interactions occur in conjunction with other modes of activity within the broader behavioral domains of parenting and parent–child relationships. Although the current analysis is limited to a consideration of the co-occurrence of parents' ideas and parent–child interactions, it will ultimately be important to discern how other modes of activity also figure into complex and multifaceted patterns of culturally meaningful activity.

As a form of social engagement, parent–child interactions are a mode of symbolic activity that clearly involves social processes. Based on an interactive perspective (Užgiris 1989), modes of social interaction are taken to be mutually constructed through the ongoing and bidirectional regulation of the contributing participants. Individual processes are also involved in the bidirectional regulation and structuring of parent–child interactions as both parent and child contribute to the ongoing flow of their interactions in terms of their own competencies and frameworks. As noted earlier, a parent's individual contributions to the structuring of parent–child interactions may also include varied factors ranging from his/her own childhood experiences to his/her current emotional state. In addition, parent–child interactions are shaped by cultural representations of parenting and parent–child relationships which parents construct as they engage in varied sociocultural activity settings. Ultimately, the development of individual competencies occurs as parents and children actively participate in social interactions over time, which in turn, contribute to the changing dynamics of parent–child interactions (e.g. Fogel 1993, Rogoff 1990, Užgiris 1989). This view of parent–child interactions reveals how they are not a purely social phenomenon, but involve varied kinds of reciprocal interchanges among individual, social and cultural processes.

Rather than conceptualizing parents' ideas as reified and static entities, the construction of parental ideas may also be viewed as a form of symbolic activity that parents engage in just as they actively engage in interactions with their children. As modes of activity, parents' ideas are constituted through individual constructive processes which are shaped by cultural representations of parenting and parent–child relationships. That is, parents interpret, transform or appropriate cultural representations of parenting and parent–child relationships as they construct their own ideas. Parents' personal constructions can, in turn, contribute to cultural change through ongoing social interactions in varied kinds of activity settings. Parents' ideas are also shaped by social interactions, including parent–child interactions. Moreover, when parents articulate their parental ideas as participants in developmental psychology studies, the construction of their ideas involves the dynamics of social interactions with the researcher. In these varied ways, parents' ideas are not taken to be the property of isolated individuals but instead are understood in terms of constantly interacting individual, social and cultural processes.

The current approach holds that, as two modes of activity that often co-occur in the lives of many parents and their children, particular combinations of parental ideas and modes of parent–child interaction constitute wider patterns of culturally meaningful symbolic activity that reflect cultural representations of parenting and parent–child relationships. In this way, parents' ideas and parent–child interactions represent parts of a wider system of cultural significance and thus may take on new meaning in relation to each other within a particular cultural context. Therefore, to understand how certain combinations or co-occurrences of parental ideas and parent–child interactions form coherent patterns, it is necessary to interpret them in relation to each other and in relation to cultural representations of parenting and parent–child relationships.

It is interesting to note that Kohn (1963), who was one of the first social scientists to investigate some of the interrelations between parents' values and parent–child interactions, did not only try to discern whether specific parental values are predictive of or correlated with specific modes of parent–child interactions. Instead, he also sought to interpret the meaning of co-occurring parental values and child-rearing strategies in relation to the parents' sociocultural circumstances, specifically the fathers' occupations. This kind of investigation assumes that co-occurring parental ideas and parent–child interactions are interrelated. To interpret the meaning of this co-occurrence, it is necessary to consider how these modes of activity form coherent patterns of culturally meaningful activity in relation to wider cultural representations.

Adolescent mothers' and older mothers' ideas and interactions with their children

The current approach to the interrelations between parents' ideas and parent–child interactions informed an interpretive study of the meaning of adolescent mothers' and older mothers' ideas and interactions with their children in relation to cultural representations of parenting and parent–child relationships. Insofar as parents' ideas and parent–child interactions are taken to be linked together by cultural representations of parenting and parent–child relationships, it is necessary to consider some aspects of the American cultural context in which these adolescent and older mothers live (Raeff 1996).

In the United States, there are general values and representations regarding parenting, parent–child relationships and child development that constitute elements of a common experience for adolescent mothers and older mothers. Within this context, women are typically responsible for childcare, and motherhood is viewed as a permanent adult social role that involves caring for a child's physical, social, and psychological well-being (Hays 1996). Generally speaking, some common American cultural goals of development include fostering children's independent achievements, and aiding them in the acquisition of social skills (Raeff 1997a, 2000). In addition to fostering these aspects of development, motherhood also ideally involves being part of a strong and fulfilling interpersonal relationship with another human being.

Because motherhood is typically viewed as a normative adult social role, some aspects of the parenting experience may be unique to adolescent mothers in the United States. Although adolescent mothers in the United States come from varied ethnic backgrounds, they all bear and raise their children in the context of wider common cultural expectations of the adolescent life-phase. Within this wider cultural context, adolescence is generally viewed as a transitional life-phase between childhood and adulthood (Offer, Ostrov, Howard and Atkinson 1988), when adolescents are struggling to construct their identities both as separate individuals and in relation to others' social expectations (Erikson 1968). This prevailing conceptualization of adolescence suggests that parenthood is not an appropriate role for adolescents, and thus many adolescent mothers may experience difficulties in integrating the role of motherhood into their identities and future life plans (Raeff 1994). In addition, insofar as adolescents are focusing on constructing their identities, they may be relatively self-oriented and less likely than older mothers to view their children as interaction partners. Adolescent mothers may also be less likely than older mothers to consider their children's perspectives.

At the same time, however, the experience of young motherhood may be different for some adolescent mothers in relation to other cultural values and representations. For example, some studies suggest that adolescent motherhood is not necessarily viewed negatively within some American ethnic groups (De Cubas and Field 1984, Wasserman, Brunelli, Rauh and Alvarado 1994). In addition, families of varied ethnic backgrounds who come to accept an adolescent's pregnancy are sources of support to the adolescent mother and her child (Furstenberg Jr., Brooks-Gunn and Chase-Lansdale 1989). It is also now widely recognized that interpersonal connections play a central role in female identity development (Gilligan 1982, Gilligan, Lyons and Hammer 1990), suggesting that motherhood may provide a way for adolescent mothers to establish and maintain a close and long-lasting interpersonal relationship.

It is important to point out that there have certainly been many studies of adolescent motherhood, including research on their interactions with their children, as well as on their ideas about parenting, parent–child relationships and child development (Brooks-Gunn and Chase-Lansdale 1995, Raeff 1994, 1996). In much of this research, age is typically conceptualized as an individual characteristic of the mothers that directly influences their behavior. However, within the current perspective, where individual, social, and cultural factors do not exist in isolation from one another, parental age is taken to be a culturally meaningful characteristic whose significance is derived from cultural life-phase expectations and cultural representations of parenting and parent–child relationships. Thus, adolescent and older mothers may construct different parental ideas and parent–child interactions not because of age differences alone, but because parents of different ages live and act in different positions vis-à-vis varied cultural representations of parenting and parent–child relationships.

These varied representations of parenting and parent–child relationships for adolescent mothers and older mothers may be enacted and reflected in varied ways as adolescent mothers and older mothers construct their parental ideas and interact with their children. Previous research has pointed to the existence of variability among adolescent mothers' ideas (Raeff 1994, 1996), and variability among the adolescent mothers' interactions with their children is expected because variability characterizes the adolescent life-phase. Such variability is also expected because adolescents are taking on the maternal role in relation to varied, sometimes conflicting, cultural representations of young motherhood. In contrast, similarities among the older mothers are likely to characterize their parental ideas, as well as their interactions with their children. Thus, one pattern of parental ideas and parent–child interactions is likely to characterize the older mothers and their children, whereas several patterns may be characteristic of the adolescent mothers and their children.

Participants and procedure

Data from twelve primiparous adolescent mothers and their children, and nine primiparous older mothers and their children will be presented. The adolescent mothers were between sixteen and twenty years old (M = seventeen years), and none of them had completed high school when their children were born. Their children were five boys and seven girls between twelve and nineteen months old

(M = fifteen months). All the adolescent mothers were on welfare, and they all lived with their children in various living arrangements. That is, six lived in their parental homes; two lived with their children's fathers; three lived in supervised housing; and one lived alone. Eleven of the adolescent mother–child pairs were participants in school-based care programs designed to help the mothers finish high school or earn their high school equivalency diplomas. One adolescent mother was in the process of entering an equivalency program. Although the ethnic backgrounds of the adolescent mothers were not straightforward, all were either born in the United States or acculturated. That is, five were European-American; one had a European-American mother and a father of Puerto Rican heritage; one was African-American; two had African-American fathers and European-American mothers; two had parents of Puerto Rican heritage, were born in the United States, and English was their primary language; and one came with her mother to the United States from Puerto Rico at the age of four, and her primary language was English. Despite their ethnic heterogeneity, all the adolescent mothers were constructing their parental ideas and modes of parent–child interactions in relation to the common adolescent cultural context discussed above.

All the older mothers had completed high school prior to having children, and they ranged in age from twenty-two to thirty-nine years old (M = twenty-seven years). Eight were European-American, and one had a European-American mother and African-American father. Their children were five boys and four girls between twelve and nineteen months old (M = fourteen months). To match the adolescent mothers in terms of expected education and income as much as possible, none of the older mothers had completed more than two years of college; one was a homemaker; five were employed in unskilled jobs; and three were receiving welfare. All of the older mothers lived with their children in various living arrangements. That is, one was separated from her husband, the child's father, and lived alone; three were married to and living with their children's fathers; two were unmarried and living with their children's fathers; and three lived alone.

All of the mother–child pairs came to a university child study area for two sessions on two separate days. Videotaped observations of the mothers and their children while they played with a set of age-appropriate toys that were provided for them were conducted. The mothers and children were told to play together as they would normally. In addition, semi-structured interviews were conducted with the mothers. The interviews covered a wide range of issues that focused on the mothers' experiences of motherhood and how they conceptualized their responsibilities as mothers (see also Raeff 1996).

Play interactions

Based on the position that interpersonal interactions are mutually constructed and regulated, the play interactions were coded continuously according to dyadic states that characterize both the mother's and the child's behavior in relation to each other. The minimum duration of a dyadic state was set at two seconds, and five dyadic states were analyzed (see Table 2.1).

For each dyad, the proportion of time spent in each dyadic state was calculated. Because all of the dyads spent most of their time in states of Mutual Engagement, Partial Engagement, and Mother Attending, the interaction results will be presented in terms of these three dyadic states.

Reliability for these categories was obtained with two independent judges. Inter-rater agreement for second-by-second coding of the dyadic states was 93.83%. The inter-rater reliability for the beginnings and endings of these dyadic states were 94.4% and 92.5% respectively.

As a group, the adolescent mother–child dyads spent a mean of 40.7% of their time in Mutual Engagement. They spent a mean of 29.2% of their time in Mother Attending, and a mean of 18.7% of their time in Partial Engagement. Although a preponderance of Mutual Engagement characterized the adolescent mother–child pairs as a group, individual variability among them was also evident. That is, six of the dyads spent most time in Mutual Engagement; four dyads spent most time in Mother Attending; one dyad spent most time in Partial Engagement; and one dyad spent equal time in Mother Attending and Partial Engagement.

During the play interactions, the older mother–child dyads typically spent most of their time in Mother Attending (M = 57.6%). They spent a mean of 24.3% of their time in Mutual Engagement, and a mean of 13.7% of their time in Partial Engagement. As expected, variability was not characteristic of this group insofar as all nine of the older mother–child pairs spent most of their play time in Mother Attending.

Based on their play interactions, the individual mother–child dyads were also grouped according to the dyadic state in which they spent most time, and two main interaction groupings emerged. That is, one grouping was made up of six adolescent mother–child dyads who spent most of their play interaction time in

Table 2.1 Definitions of dyadic state categories

Dyadic state	Definition
MUTUAL ENGAGEMENT	Mother and child are mutually engaged in an object-mediated or interpersonal activity.
PARTIAL ENGAGEMENT	Mother and child are negotiating or pursuing different interests as they simultaneously partially attend to one another.
MOTHER ATTENDING	The mother focally attends to the child who is engaged in his/her own activity.
CHILD ATTENDING	The child focally attends to the mother who is engaged in her own activity.
SEPARATE ACTIVITIES	Mother and child are not attending to one another, and each is engaged in a different activity on his/her own.

the dyadic state of Mutual Engagement. A second grouping was made up of four
adolescent mother–child dyads and all nine older mother–child dyads who spent
most of their play interaction time in the dyadic state of Mother Attending. The
remaining two adolescent mother–child dyads' play interaction times were
characterized in different ways, i.e. one spent most time in Partial Engagement
and one spent most time in Partial Engagement and Mother Attending.

Interviews

All of the interviews were transcribed and then coded according to thematic units
that were further subdivided into various dimensions. For current purposes, the
following three thematic units and their dimensions were analyzed:

1   *Conceptions of the child*

   (a)   The child as a being *on* whom one acts: the child is viewed as someone
         who requires mostly physical caretaking.
         Interview example: "I give her baths. And change her diapers. I buy her
         clothes. I buy her diapers."
   (b)   The child as a being *with* whom one interacts: the child is viewed as
         someone with whom one can establish an interpersonal relationship.
         Interview example: "We do things. We have fun together. We play a lot.
         And he always likes me to read to him."

2   *Conceptions of parenting responsibilities*

   (a)   Child-centered: taking the child's perspective into account.
         Interview example: "No matter what you're doing. No matter what you
         think you have to do. You know that if the baby wants you, it's more
         important than what you're doing."
   (b)   Not child-centered: not considering the child's perspective.
         Interview example: "It's not easy being a mother at a young age. 'Cause
         you have to go to school, you have to wake up early and take a shower
         and do your hair. 'Cause that's a girl's best thing in life, to do your hair."

3   *Conceptions of the future*

   (a)   Inclusion: including the child in discussions of future aspirations.
         Interview example: "One thing in the future, I want to be higher up in
         my job. To be able to have a house. Uhh. Save money, which I'm doin'
         right now for him [her son] for college."
   (b)   Exclusion: excluding the child from discussions of future aspirations.
         Interview example: "I want a house. I want to have a nice job. I want to
         drive around in a nice car. That's just about it."

Inter-rater reliability for these thematic unit categories was 88.9%.
   Individual mothers' statements for the "conceptions of the child" thematic unit
were proportionalized to yield an overall classification of On or With for each

mother. As expected, and in keeping with previous research, the adolescent mothers tended to express more varied ideas about motherhood and their relationships with their children than did the older mothers. Within group analyses showed that five of the adolescent mothers tended to view their children as beings on whom they act, and seven tended to view their children as people with whom they interact. There was no variability among the older mothers as all nine of the older mothers tended to view their children as people with whom they interact.

With respect to the Conceptions of Parenting Responsibilities thematic unit, the older mothers were more likely than the adolescent ones to take their children's perspectives into account. Individual mothers' statements were proportionalized to yield an overall classification of Child-Centered or Not Child-Centered for each mother. Based on these individual analyses, eight adolescent mothers were classified as Child-Centered and four adolescent ones were classified as Not Child-Centered. In contrast, all nine older mothers were classified as Child-Centered.

When considering their future aspirations, eight adolescent mothers and all nine of the older ones included their children as they discussed their futures. Four adolescent mothers focused exclusively on themselves, and did not mention their children as they discussed their future plans.

Based on these three thematic unit dimensions, the adolescent mothers and older mothers were grouped individually according to constellations of parental ideas that emerged from the data. For the sake of clarity and brevity, these thematic unit dimensions of parents' ideas will be referred to as On/With, Child-Centered/Not Child-Centered, and Inclusion/Exclusion. One main constellation of parental ideas, "With, Child-Centered, Inclusion", characterized the ideas of six adolescent mothers and all nine older mothers. A second constellation of parental ideas included three adolescent mothers whose ideas were categorized as "On, Not Child-Centered, Exclusion". The remaining three adolescent mothers expressed parental ideas that were categorized as "On, Not Child-Centered, Inclusion", "With, Child-Centered, Exclusion", and "On, Child-Centered, Inclusion" respectively.

Linking parents' ideas and parent–child interactions

Three main combinations or patterns of parental ideas constellations and play interaction groupings were identified, and they are depicted in Table 2.2. The first pattern is made up of five adolescent mother–child pairs who spent most of their play time in Mutual Engagement. The parental ideas for these adolescent mothers were classified as "With, Child-Centered, Inclusion". A second pattern is made up of two adolescent mother–child pairs who spent most of their play time in Mother Attending, and these mothers' ideas were classified as "On, Not Child-Centered, Exclusion". The third pattern is made up of all nine older mother–child pairs and one adolescent mother–child pair who spent most of their play time in Mother Attending, and these mothers' ideas were classified as "With, Child-Centered, Inclusion".

Table 2.2 Combinations of play interactions and parents' ideas

Dyads	Characteristic mode of play interactions	Parents' ideas constellation
5 adolescent mother–child dyads	Mutual Engagement	With, Child-Centered, Inclusion
2 adolescent mother–child dyads	Mother Attending	On, Not Child-Centered, Exclusion
9 older mother–child dyads 1 adolescent mother–child dyad	Mother Attending	With, Child-Centered, Inclusion

At first glance, these combinations of parent–child interactions and constellations of parental ideas seem to indicate that they are related haphazardly insofar as one interaction grouping may be related to different parental ideas constellations. That is, for the adolescent mother–child pairs, Mother Attending occurred in conjunction with the "On, Not Child-Centered, Exclusion" constellation of parental ideas. For the older mother–child pairs, Mother Attending also occurred in conjunction with the "With, Child-Centered, Inclusion" constellations of parental ideas. The findings also reveal that, for the adolescent mother–child pairs, the parental ideas constellation "With, Child-Centered, Inclusion" occurred in conjunction with a preponderance of Mutual Engagement, as well as with a preponderance of Mother Attending during the play interactions of the older mother–child pairs. From a traditional approach to the inter-relations between parents' ideas and parent–child interactions, these combinations seem to be inconsistent. Indeed, one would be hard pressed to predict the structuring of parent–child interactions based on knowledge of parental ideas or vice versa. However, the current interpretive approach provides a way to understand these combinations of parental ideas and parent–child interactions as coherent patterns of culturally meaningful activity by considering them in terms of the cultural context in which they are particularized.

The Mutual Engagement play grouping in relation to the parental ideas constellation "With, Child-Centered, Inclusion" is comprised only of adolescent mother–child dyads. This combination of parental ideas and parent–child interactions may be viewed as constituting a pattern of culturally meaningful activity that reflects the adolescent mothers' orientations towards establishing interpersonal connections with their children. These mothers who treat their children as interaction partners, who consider their children's perspectives, and who include their children in their life plans, are also adolescents in the midst of making the transition from childhood to adulthood. Thus, establishing Mutual Engagement with a young child may be a way of enacting the more childlike aspects of this transition while at the same time reflecting the adolescent mothers' abilities to think beyond themselves as they care for and nurture their children. The co-occurrence of Mutual Engagement and "With, Child-Centered, Inclusion" also reflects cultural representations that adolescence is a transitional life-phase of identity construction during which establishing interpersonal relationships and caring for others is an important part of female identity development.

Mother Attending during play time, in relation to the parental ideas constellation "On, Not Child-Centered, Exclusion," is also composed only of adolescent mothers. Its coherence or unity as a pattern of culturally meaningful activity can be interpreted as reflecting and enacting cultural representations of adolescence that do not encourage adolescent motherhood. The preponderance of Mother Attending, in conjunction with this constellation of parental ideas for adolescent mother–child pairs, reflects the self-focus of adolescence. It further reflects disengagement between the mothers and their children, as the mothers struggle to handle motherhood and constructing their identities during a life-phase that is typically deemed culturally incompatible with parenthood.

Mother Attending during play time was also related to the "With, Child-Centered, Inclusion" constellation of parental ideas mostly for the older mothers and their children. This combination of mother–child interactions and parental ideas reflects cultural representations of parenthood as a permanent adult role that involves establishing and maintaining a fulfilling interpersonal relationship with another individual. As a pattern of culturally meaningful activity, this combination also reflects the enactment of American cultural values regarding the importance of both establishing interpersonal connections with and fostering independence in children who are treated as separate individuals with their own points of view and goals.

The finding that Mother Attending occurs in tandem with two different parental ideas constellations, and that the "With, Child-Centered, Inclusion" parental ideas constellation occurs in tandem with two parent–child interaction groupings, suggests that the meaning of each mode of activity is not necessarily fixed. In this way, Mother Attending is an aspect of different patterns of culturally meaningful activity, and thus takes on a different meaning as part of a larger whole. Similarly, the meaning of the parental ideas constellation "With, Child-Centered, Inclusion" is not fixed. In relation to adolescent mother–child interactions and in relation to older mother–child interactions, this constellation of parental ideas is part of different patterns of culturally meaningful activity, reflecting different cultural representations of parenting and parent–child relationships. Thus, the current interpretive approach points to how some modes of human activity can take on a new significance in relation to other modes of activity, and in relation to cultural representations of being and behaving.

It is important to note that four adolescent mother–child dyads could not be categorized according to the play interaction groupings and parental ideas constellations just discussed. One adolescent mother–child pair spent most of their play time in Partial Engagement, and the mother's ideas were categorized as "On, Not Child-Centered, Exclusion". Another adolescent mother–child pair split most of their play time between Partial Engagement and Mother Attending, and the mother's ideas were classified as "On, Not-Child Centered, Inclusion". One adolescent mother–child dyad spent most of their play time in Mutual Engagement, and the mother's ideas were classified as "On, Child-Centered,

Inclusion". Finally, one adolescent mother–child pair spent most of their play time in Mother Attending, and this mother's ideas were classified as "With, Child-Centered, Exclusion." In effect, the difficulty in characterizing these dyads may constitute another pattern of culturally meaningful activity that can be interpreted as reflecting or enacting cultural representations that the adolescent life-phase is transitional and characterized by variability. As these dyads continue to construct their modes of interaction, and as the mothers continue to construct their identities, they may eventually come to resemble the other adolescent mother–child pairs. Longitudinal research is required to clarify how the ongoing construction of parent–child interactions and parental ideas are intertwined to constitute changing patterns of culturally meaningful activity.

As children interact with their parents, the patterns of culturally meaningful activity elucidated in this study constitute part of their developmental experiences, and provide them with different opportunities for individual development. By understanding the culturally constituted meaning of aspects of children's developmental experiences, we can, in turn, make better inferences about the varied expectations that the children of adolescent and older mothers may have for the structuring of interpersonal interactions and relationships. For example, as we have seen, the occurrence of Mother Attending takes on a different meaning in conjunction with different constellations of parents' ideas, and thus is part of a different developmental context for the adolescent mothers' children and for the older mothers' children. Thus it is likely that even though both groups of children participated in parent–child interactions that are characterized by a preponderance of Mother Attending, they might have different expectations regarding the availability and consideration of social partners. More research is required to discern how children construe these varied developmental experiences in terms of individual, social and cultural processes in different activity settings over time.

In addition, longitudinal research to discern changes in parents' ideas and the structuring of parent–child interactions would provide important information regarding the ongoing dynamics of the two modes of activity in and of themselves. Furthermore, such longitudinal research would also elucidate the changing dynamics of their co-occurrences, and the patterns of culturally meaningful activity that they constitute. Continuing to investigate parents' ideas and the structuring of parent–child interactions in relation to cultural representations of parenting and parent–child relationships will also further our understanding of how culture shapes individual and social processes, as well as how individual and social processes contribute to the ongoing dynamics of cultural change.

The current interpretive approach also points to varied other directions for future research that have implications for the interrelations among individual, social and cultural processes in development. For example, it should prove useful to investigate the intersecting roles of varied individual, social and cultural processes in the construction of parents' ideas and the structuring of parent–child interactions more precisely. Although there is a vast amount of research on these issues, many studies of parent–child interactions tend to treat individual, social and cultural factors separately, as they are designed to investigate the effects of "individual" parental variables (e.g. maternal depression, parental marital status) on parent–child interactions. Similarly, some research in this area has focused on how culture shapes the construction of different parental ideas and modes of parent–child interaction. However, less attention is then given to how cultural processes operate in conjunction with individual and social processes, as parents actively construct their parental ideas and interact with their children. A promising approach to understanding the intersection among individual, social and cultural processes involves explicating how individual reasoning processes operate as parents actively construct their parental ideas in relation to cultural representations that are enacted through social interactions (Valsiner and Litvinovic 1996).

The current interpretive approach provides a way to make sense of some of the complexities of parents' ideas and the structuring of parent–child interactions. It also facilitates understanding the cultural significance of different combinations of parental ideas and parent–child interaction groupings. An interpretive approach further points to how the co-occurrence of parents' ideas and parent–child interactions can be meaningful and coherent, even if parents' ideas and the structuring of parent–child interactions are not statistically correlated or predictive of one another. Insofar as there are different types of parental ideas and different dimensions of parent–child interactions, it may prove useful to synthesize an interpretive approach with traditional approaches that focus on correlating specific parental ideas with concomitantly specific dimensions of parent–child interactions. Ultimately, the promises of this area of inquiry are likely to be realized through approaches that account for individual, social, and cultural complexities, as well as for the ongoing dynamics of parents' ideas and the structuring of parent–child interactions.

Acknowledgements

I gratefully thank the mothers and children who participated in this study. And I thank Cristina Ramirez and Angela Wiley for their reliability help. Most of all I am deeply indebted to Ina Č. Užgiris, without whom the ideas expressed in this chapter would never have been realized. For me, her simultaneously patient and challenging guidance serves as an ongoing foundation for trying to understand the complexities of human culture, behavior, and development.

References

Ajzen, I. (1996) "The Directive Influence of Attitudes on Behavior" in Gollwitzer, P. M. and Bargh, J. A. (eds.) *The Psychology of Action*. New York: The Guilford Press.

Brooks-Gunn, J. and Chase-Lansdale, P. L. (1995) "Adolescent Parenthood" in Bornstein, M. (ed.) *Handbook of Parenting, vol. 3*.

D'Andrade, R. G. (1984) "Cultural Meaning Systems" in Shweder, R. A. and LeVine, R. A. (eds.) *Culture Theory*. Cambridge: Cambridge University Press.

De Cubas, M. and Field, T. (1984) "Teaching Interactions of Black and Cuban Teenage Mothers and Their Infants", *Early Child Development and Care, 16*: 41–56.

Elias, M. and Ubriaco, M. (1986) "Linking Parental Beliefs to Children's Social Competence: Toward a Cognitive Behavioral Assessment Model" in Ashmore, R. D. and Brodzinsky, M. (eds.) *Thinking About the Family: Views of Parents and Children.* Hillsdale, NJ: Lawrence Erlbaum Associates.

Erikson, E. H. (1968) *Identity: Youth and Crisis.* New York: W. W. Norton.

Fogel, A. (1993) *Developing Through Relationships.* Chicago: University of Chicago Press.

Furstenberg, F. F., Jr., Brooks-Gunn, J. and Chase-Lansdale, L. (1989) "Teenaged Pregnancy and Childbearing", *American Psychologist, 44*: 313–320.

Geertz, C. (1973) *The Interpretation of Cultures.* New York: Basic Books.

Gilligan, C. (1982) *In a Different Voice.* Cambridge: Harvard University Press.

Gilligan, C., Lyons, N. P. and Hammer, T. J. (1990) *Making Connections.* Cambridge, MA: Harvard University Press.

Goodnow, J. J. (1985) "Change and Variation in Ideas about Childhood and Parenting" in Sigel, I. E. (ed.) *Parental Belief Systems*, pp. 235–270. Hillsdale, NJ: Lawrence Erlbaum Associates.

—— (1988) "Parents' Ideas, Actions, and Feelings: Models and Methods from Developmental and Social Psychology", *Child Development, 59*: 286–320.

—— (1995) "Parents' Knowledge and Expectations" in Bornstein, M. (ed.) *Handbook of Parenting, vol. 3.*

Goodnow, J. J. and Collins, W. A. (1990) *Development According to Parents.* Hillsdale, NJ: Lawrence Erlbaum Associates.

Hampshire, S. (1959/1983) *Thought and Action.* Notre Dame, Indiana: University of Notre Dame Press.

Harkness, S. and Super, C. M. (eds.) (1996) *Parents' Cultural Belief Systems.* New York: The Guilford Press.

Hays, S. (1996) *The Cultural Contradictions of Motherhood.* New Haven: Yale University Press.

Holden, G. W. (1995) "Parental Attitudes Towards Childrearing" in Bornstein, M. (ed.) *Handbook of Parenting, vol. 3.*

Holden, G. W. and Edwards, L. A. (1989) "Parental Attitudes Toward Childrearing: Instruments, Issues, and Implications", *Psychological Bulletin, 106*: 29–58.

Kohn, M. L. (1963) "Social Class and Parent–Child Relationships: An Interpretation", *The American Journal of Sociology, 68*: 471–480.

LeVine, R. A. (1984) "Properties of Culture: An Ethnographic View" in Shweder, R. A. and LeVine, R. A. (eds.) *Culture Theory.* Cambridge: Cambridge University Press.

Lightfoot, C. and Valsiner, J. (1992). "Parental Belief Systems Under the Influence: Social Guidance of the Construction of Personal Cultures" in Sigel, I. E., McGillicuddy-DeLisi, A. V. and Goodnow, J. J. (eds.) *Parental Belief Systems: The Psychological Consequences for Children.* Hillsdale, NJ: Lawrence Erlbaum Associates.

McGillicuddy-DeLisi, A. V. (1982) "Parental Beliefs About Developmental Processes", *Human Development, 25*: 192–200.

McGillicuddy-DeLisi, A. V. and Sigel, I. E. (1995) "Parental Beliefs" in Bornstein, M. (ed.) *Handbook of Parenting, vol. 3.*

Miller, S. A. (1988) "Parents' Beliefs about Children's Cognitive Development", *Child Development, 59*: 259–285.

Mills, R. S. L. and Rubin, K. H. (1992) "A Longitudinal Study of Maternal Beliefs About Children's Social Behaviors", *Merrill-Palmer Quarterly, 38*: 494–512.

Murphey, D. A. (1992) "Constructing the Child: Relations Between Parents' Beliefs and Child Outcomes", *Developmental Review, 12*: 199–232.

Offer, D., Ostrov, E. Howard, K. I. and Atkinson, R. (1988) *The Teenage World.* New York: Plenum.

Raeff, C. (1994) "Viewing Adolescent Mothers on Their Own Terms. Linking Self-Conceptualization and Adolescent Motherhood", *Developmental Review, 14*: 215–244.

— (1996) "A Cultural Analysis of Maternal Self-Conceptions", *Journal of Applied Developmental Psychology, 17*: 271–306.

— (1997a) "Individuals in Relationships: Cultural Values, Children's Social Interactions, and the Development of an American Individualistic Self", *Developmental Review, 17*: 205–238.

— (2000) "European-American Parents' Ideas About Their Toddlers' Independence and Interdependence", *Journal of Applied Developmental Psychology, 21*: 183–205.

Rogoff, B. (1990) *Apprenticeship in Thinking.* New York: Oxford University Press.

— (1995) "Observing Sociocultural Activity on Three Planes: Participatory Appropriation, Guided Participation, and Apprenticeship" in Wertsch, J. V., Rio, P. D. and Alvarez A. (eds.) *Sociocultural Studies of Mind.* Cambridge: Cambridge University Press.

Searle, J. R. (1983) *Intentionality.* Cambridge: Cambridge University Press.

Shweder, R. A. (1990) "Cultural Psychology – What Is It?" in Stigler, J. W., Shweder, R. A. and Herdt, G. (eds.) *Cultural Psychology.* Cambridge: Cambridge University Press.

Shweder, R. A., Jensen, L. A. and Goldstein, W. M. (1995) "Who Sleeps by Whom Revisited: A Method for Extracting the Moral Goods Implicit in Practice", *New Directions for Child Development, 67*: 21–39.

Sigel, I. E. (1985) "A Conceptual Analysis of Beliefs" in Sigel, I. E. (ed.) *Parental Belief Systems.* Hillsdale, NJ: Lawrence Erlbaum Associates.

— (ed.) (1985) *Parental Belief Systems.* Hillsdale, NJ: Lawrence Erlbaum Associates.

Sigel, I. E., McGillicuddy-DeLisi, A. V. and Goodnow, J. J. (eds.) (1992*). Parental Belief Systems.* Hillsdale, NJ: Lawrence Erlbaum Associates.

Užgiris, I. Č. (1996) "Together and Apart: The Enactment of Values in Infancy" in Reed, E. S., Turiel, E. and Brown, T. (eds.) *Values and Knowledge.* Mahwah, NJ: Lawrence Erlbaum Associates.

— (1989) "Infants in Relation: Performers, Pupils, and Partners" in Damon, W. (ed.) *Child Development Today and Tomorrow.* San Francisco: Jossey-Bass.

Valsiner, J. and Litvinovic, G. (1996) "Processes of Generalization in Parental Reasoning" in Harkness, S. and Super, C. M. (eds.) *Parents' Cultural Belief Systems.* New York: The Guilford Press.

Wasserman, G. A., Brunelli, S. A., Rauh, V. A. and Alvarado, L. E. (1994) "The Cultural Context of Adolescent Childrearing in Three Groups of Urban Minority Mothers" in Lamberty, G. and Coll, C. G. (eds.) *Puerto Rican Women and Children.* New York: Plenum.

Wertsch, J. V. (1995) "The Need for Action in Sociocultural Research" in Wertsch, J. V., Rio, P. D. and Alvarez, A. (eds.) *Sociocultural Studies of Mind.* Cambridge: Cambridge University Press.

— (1991) *Voices of the Mind.* Cambridge, MA: Harvard University Press.

3 Environmental chaos, development and parenting across cultures

Theodore D. Wachs and Feyza Çorapçi

With the publication and expansion of Bronfenbrenner's structural model of the environment (Bronfenbrenner 1989, 1999), there has been an increasing recognition by developmental researchers that parent–child transactions are imbedded in a complex hierarchical environmental structure composed of multiple linked, intersecting layers. This structure is documented in Fig. 3.1.

Given existing knowledge on the linked structure of the environment, a critical question is the degree to which developmental outcomes are a function of the intersection of multiple levels of the child's overall environmental context (Wachs 1999). In the present chapter we will address this question with specific reference to the intersection of the proximal social microsystem (e.g. the family) with two other aspects of the environmental context of the child. The first aspect involves the all-too-often overlooked other major domain of the child's microsystem, namely the proximal physical environment. The second aspect involves the cultural macrosystem within which the child's environmental microsystem is nested.

The physical microenvironment: characteristics and consequences

Bronfenbrenner (1989: 227) has defined the microsystem as follows: "A pattern of activities, roles and interpersonal relations experienced by the developing person in a given face-to-face setting with particular physical and material features and containing other persons with distinctive characteristics of temperament, personality and systems of belief".

For the most part, research on the influence of microsystem characteristics has focused on the role of caregiver activities, beliefs and interpersonal relations, as exemplified by the multiple studies on parent–child transactions and children's development (Bradley 1999, Wachs 1992). Far less emphasis has been given to the "physical and material features" of the child's context, which are also an essential feature of Bronfenbrenner's definition of the microsystem (Wohlwill and Heft 1987). Conceptually, three major dimensions appear to define the physical microenvironment: first, *spatial characteristics* as seen in terms of features such as open or closed space or crowding; second, "*affordance*" *characteristics*, such as play materials that promote specific uses; third, "*affordanceless*" environmental features

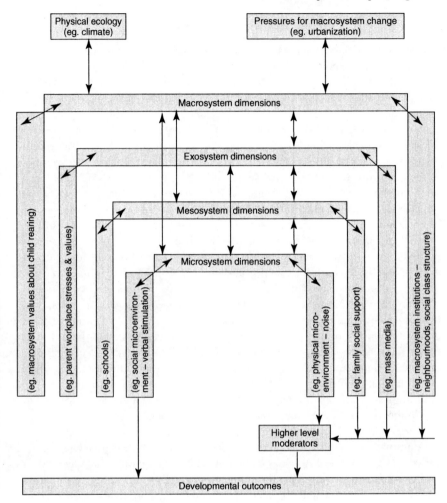

Double headed arrows refer to bidirectional levels of influence across the environment. Single headed arrows refer to direct or mediating influences of the environment upon development.

Figure 3.1 Bronfenbrenner's structural model of the environment

Figure taken from Theodore D. Wachs, *The Nature of Nurture*, p. 41, copyright © Sage: 1992. Reprinted by permission of Sage Publications, Inc.

involving non-specific background stimulation such as noise (Wachs 1992). Research has documented the developmental consequences of variations in both affordance based aspects of the physical environment such as the availability and responsivity of stimulus objects in the child's environment (Bradley *et al.* 1994, Evans, Kliewer and Martin 1991), as well as spatial characteristics such as the proximity of physically dangerous objects or contexts such as open fires (Woodson and da Costa Woodson 1984).

Environmental chaos and development

One aspect of the physical microenvironment that has been of particular interest to environmental researchers is what has been called "environmental chaos" (Matheny *et al.* 1995). Environmental chaos is a summary term encompassing spatial and affordanceless features of the physical microsystem. As defined, environmental chaos refers to microsystem contexts such as the home, day care center or school, which are characterized by high noise levels, high levels of density or crowding, high-context traffic patterns (many people coming and going) and a lack of physical and temporal structure (few regularities or routines in the environment, little is scheduled, nothing has its place, Wachs 1989). It is important to note that even though chaos is considered to be an aspect of the physical microsystem, environmental features summarized under the dimension of environmental chaos include both people and physical characteristics. The rationale for this inclusion is based upon a reconceptualization of what is meant by the physical microsystem, which was originally defined only on the basis of inanimate (object) characteristics (Wohlwill and Heft 1987). Integrating both the spatial and affordanceless dimensions into the classification of environmental domains allowed animate objects such as people to contribute to what was defined as environmental chaos, if the persons in the child's environment were primarily non-responsive to the child's actions and functioned as background rather than focal sources of stimulation (Wachs 1989). Evidence indicating that inanimate, non-responsive, background aspects of the environment (e.g. noise) and animate, non-responsive, background aspects of the environment (e.g. crowding) show similar patterns of relations to parental behavior and child developmental outcomes supports our defining chaos on the basis of both animate and inanimate physical microsystem characteristics (Wachs 1992).

A number of studies have linked microsystem environmental chaos to a variety of problematical developmental outcomes. Examples of these are shown in Table 3.1. For the most part the studies listed in Table 3.1 either relate direct observations of ambient levels of noise and crowding in children's homes to various developmental outcomes (e.g. studies by Cohen, Heft, Matheny and Wachs), or look at performance variability as a function of distance of children's homes or schools from major noise sources such as airports or subway trains (e.g. studies by Bronzaft, Bullinger, Evans and Hambrick-Dixon). However, homes and schools are not the only types of chaotic proximal environments that children encounter. Another microsystem context characterized by chaos and crowded conditions is homeless shelters. Especially, with recent increases in homelessness, the impact of shelter life on children and parents is becoming a growing area of environmental research. While homelessness covaries with a variety of developmental risk factors such as an increased risk for illness and poor nutrition, studies also indicate that high density in shelters contributes to a variety of behavior problems in children including internalizing behavior problems as well as academic problems (Buckner, Bassuk, Weinreb and Brooks 1999).

Table 3.1 Aspects of children's development that are sensitive to environmental chaos

Environmental chaos related to	References
Cognition	
Lower cognitive performance	Gottfried and Gottfried (1984), Wachs, (1979), Wachs, Užgiris and Hunt (1971)
Altered attentional patterns	Cohen, Glass and Singer (1973), Glenn, Nerborne and Tolhurst (1978), Hambrick-Dixon (1988), Heft (1979)
Poor performance on reading or on tasks assessing components of reading skills	Bronzaft and McCarthy (1975), Evans, Hygge and Bullinger (1995), Haines *et al.* (2001), Maxwell and Evans (2000)
Reduced use of communication to gain adult attention	Wachs and Chan (1986)
Temperament	
Greater likelihood of child having a difficult temperament	Matheny and Phillips (2001), Matheny *et al.* (1987), Wachs (1988)
Greater difficulty in maintaining neonatal state control	Als (1992)
Reduced frustration tolerance	Moch-Sibony (1981)
Motivation	
Reduced mastery motivation	Wachs (1987)
Increased risk of learned helplessness	Bullinger *et al.* (1998), Evans *et al.* (1995), Maxwell and Evans (2000)
Behavioral problems	
Increased risk of behavioral disturbance	Maxwell (1996)
Biomedical consequences	
Increased risk of childhood injuries	Matheny (1986)
Increased risk of elevated blood pressure	Evans, Bullinger and Hygge (1998), Evans *et al.* (1995)
Greater cardiovascular reactivity under stress conditions	Johnston-Brooks *et al.* (1998)

Overall, the evidence indicates that one measure of the physical microenvironment, environmental chaos, appears to have a consistent and negative impact upon children's development across a variety of domains. In interpreting the results from Table 3.1, what must be stressed is that the developmental impact of environmental chaos may vary as a function of either individual characteristics or other contextual characteristics. For example, there is a consistent body of evidence indicating that children with difficult temperaments or children with behavior problems may be particularly sensitive to environmental chaos (Langmeier and Matejeck 1975, Loo 1978, Matheny and Phillips 2001, Wachs 1987, Wachs and Gandour 1983). Evidence also suggests that males and females may show different types of reaction patterns when faced with environmental chaos (Evans *et al.* 1998). Contextually, the impact of environmental chaos also may vary depending upon the individual's level of access to non-chaotic environmental contexts (Draper 1973, Fagot 1977, Saegert 1982). In addition, environmental chaos has been found to lead to deterioration of an individual's social support networks, which in turn results in more problematical outcomes for the individual (Evans *et al.* 1989, Lepore, Evans and Schneider 1991). On the other hand, perceived self-control along with high social support appears to reduce the stress of crowding (Sinha and Nayyar 2000). Further, different aspects of environmental chaos also may cumulate to exert a stronger impact upon individual development than aspects of chaos taken in isolation. For example, children from low SES families are found to be significantly more affected by high-density living conditions when family turmoil is high than when family turmoil is relatively low (Evans and Saegert 2000).

Environmental chaos and development in different cultures

For the most part the research findings documented in Table 3.1 have been carried out using children living in Western developed countries. Within the framework of Bronfenbrenner's structural model, as shown in Fig. 3.1, higher-order levels of the environment such as culture can act to moderate the impact of lower-order levels such as microsystem chaos. Data from anthropological studies suggest that there may be culture-specific environmental characteristics that can act to attenuate the impact of environmental chaos (Konner 1977). It is thus essential to ask whether the same pattern of increased risk of developmental problems associated with exposure to a chaotic environment also holds in developing countries or in non-Western cultures.

While research is limited and there are exceptions (Fagot 1977, Liddell 1994), evidence generally indicates similar patterns of findings relating environmental chaos to developmental outcomes in both Western developed and non-Western developing countries. Specifically, aspects of environmental chaos have been negatively associated with measures of cognitive, social or motivational competence in *South Africa* (Goduka, Poole and Aotaki-Phenice 1992, Liddell and Kruger 1987, 1989), *Israel* (Shapiro 1974), *Egypt* (Wachs *et al.* 1993), *India* (Evans *et al.* 1998), and *Nigeria* (Ani and Grantham-McGregor 1998). In addition, in less developed countries measures of environmental chaos have also been found to adversely impact upon children's biological outcomes, such as increased morbidity (Pearce 1996) and higher levels of blood pressure (Evans *et al.* 1998). Going beyond the family environment, research also indicates that Indian children living in more chaotic residential areas are more likely to develop a reduced sense of personal control over their environment (Regani 2000). Given the general consistency of findings across cultures, a second critical question involves understanding what processes act to mediate relations between environmental chaos and children's development.

Processes underlying chaos-development relations

The similarity of findings indicating a consistent and negative influence of environmental chaos upon children's development in both Western and non-Western cultures may be the result of similar underlying cross-cultural process mechanisms. Such process mechanisms mediate how variability in levels of environmental chaos translates into variability in developmental outcomes. Within the terms of this explanatory framework it is critical to assess what these common process mechanisms may be.

Environmental chaos and attention

One process that has been put forward to explain chaos–development relations involves environmental chaos acting to inhibit *either* children's attention to developmentally facilitative aspects of their environment *or* their ability to discriminate meaningful from less meaningful environmental cues (Deutsch 1964, Evans and Cohen 1987). There are a number of studies that report declines in attentional or discriminative capacities as a function of exposure to environmental chaos (Cohen, Glass and Singer 1973, Glenn *et al.* 1978, Heft 1979, Nober and Nober 1975). Although there has been little non-Western research on the chaos–attention hypothesis, studies have found an interactive effect of crowding and nutrition upon measures of alertness in Egyptian toddlers (Rahmanifar *et al.* 1993) and Jamaican schoolchildren (Grantham-McGregor *et al.* 1998). However, there are other studies that report a pattern of complex, not easily interpretable interactions between environmental chaos and type of outcome measure used, test conditions, gender and race (Blue and Vergason 1975, Cohen *et al.* 1986, Hambrick-Dixon 1986, 1988). The complex pattern of interactions reported by some studies suggests that not all of the cross-cultural similarities in developmental consequences associated with exposure to environmental chaos can be attributed solely to fundamental deficits in attentional or discrimination processes. Directly supporting this conclusion Evans and Maxwell (1997) have reported that noise-related decrements in speech perception only partially account for the negative influence of noise upon children's reading performance.

Environmental chaos and parenting

In addition to fundamental deficits in attention or discrimination, there is another proposed explanatory framework for understanding processes underlying the influence of environmental chaos upon child development. Interestingly, this alternative framework is one that would predict that there should be greater cross-cultural differences in the developmental impact of environmental chaos than is currently seen in the literature. We refer here to the hypothesis that environmental chaos acts both to inhibit the occurrence of developmentally facilitative transactions between children and their caregivers, and to promote the occurrence of developmentally inhibiting caregiver–child transactions (Booth 1985, Ekblad 1993, Wachs 1992). Developmentally facilitative transactions are those that promote cognitive or behavioral patterns that are viewed as desirable within a given culture, while developmentally inhibiting transactions are those that promote culturally undesirable patterns. Within this explanatory framework it is the chaos-driven patterns of developmentally facilitative or developmentally inhibiting parent–child transactions that are directly responsible for lower developmental competence.

In terms of its pattern of linkages with facilitative or inhibitory parental behavior patterns environmental chaos may operate in a somewhat different, more bidirectional, way than do other dimensions of the physical environment. Traditionally, outcomes associated with high affordance related object aspects of the physical environment, such as provision of books or age-appropriate play materials, have been viewed as due to caregivers using such objects in developmentally appropriate or inappropriate ways (Sutton-Smith 1986), with little emphasis on how object availability or object characteristics influence the nature of parental behaviors. In contrast, for low affordance aspects of the environment such as environmental chaos, it seems clear that while parental structuring of the environment can accentuate or attenuate the level of environmental chaos, level of environmental chaos in turn can also influence parental behavioral patterns.

Studies shown in Table 3.2 relate measured aspects of the child's physical environment, such as rooms/persons ratio to either child or parent report (e.g. Gove, Hughes and Galle 1979, Saegert 1982) or to directly observed measures of parent–child relations (e.g. Gottfried and Gottfried 1984, Wachs 1993). As seen in Table 3.2, evidence directly supporting the hypothesis that living in chaotic homes adversely influences the pattern of parent–child relations comes from a number of studies done in Western developed countries. Similarly, parents living in chaotic homeless shelters report high levels of distress due to limited privacy, lack of control over their children's daily routine and interference with their discipline style by other residents or staff members (Lindsey 1998).

Why high levels of home chaos act to adversely influence patterns of parent–child transactions is a critical issue for further research. Recently collected evidence on this question from our research program indicates that although home chaos adversely impacts upon some aspects of parental mood and feelings of efficacy, alterations in mood or efficacy do not act to mediate links between chaos and parental behavior (Çorapçi and Wachs, 2002). However, linkages between environmental chaos and patterns of developmentally facilitative or inhibitory parent–child transactions may be mediated by chaos leading to greater levels of family conflict (Saegert 1982), poor marital relations and a greater sense of parental fatigue (Gove *et al.* 1979), greater sensitivity to daily stress (Lepore, Evans and Palasane 1991), lower levels of perceived support (Lepore, Evans and Schneider 1991), or deterioration in cognitive processes such as difficulty in decision-making and attending to social information (Bruins and Barber 2000, Evans, Rhee, Forbes, Allen and Lepore 2000).

Table 3.2 Linkages between environmental chaos and measures of caregiver–child transactions

Linkage patterns	References
Infants and toddlers	
Environmental chaos associated with caregivers who are:	
Less responsive, less involved	Çorapçi and Wachs (2002)
Less vocally stimulating, less likely to show or demonstrate object and more likely to interfere with exploration.	Gottfried and Gottfried (1984), Hannan and Luster (1990), Matheny *et al.* (1995), Ricciuti and Thomas (1990), Shapiro (1974), Wachs (1986, 1989, 1993), Wachs and Camli (1991), Wachs and Desai (1993)
Preschool and school-age children	
Environmental chaos associated with caregivers who are:	
More likely to use physical punishment and less likely to monitor child's activities.	Booth (1985), Gove *et al.* (1979), Saegert (1982)

Does culture moderate chaos–parent relations?

While there is consistent evidence from studies done in developed Western countries showing a negative impact of home chaos upon quality of parent–child relations there are a number of reasons to assume that such relations may be moderated by cultural influences. Culturally driven parental norms, preferences, coping strategies, or values and belief systems can all act to influence the degree to which parents or caregivers perceive their environment as chaotic or not (Baldassare 1981, Evans *et al.* 2000, Gillis, Richard and Hagan 1986, Jain 1987, Stokols 1978). For example, whether high levels of sound are viewed as aversive noise can vary as a function of culturally based preferences for different types of sounds (Leff 1978) or for preferred levels of exposure to audiovisual stimulation (Anderson 1972, Boykin 1978). It has also been suggested that after a certain level of person density has been reached further crowding will have little impact on caregiver or child behaviors (Liddell 1994). Some cultures may exceed this density threshold. Thus, families who live in densely populated cities in non-Western cultures such as Hong Kong or India typically have households where there are 2–4 persons per room; such density levels would be highly unlikely for most families living in North America (Evans *et al.* 1998, Fuller, Edwards, Vorakitphokatorn and Sermsri 1993).

Studies have also identified a number of culturally driven coping strategies that can act to moderate the impact of environmental chaos upon family functioning. Culturally based traditions of extended families living in one household can serve to promote the availability of multiple caregivers for young children, such as older siblings or grandparents (Munroe and Munroe 1971, Valsiner 1989, Whiting 1977). Other culturally based "buffering" strategies that have been identified include an emphasis on interpersonal cooperation and reduced public display of emotionality (Anderson 1972, Hwang 1979), as well as implicit "rules" governing space utilization and social organization (Altman and Chemers 1980). Evidence further indicates that while density can be objectively assessed using indices such as rooms to people ratio, feelings of being crowded in dense environments are subjective and appear to depend upon culturally based social values about the appropriate level of physical distance between people (Jain 1987, Merry 1987). Thus, while perceptions of being more crowded are related to greater physiological reactivity, the relation between perception and physiology does not appear to reflect a simple linear function (Schaeffer *et al.* 1988)

Given the above data we are faced with a paradox. Similar patterns of relations are found between environmental chaos and children's development in Western and non-Western cultures. For Western cultures one validated explanatory framework involves the detrimental impact of environmental chaos upon caregiver–child transactions, perhaps as a function of chaos leading to greater family conflict or poorer parental emotional well-being (Evans and Saegert 2000). However, other evidence has identified a number of culturally driven factors that could potentially act to moderate the impact of environmental chaos upon parent–child transactions, family conflict or parental emotional well-being. The operation of such moderators would lead to the prediction that we should find different linkage patterns between environmental chaos and child development in different cultures. As discussed above this prediction generally has not been confirmed. Is it possible that the impact of environmental chaos upon family and adult functioning is consistent across cultures, in spite of different social norms, coping strategies and beliefs? Evans (personal communication, April 2000) has suggested that while there are well documented cross-cultural differences in preferred personal space and perceptions of crowding, these differential preferences and perceptions may not directly translate into individual behavioral differences. Supporting this suggestion, evidence indicates that among the different ethnic groups in the United States, Vietnamese-Americans and Mexican-Americans have a higher threshold for perceiving their home as crowded in comparison to Anglo-Americans and African-Americans. However, the difference in perceptions of crowding did not implicate tolerance to crowding. Higher household density was found to be related to higher psychological distress among individuals from these ethnic groups, independent of their acculturation level (Evans, Lepore and Allen 2000).

If cross-cultural differences in perception of chaos do not automatically translate into different behavioral patterns this suggests a possible explanation for the paradox we have described above. Specifically, if a similar pattern of linkages between environmental chaos and parent–child transactions, family functioning or parental emotional well-being can be found in both non-Western developing countries and Western developed countries, this would go a long way towards understanding why there are similar patterns of relations between chaos and children's development across cultures. We turn to this question in the next section of this chapter.

Chaos and parent–child transactions in different cultures

Research investigating the influence of environmental chaos upon patterns of parent–child transactions in non-Western countries is relatively sparse. Table 3.3 presents the major studies relating environmental chaos (primarily high-density living conditions) to patterns of parent–child transactions in non-Western countries. What is most obvious from the pattern of results shown in Table 3.3 is the importance of the age of the child as a potential moderator.

As shown in Table 3.3 evidence indicates that African infants in high-density households were held more often, and were responded to more quickly and positively than were infants in low-density households. Underlying this pattern of relations is the fact that although mothers in high-density African households were generally not available to the baby, the mothers' lack of involvement was more than compensated for by the high rate of caretaking activities performed by older siblings in these households.

The pattern of older sibs acting to buffer infants in the family against the detrimental impact of environmental chaos upon mother–child transactions does not appear to extend beyond the infancy period. As also shown in Table 3.3, studies relating environmental chaos to quality of parenting with preschool and school-age children in non-Western countries are consistent with results from Western developed countries, in terms of indicating an association of environmental chaos with harsher parental discipline and lower parental

Table 3.3 Effects of environmental chaos on caregiver–child transactions in non-Western cultures

Environmental chaos associated with caregivers who are:	Subjects	References
Infants		
More responsive	Kalahari hunter-gatherers in *Southwest Africa*, Logoli households in *East Africa*	Konner (1977), Munroe and Munroe (1971)
More likely to show physical contact	Kalahari hunter-gatherers in *Southwest Africa*	Konner (1977)
Preschool and school-age children		
More likely to use discipline or highly controlling behavior	Children in *Egypt* Families in *Bangkok* Families in *India*	Youssef et al. (1998) Fuller et al. (1993) Evans et al. (1998), Whiting and Edwards (1988)
Less likely to monitor child's activities	Residents in *Hong Kong*	Mitchell (1971)
Less likely to express warmth and hostility	Multiple societies in non-Western cultures	Minturn and Lambert (1964)
More likely to be permissive	Multiple societies in non-Western cultures	Minturn and Lambert (1964), Munroe and Munroe (1980)

monitoring. The lower levels of warmth and the greater permissiveness shown by parents in chaotic households in non-Western countries (see Table 3.3) may be analogous to the lower parental involvement reported in studies relating environmental chaos to parent–child transactions in Western populations. The one area where consistency does not appear involves the lower levels of parental hostility in more chaotic homes in non-Western cultures which, up to the present, has not been reported as occurring in studies in Western developed countries. There does not appear to be an obvious explanation for this difference in findings.

Two interpretations have been made regarding the pattern of relations between environmental chaos and parent–child transactions in non-Western or developing countries. Minturn and Lambert (1964) have suggested that a policy of laissez-faire rather than emotional control differentiates multifamily households from nuclear households in non-Western cultures. The lower levels of parental hostility and warmth referred to in Table 3.3 may be viewed as an index of lower parental involvement in more chaotic homes. In line with the laissez-faire view, Mitchell (1971) has suggested that high household density in Hong Kong reduces the amount of surveillance parents have over their children. Mitchell further argues that lack of supervision by parents might be the cause of many social problems of youth in high-density slum communities around the world.

Alternatively, Insel and Lindgren (1978) have concluded that in crowded households *authoritarian* child-rearing values dominate. These authors suggest that behavior and adjustment problems that are more prevalent in overcrowded families are more likely to be controlled by parental strictness. As shown in Table 3.3, studies in Egypt, Thailand and India (Evans *et al.* 1998) have yielded results that are consistent with Insel and Lindgren's hypothesis. Within this framework, as a result of greater parental strictness, parent–child conflict emerges as a common mediator across cultures to explain the negative effects of chaotic environments on children's well-being (Evans *et al.* 1998).

While these two interpretations appear contradictory, in reality the evidence seems to suggest that parental laissez-faire permissiveness and authoritarian values may *coexist* in chaotic homes in both Western and non-Western cultures. As seen in Tables 3.2 and 3.3, chaotic home environments are associated with lower parental involvement and monitoring, as well as with higher parental discipline and interference. An important question is what maintains the coexistence of such radically different parental rearing styles in chaotic homes? Although little data are available on this question, observations of family patterns in crowded households suggest that there is a low tolerance for child behavior that disrupts family routines, such as aggression between playmates (Kagitcibasi 1988). Based on what is clearly a limited database we offer the following speculative hypothesis. High levels of ambient chaos act to reduce the ability of caregivers to support or monitor their children's activities. Thus, in chaotic homes in both Western and non-Western cultures, caregivers will be uninvolved, as long as children's actions do not disturb ongoing family activities and thus increase the level of chaos. When children's actions do disrupt family functioning the caregiver's response is more likely to involve overly punitive reactions and authoritarian discipline as a means of restoring order and reducing both chaos and the stress associated with increased chaos.

Environmental chaos and adult emotional well-being

Table 3.4 presents the studies on environmental chaos and its effects on adult well-being in non-Western cultures. Integrating the results of studies done in Thailand, Japan, India and Bangladesh there seems to be considerable agreement that objective crowding (persons per room) produces psychological distress through subjective crowding, specifically through the perception or experience of being crowded. Psychological distress includes unhappiness, irritability, and heightened vulnerability to the demands of minor social hassles. As also shown in Table 3.4, chaos-induced adult psychological distress can also result from the breakdown of social support systems and a lack of perceived control. These results suggest a common mediating process in both Western and non-Western cultures underlying the relation of environmental chaos to quality of parenting and to problematic developmental outcomes for children. A conceptual framework integrating evidence on environmental chaos, caregiver emotional well-being, caregiver–child relations and child outcomes is shown in Fig. 3.2. As seen in Fig. 3.2, high levels of environmental chaos lead to increased levels of caregiver stress. How this increased level of caregiver stress translates into caregiver–child rearing patterns depends partly on the behavior shown by the child, which also influences patterns of caregiver reactivity. Parental behavior patterns in turn directly (low involvement) or indirectly (harsh discipline) feed back onto ambient levels of home chaos.

Culturally sensitive moderators of chaos → parenting linkages

While the conceptual framework shown in Fig. 3.2 suggests common underlying processes mediating relations between microsystem chaos and child development across cultures, it is important to also recognize the potential operation of unique moderators that operate only in some cultures. The formal role assigned to older siblings as caretakers of younger siblings may serve as an important cultural moderator on the impact of environmental chaos upon parent–child transactions, particularly in non-Western cultures. In such cultures, even when environmental chaos acts to reduce the level of maternal caregiving involvement, older sibling involvement in caregiving can act to compensate for the unavailability of the mother. A second potential moderator involves living arrangements. Living with unrelated families in the same household appears to be more common in developing countries than is the case in Western cultures. In Egypt, families sharing an apartment with strangers were more likely to discipline their children physically than either families sharing an apartment with relatives or families living in a separate apartment (Youssef *et al.* 1998). Likewise in Hong Kong, when the dwelling unit was shared with unrelated families, levels of hostility among the residents were high (Mitchell 1971). Whether the social composition of the

Table 3.4 Effects of overcrowding on physical and psychological health in non-Western cultures

Study	Subjects	Methodology	Results
Cheung, Leung, Chan and Ma (1998)	122 residents in bedspace apartments in Hong Kong	Structured interview questions to measure psychological/physical well-being and social support Satisfactory reliability (α's range from .53 to .89)	The perception of the adverse environment directly affected feelings of depression (R = .35; p < .05), loneliness (R = .2; p < .05), social support (R = −.2; p < .05) and social problems R = .2; p < .05), but not self-assessed health and morbidity. Mean residential density was not related to residents' physical and psychosocial health
Evans, Palsane, Lepore and Martin (1989)	175 male heads of households in Pune, India with a crowding index of 2.81 persons per room. The sample represents the urban poor and lower class in India	Social Support Scale and a modified version of the Psychiatric Epidemiology Research Interview as a psychological symptoms scale with extensive pilot testing (α's were reported as .91 and .77, respectively)	High residential density was associated with greater psychological distress (r = .20; p < .05) and lower social support (r = .0.39; p < .05)
Fuller, Edwards, Vorakitphokatorn and Sermsri (1996)	2017 subjects living in Bangkok, with a mean crowding index of 2.1 per room	Focus group interviews Psychological well-being survey: Cronbach's alphas for the subscales range from 0.62 to 0.84. Evidence for construct validity was obtained by comparing the scale scores to the scale developed by Gove and Hughes (1983)	Subjective crowding was related to several aspects of psychological well-being, including psychological distress (r = 0.4; p < .001), unhappiness (r = 0.45; p < .001), irritability (r = 0.26; p < .001), and the contemplation of suicide (r = 0.21; p < .001)
Lepore, Evans and Palsane (1991)	175 male heads of households in Pune, India	Interview and surveys (α's were reported as .86 and .77 for each scale)	Residents of high-density homes were more susceptible to psychological distress than their lower counterparts from low-density homes

Study	Subjects	Methodology	Results
Mitchell (1971)	Residents in urban Hong Kong	Large-scale surveys	The index of emotional illness and hostility was related positively to the floor level of residence and to the presence of non-related families in the same household. Especially living in the upper floors with non-kinsmen had negative effects on emotional health of individuals
Ruback and Pandey (1991)	167 married couples in Allahabad, India, with a mean crowding index of 2.32 persons per room	Observation and survey Interobserver reliabilities ranged from .55 to .97 , α's ranged from .60 to .87 for different scales	Individual's control over the environment affects physical ($r = -.26$; $p < .001$) and mental health ($r = -.43$, $p < .001$) as well as interpersonal relations ($r = .18$; $p < .05$)
Ruback, Pandey and Begum (1997)	116 pedestrians in Old Delhi, 362 pedestrians in New Delhi and 430 pedestrians in Dhaka	20-item questionnaire on affective measures and perceived control Reliability and validity data of the measures are not reported	In all cities respondents who reported more perceived control also reported feeling better ($r = .25$; $p < .001$), having fewer symptoms ($r = -.1$; $p < .01$), and being less upset by noise ($r = -.17$; $p < .001$), air pollution ($r = -.09$; $p < .05$), and crowding ($r = -.16$; $p < .001$)
Saito, Iwata, Hosokawa and Ohi (1993)	421 households in a community consisting of buildings of aggregated dwelling units in Tokyo, Japan.	28-item general health questionnaire 12-item physical health questionnaire Reliability and validity data of the measures are not reported.	Living in the high floor levels was associated with greater physical health problems, whereas dissatisfaction with the plan of the house and annoyance by indoor/outdoor noise were associated with poor psychological health.

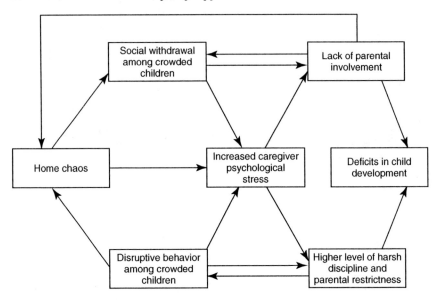

Figure 3.2 Hypothesized linkage pattern between environmental chaos and children's development

household acts to moderate the negative effects of environmental chaos on family relations in Western developed countries is, as yet, an unanswered question.

Further, evidence from studies in the United States indicates that work stress for both fathers (Repetti 1994) and mothers (Repetti and Wood 1997) can act to adversely influence the quality of parent–child relations. Although only limited empirical evidence is available, the role conflict experienced by employed mothers with traditional belief systems appears to be a link between environmental chaos and developmentally inhibiting parent–child transactions that may be particularly important in non-Western cultures (Ilyas 1990). With the changing status of women (Engle 1991, Sinha 1988) and the changing roles for children as a result of urbanization and industrialization in non-Western societies (Kağitçibaşi 1996), mothers may be forced to assume multiple roles. Employed mothers in developing or non-Western countries are more likely to have to deal with large families and a lack of child help with family tasks. As a result these women may be confronted with greater demands to fulfill multiple role obligations inside and outside the home than are either non-employed mothers in these countries or even employed mothers in Western developed countries (Ilyas 1990, Saito *et al.* 1993). For example, in India the rate of paternal involvement in child-rearing activities did not differ in families where both parents were employed as opposed to economically comparable families where only the father was employed (Roopnarine *et al.* 1992). What these results indicate is that the demands of employment did not reduce the mother's level of in-home obligations. Similarly, working mothers in Bangladesh reported greater home–career conflict and difficulties in child rearing in the absence of reliable persons for taking care of home and children (Ilyas 1990). These findings further suggest that the conceptual framework shown in Fig. 3.2 may need to be modified in those non-Western cultures or developing countries undergoing urbanization/industrialization, where traditional family caregiving models may be breaking down.

Future directions

In this chapter we have reviewed the available literature on environmental chaos, children's development and caregiver–child transaction patterns in both Western and non-Western countries. In the final section of this chapter we will discuss the implications of this research for developmental theory, as well as indicate future directions to further enhance our understanding of the influence of environmental chaos on family relations across different cultures.

Implications of cross-cultural chaos research for contextual theory

As seen in Fig. 3.1, while the microsystem (e.g. the family) and the macrosystem (e.g. culture) form distinct and different levels of the environment, they are linked to each other. One of the implications of this linkage between different levels of the environment is seen in the hypothesis that culture will act to moderate the impact of parental or caregiver rearing practices on children's development. This hypothesis is central to many of the current theoretical approaches to conceptualizing environment and the impact of the environment upon individual development (e.g. Bronfenbrenner and Ceci 1994, Super and Harkness 1999). Although a number of studies have shown how the nature or impact of the family social environment varies across different cultures, the overall pattern of evidence is not consistent (Wachs 1996). For example, while some studies indicate that relations between parental rearing strategies and children's school performance vary as a function of ethnic–cultural background (e.g. Steinberg, Dornbusch and Brown 1992), other studies find the converse, namely similar pattern of relations across cultures between parental stimulation patterns and children's cognitive development (e.g. Bornstein *et al.* 1990; Ogilvy 1990).

For the most part discussions on the discrepancy between environmental theory and environmental research over the question of cross-cultural moderation have been restricted to the child's social–interpersonal environment. What our review has shown is that this discrepancy also is seen when we look at relations between environmental chaos and parenting across different cultures. Theoretically, culture should act to moderate such relations. Empirically, the results do not fit what theory predicts.

It could be argued that the results from studies that fail to show cross-cultural moderation can be attributed to methodological problems that result in an inability to detect existing differences (e.g. low statistical power). However, our reading of the literature indicates that not all studies have such flaws. It also could be argued that the inconsistencies described above are artifactual, and that whether or not results are consistent with the hypothesis that culture will act to moderate the impact of parental rearing practices will depend on how culture is defined in a given study. We do not find this argument to be helpful as a way of explaining the inconsistency of findings in this area. Given the multiple definitions of culture that are available any number of post-hoc explanations could be generated, depending on which definition of culture was chosen. Further, underlying many of the current approaches to conceptualizing culture is the basic assumption that parental practices, rearing beliefs and goals will vary depending upon cultural goals and features (Super and Harkness 1999), so that we should expect moderation of physical or social microsystem influences regardless of the specific definition of culture used. An alternative viewpoint argues for "universal" parenting behaviors based on innate, evolution-driven patterns of reactivity to species-typical childhood behavioral patterns (Papousek and Papousek 1991). Assuming a common biological heritage, within this framework we should not expect moderation. The current evidence indicating both cross-cultural consistencies and inconsistencies in the impact of parental rearing practices does not lend strong support to either of these viewpoints.

The discrepancy between environmental theory and environmental research over the question of cross-cultural moderation may be one of the most essential questions currently facing environmental researchers (Wachs 1996). Discussion on ways of dealing with this discrepancy is one issue we will deal with in the final section of this chapter.

Methodological issues

What should be obvious to the reader is the relatively small number of studies in the area of chaos, child development and caregiver–child transactions, particularly in non-Western cultures. Not only are more studies needed, but it is our conclusion that future studies need to correct certain methodological problems seen in earlier studies, as well as address a number of persistent methodological issues. Current research on environmental chaos has avoided many of the methodological problems seen in earlier studies, such as a lack of control for socioeconomic status. However, a number of methodological problems remain. Certainly, there needs to be an expansion of the number of cultures studied, as well as more systematic cross-cultural comparisons using comparable yet culturally relevant methodologies. What this means, in part, is going beyond comparison of two or more "cultures" and providing detailed information on the chaos relevant features of the chosen cultures, so that we can begin to understand what about a given culture is acting to accentuate or attenuate the impact of environmental chaos upon children's development and parent–child relations. For example, how will the impact of environmental chaos play out in a culture that is faced with increasing industrialization/urbanization as opposed to in a more traditional culture? To what extent do deeply held cultural values such as collectivism versus individualism, or passive acceptance of what the environment offers versus acting to change the environment, influence the impact of environmental chaos upon children or caregivers? Ultimately, whether we find consistencies or inconsistencies in regard to cultural moderation of the influence of parental rearing practices or environmental chaos may depend on how similar or dissimilar are the cultures studied in regard to values, beliefs and goals that impact upon what parents do and believe. However, while there is ample evidence available on cultural similarities and differences in parental rearing practices and goals, there is virtually no available evidence available that makes use of cultural similarities or differences to predict whether the impact of environmental chaos (or parenting rearing practices) will vary or be similar across given cultures (Wachs 2000).

Detailed descriptions of cultures need to be linked to equally detailed descriptions of the specific microsystems inhabited by children living within a given culture. One critical question in this area is the extent to which the detrimental impact of environmental chaos is accentuated as a function of other microsystem stressors encountered by children and their caregivers. For example, as noted by Evans and Saegert (2000), the likelihood of having to deal with environmental chaos is increased in low income families. Also, the degree of satisfaction with living quarters and achieved privacy were found to be important determinants to decrease feelings of crowding and other adverse psychological effects in Hong Kong (Chan 1999). Studies providing detailed descriptive information on the macrosystem (culture) and microsystem characteristics encountered by children are a necessary first step toward understanding why cultural moderation of the impact of environmental chaos does or does not occur.

In practice, what the above suggestions involve is going beyond commonly utilized survey or interview methods for data collection. Future studies need to integrate these methods along with repeated observational assessments to assure a thorough assessment of the multiple levels encompassing the child's environment. The emphasis here is on *integration of measures*. For example, combining objective observational data on factors such as household density and sound level with interview data on more subjective aspects of the environment, such as caregivers' culturally driven feelings of perceived control over their environment, will produce a far more illuminating set of findings than either observational or interview data taken in isolation. In non-Western countries where there is increasing urbanization or industrialization, we may need to integrate not only objective measures of chaos but also the mothers' subjective perception of the degree of role conflict they are encountering as a result of demands from both a crowded chaotic environment as well as from their non-family work environment. In addition, it would also be desirable to collect data from multiple sources (e.g. children, parents, other family or non-family caregivers and teachers) in order to construct a more detailed picture of the characteristics of the child's environments and his/her developmental competencies. For example, to what extent will the influence upon children's development of the level of home chaos be accentuated or attenuated by the level of chaos in non-home settings that the child encounters? The overall goal in future chaos–development research should be an integration across the multiple levels of the caregiver's and child's objective (observed) and subjective (perceived) environments. Such integration would allow us to obtain a detailed understanding of not only the level of chaos in the child's environment but also how and why the child and significant others react to such chaos.

Expanding the field of study

Our review has suggested the possibility of culturally unique moderators of environmental chaos, such as social composition of the household and the role assigned to the siblings as caretakers. However, the number of studies investigating the role of culturally unique moderators is limited. We need more research on potentially culturally unique moderators if we are to understand whether the influence of environmental chaos upon children's development, and the processes underlying such influences, are truly similar across cultures. For example, relatively little research has been carried out on specific strategies used to cope with environmental chaos and the long-term implications of these strategies for parent–child transactions in Western and non-Western countries. As noted by Evans *et al.* (1998), one way people cope with crowded living conditions is by withdrawing from others. Thus, residents of higher-density homes are more likely to want to be left alone and filter out social information than do their low-density counterparts (Evans *et al.* 2000). If this coping strategy becomes overgeneralized, a caregiver may avoid social interactions with younger children. How this scenario plays out in cultures where social interactions are highly valued seems an important question if we are to understand the link between macrosystem and microsystem influences on the developing child.

Another potentially important cultural moderator involves parental belief systems about their level of control over their environment. In situations such as living in a chaotic home environment in a low-income neighborhood, where there are high levels of uncontrollable environmental stress, parents may develop an increased level of learned helplessness that can compromise their ability to deal effectively with their offspring (Evans and Saegert 2000). However, individuals from different cultures vary in the level of attributions they make about the controllability of events and the strategies they use to deal with uncontrollable events (Kağitçibaşi 1996). Culturally based differences in control attribution may result in culturally based differences in levels of susceptibility to chaos-driven learned helplessness, as well as in the strategies that parents use in situations that are perceived as being beyond their direct control. Belief and attribution systems may act to influence the quality of child-rearing in chaotic environments. As a result it is important to assess culturally based differences in parental belief systems that may act to influence how caregivers in different cultures react to environmental chaos. Given the increasing levels of forced migration in some areas of the world one potentially important area of research would involve the reactions of displaced parents in different cultures to being forced to live in chaotic shelter environments, and the impact of parental reactions on child development in these environments.

In addition, research on the moderating impact of culture upon the impact of environmental chaos has usually focused just on the family microenvironment of the child. Little systematic research has been done involving characteristics or influences of physical microenvironment chaos upon other microsystem domains. Stevenson and Lee (1990) have argued that cultural values centering around the need for effort and the value of education serve to buffer the academic performance of Asian children from the potential negative consequences of overcrowded classrooms. While logically compelling, this argument must be regarded as a hypothesis in need of testing. Finally, as discussed earlier, available studies conducted in non-Western countries suggest that chaos need not inhibit developmentally facilitative transactions between infants and caregivers where older siblings act to compensate for the unavailability of the mother. However, as also discussed earlier, developmental deficits are seen even in those cultures where such substitute caregiving occurs. If we assume that developmental deficits are the result of caregiving deficits how can we deal with this discrepancy? Following from the work of Evans, Maxwell and Hart (1999), one potential explanation may be that the quality of parent–child transactions may be as important as the quantity of such transactions. Specifically, Evans *et al.* (1999) report that the diversity and sophistication of caregiver–infant verbal interactions in crowded households is as important for infants' cognitive development as is the rate of caregiver verbal responsivity. Although there are cultures where siblings take over the infant caregiving role from mothers in chaotic households, is the quality of the caregiving and stimulation provided by siblings comparable to that given by adult caregivers? Available evidence from Western or developed countries suggests that older siblings can serve as social models, thus facilitating the socialization of younger siblings in areas such as learning social roles (Lewis and Feiring 1998, Morelli and Tronick 1991, Rogoff *et al.* 1991). Evidence also illustrates how, by serving as play partners, older siblings can act to facilitate younger siblings' exploration of the environment (Samuels 1980). Similar sibling effects are also seen in developing or non-Western cultures (Watson-Gegeo and Gegeo 1989, Zukow-Goldring 1989). However, it is also important to note that the care of infants requires a certain level of cognitive, emotional and social skills on the part of the older sibling. Evidence indicates that older siblings appear to be less skilled than adults in promoting developmentally facilitative interchanges such as contingent responsivity, turn-taking or language-focused interactions in both non-Western (Whiting and Edwards 1988) and Western cultures (Jones and Adamson 1987, Vandell and Wilson 1987). Further, in developing countries extensive caregiving by preteen siblings can increase the risk of poor nutritional status in younger siblings during the first three years of life (Engle 1991). The widespread use of sibling caregiving in many cultures (Whiting and Edwards 1988), and the available evidence questioning the adequacy of sibling caregiving, suggests the importance of measuring both quality and quantity of sib caregiving in future studies assessing the impact of environmental chaos upon children's development in different cultures. It is also important to note that such studies should not be restricted just to non-Western contexts. While much of the concern over the use of sibling caregivers involves children living in non-Western or developing countries, sibling caregiving is an issue that is becoming quite important in Western countries with the rising number of two-wage earner families unable to meet the expenses of after-school care for their children (Zukow-Goldring 1995).

Applied directions

Research findings focusing on the linkages between environmental chaos and parent–child transactions have the potential to lead to interventions to enhance the development of children and to empower parents in chaotic homes. Many of the potential applications are derived from Bronfenbrenner's (1989) ecological perspective on development. For example, in traditional cultures where childcare is assumed to be the mother's task (Ilyas 1990, Roopnarine *et al.* 1992, Saito *et al.* 1993), maternal employment status seems to be associated with home–career conflict and concern about how and where to raise children. As noted earlier, employed women in traditional cultures with large households suffer from role stress, which in turn seems to impair their parenting behavior. Not surprisingly, there has been an increased emphasis on expanding resources for day care facilities to help employed mothers deal better with these concerns. As childcare outside of the home increases, the quality of these care facilities becomes a crucial issue. Studies examining the effects of crowding in both home and day care settings point out that negative consequences of environmental chaos are exacerbated by the combination of these two settings for children's development (Maxwell 1996). Effective social policies should focus on expanding high-quality, low-chaos, culturally appropriate alternative childcare systems in developing countries undergoing urbanization and industrialization, to reduce mothers' home–career conflict.

Along the same lines, studies have noted the importance of maternal education as a buffering factor in overcrowded homes (Shapiro 1974, von der Lippe 1999). Based on observations of maternal behavior and self-report, results from a recent study by von der Lippe (1999) indicated that the use of authoritative style of child rearing and teaching styles associated with higher cognitive competence were more frequently noted among highly educated Egyptian mothers living in overcrowded homes than among their low-educated counterparts. These results imply that opportunities for increased maternal education could be a valuable tool to increase mothers' ability to develop effective coping skills to deal with environmental chaos and thus promote better parent–child transactions. In cultures where childcare is left to older siblings, childcare education programs directed at siblings may be a culturally relevant means of also promoting better coping strategies to deal with existing environmental chaos.

While the home environment constitutes an immediate proximal context of child development, children's lives in a number of non-Western countries are also embedded in macrosystem chaos, either in the form of political violence and/or forced migration (Cairn and Dawes 1996, Garbarino and Kostelny 1996, Ladd and Cairns 1996, Macksoud and Aber 1996, Straker, Mendelsohn, Moosa and Tudin 1996). Although macrosystem chaos represents a severe contextual threat to children's development, children exposed to such chaos do not necessarily suffer serious psychological consequences (Garbarino and Kostelny 1996, Straker *et al.* 1996). Specifically, the detrimental effects of macrosystem chaos on children's well-being were found to be attenuated when parents were able to maintain their daily routines and provide a supportive environment (Freud and Burlingham 1943, Garbarino and Kostelny 1996, Klingman, Sagi and Raviv 1993). These findings suggest that the impact of distal macrosystem influences is likely to interact with factors at the microenvironment level. The extent to which children's well-being and development are affected by macrosystem chaos may be determined, in part, by the physical and social aspects of the home environment. Thus, the impact of macrosystem chaos could be attenuated when children live in less chaotic homes. A more thorough investigation of this potential moderating mechanism of home environment is an important avenue of research for future studies. In such studies it also is essential to consider the possibility that the extent to which the family can function as a protective mechanism in the midst of social chaos may be a culturally determined factor. The results of this line of research are likely to have practical value. Particularly, when it is difficult or impossible to avoid macrosystem chaos, it may be possible to directly target the nature of home environment as a point of intervention in order to enhance children's well-being and prevent chaos-induced developmental problems.

Alternatively, while the above evidence suggests that stable home environments can act to moderate the impact of macrosystem chaos, not all children encountering macrosystem chaos live in stable home environments. As noted earlier, even in developed countries homeless parents and children's exposure to chaotic shelter environments place them at increased risk of increased developmentally inhibiting parenting and less adequate development. In many chaotic macrosystems children and their families are forced to live in refugee camps. More systematic research is needed across cultures on the level of chaos in these contexts and whether such chaos acts to accentuate the already detrimental consequences of macrosystem chaos. For example, research cited earlier indicates that high levels of environmental chaos can attenuate social support networks (Evans *et al.* 1989, Lepore *et al.* 1991). Looking at whether reduced social support, as a result of exposure to chaotic camps or homeless shelters, serves to mediate the detrimental consequences of macrosystem chaos is a line of research with clear theoretical and practical implications.

Conclusions

Working within an ecological theory perspective, the goal of this chapter has been to integrate and critically evaluate past and current empirical studies on environmental chaos and its relation to child development as well as to parenting behavior. Findings from the small number of studies that are available point to an unexpectedly similar pattern of relations between environmental chaos, increased risk of developmental problems and developmentally inhibiting parent–child transactions across different cultures. This similarity of findings poses a clear challenge to ecological theory, which predicts that cultural characteristics will act to moderate proximal environmental influences. However, this apparent lack of cultural moderation also provides an exciting avenue for future research to generate new hypotheses about the processes that may underlie the discrepancy between empirical data and theoretical predictions. While we are still faced with many critical questions that need to be answered about the processes that underlie the impact of environmental chaos upon children's development and caregiver behavior patterns, our current level of knowledge on this issue also suggests a number of potential intervention strategies that could act to buffer children against the impact of either microsystem or macrosystem environmental chaos. A number of these potential interventions were discussed in the present chapter, such as increased maternal educational opportunities and increased usage of culturally appropriate alternative childcare systems by working mothers. The coupling of basic research on the processes underlying the negative impact of environmental chaos on children's development and family processes with the use of interventions that flow from this research has the potential not only to advance ecological theory but also to facilitate children's development, even in the face of ongoing familial or societal environmental chaos.

Acknowledgements

The authors gratefully acknowledge Professor Gary Evans' incisive comments on a preliminary version of this chapter.

References

Aiello, J., Thompson, D. and Baum, A. (1985) "Children, Crowding and Control" in Wohlwill, J. and VanVliet, W. (eds.) *Habitats for Children* (pp. 97–124). Hillsdale: Erlbaum.

Als, H. (1992) "Individualized Family Focused Developmental Care for the Very Low Birthweight Preterm Infant in the NICU" in Friedman, S. and Sigman, M. (eds.) *The Psychological Development of Low Birthweight Children* (pp. 341–388). Ablex: Norwood.

Altman, I. and Chemers, M. M. (1980) *Culture and Environment.* Monterey, CA: Brooks Cole.

Anderson, E. (1972) "Some Chinese Methods of Dealing with Crowding", *Urban Anthropology*, *1*: 141–150.

Ani, C. and Grantham-McGregor, S. (1998) "Family and Personal Characteristics of Aggressive Nigerian Boys", *Journal of Adolescent Health*, *23*: 311–317.

Baldassare, M. (1981) "The Effects of Household Density on Subgroups", *American Sociological Review*, *46*: 110–118.

Baum, A. and Paulus, P. B. (1987) "Crowding" in Stokols, D. and Altman, I. (eds.) *Handbook of Environmental Psychology* (pp. 534–570). New York: Plenum.

Blue, M. and Vergason, G. (1975) "Auditory Discrimination in Conditions of Noise and Quiet by Black and White Disadvantaged Children", *Perceptual Motor Skills, 41*: 35–40.

Booth, A. (1985) "Quality of Children's Family Interaction in Relation to Residential Type and Household Crowding" in Wohlwill, J. and VanVliet, W. (eds.) *Habitats for Children* (pp. 145–165). Hillsdale: Erlbaum.

Bornstein, M., Azuma, H., Tamis-LeMonda, C. and Ogino, M. (1990) "Mother and Infant Activity and Interaction in Japan and in the United States", *International Journal of Behavioral Development, 13*: 267–288.

Boykin, W. (1978) "Psychological/Behavioral Verve in Academic/Task Performance", *Journal of Negro Education, 47*: 343–354.

Bradley, R. (1999) "The Home Environment" in Friedman, S. and Wachs, T. D. (eds.) *Measuring Environment Across the Life Span* (pp. 31–58). Washington, DC.: American Psychological Association.

Bradley, R., Whiteside, L., Mundfrom, D., Casey, P., Kelleher, K. and Pope, S. (1994) "Early Indications of Resilience and Their Relation to Experiences in the Home Environments of Low Birth Weight Premature Children Living in Poverty", *Child Development, 65*: 346–360.

Bronfenbrenner, U. (1989) "Ecological Systems Theory", *Annals of Child Development, 6*: 187–249.

—— (1999) "Environments in Developmental Perspective" in Friedman, S. and Wachs, T. D. (eds.) *Measuring Environment Across the Life Span* (pp. 3–30). Washington, DC: American Psychological Association.

Bronfenbrenner, U. and Ceci, S. (1994) "Nature-Nurture Reconceptualized: A Bio-Ecological Perspective", *Psychological Review, 101*: 568–586.

Bronzaft, A. and McCarthy, D. (1975) "The Effect of Elevated Train Noise on Reading Disability", *Environment & Behavior, 7*: 517–527.

Bruins, J. and Barber, A. (2000) "Crowding, Performance, and Affect: A Field Experiment Investigating Mediational Processes", *Journal of Applied Social Psychology, 30*: 1268–1280.

Buckner, J. C., Bassuk, E. L., Weinreb, L. F. and Brooks, M. G. (1999) "Homelessness and Its Relation to the Mental Health and Behavior of Low-Income School-Age Children", *Developmental Psychology, 35*: 246–257.

Bullinger, M., Hygge, S., Evans, G., Meis, M. and Mackensen, S (1998) "The Psychological Cost of Aircraft Noise for Children", *Zentralblatt fur Hygiene und Umweltmed, 202*: 127–138.

Cairns, E. and Dawes, A. (1996) "Children: Ethnic and Political Violence – A Commentary", *Developmental Psychology, 67*: 129–139.

Chan, Y. (1999) "Density, Crowding, and Factors Intervening in Their Relationship: Evidence from a Hyper-Dense Metropolis", *Social Indicators Research, 48*: 103–124.

Cheung, C., Leung, K., Chan, W. and Ma, K. (1998) "Depression, Loneliness, and Health in an Adverse Living Environment: A Study of Bedspace Residents in Hong Kong", *Social Behavior and Personality, 26*: 151–170.

Cohen, S., Evans, G., Stokols, D. and Krantz, D. (1986) *Behavior, Health and Environmental Stress*. New York: Plenum.

Cohen, S., Glass, D. and Singer, J. (1973) "Apartment Noise, Auditory Discrimination and Reading Ability in Children", *Journal of Experimental Social Psychology, 9*: 407–422.

Çorapçi, F. and Wachs, T. D. (2002). "Does Parental Mood or Self-Efficacy Mediate Relations Between Environmental Chaos and Parenting Behaviors?" *Merrill-Palmer Quarterly, 48*, 182–201.

Deutsch, C. (1964) "Auditory Discrimination and Learning", *Merrill-Palmer Quarterly, 10*: 276–296.

Draper, P. (1973) "Crowding Among Hunter Gatherers: The Kung Bushman", *Science, 182*: 301–303.

Ekblad, S. (1993) "Stressful Environments and Their Effects on Quality of Life in Third World Cities", *Environment and Urbanization, 5*: 125–134.

Engle, P. (1991) "Maternal Work and Child Care Strategies in Peri-Urban Guatemala: Nutritional Effects", *Child Development, 62*: 954–965.

Evans, G., Bullinger, M. and Hygge, S. (1998) "Chronic Noise Exposure and Physiological Response: A Prospective Study of Children Living under Environmental Stress", *Psychological Science, 9*: 75–77.

Evans, G. and Cohen, S. (1987) "Environmental Stress" in Stokols, D. and Altman, I. (eds.) *Handbook of Environmental Psychology, vol. 1* (pp. 71–610). New York: Wiley.

Evans, G., Hygge, S. and Bullinger, M. (1995) "Chronic Noise and Psychological Stress", *Psychological Science, 6*: 333–338.

Evans, G., Kliewer, W. and Martin, J. (1991) "The Role of the Physical Environment in the Health and Well-being of Children" in Schroeder, H. (ed.) *New Directions in Health Psychology Assessment* (pp. 127–157). New York: Hemisphere.

Evans, G. and Lepore, S. (1993) "Household Crowding and Social Support: A Quasi-Experimental Analysis", *Journal of Personality and Social Psychology, 65*: 308–316.

Evans, G., Lepore, S., Shejwal, B. and Palsane, M. (1998) "Chronic Residential Crowding and Children's Well-being", *Child Development, 69*: 1514–1523.

Evans, G. and Maxwell, L. (1997) "Chronic Noise Exposure and Reading Deficits: The Mediating Effects of Language Acquisition", *Environment and Behavior, 29*: 638–656.

Evans, G., Maxwell, L. and Hart, B. (1999) "Parental Language and Verbal Responsiveness to Children in Crowded Homes", *Developmental Psychology, 35*: 1020–1024.

Evans, G., Lepore, S. and Allen, K. M. (2000) "Cross-Cultural Differences in Tolerance for Crowding: Fact or Fiction?", *Journal of Personality and Social Psychology, 79*: 204–210.

Evans, G., Palsane, M., Lepore, S. and Martin, J. (1989) "Residential Density and Psychological Health", *Journal of Personality and Social Psychology, 57*: 994–999.

Evans, G., Rhee, E., Forbes, C., Allen, K. M. and Lepore, S. J. (2000) "The Meaning and Efficacy of Social Withdrawal as a Strategy for Coping with Chronic Residential Crowding", *Journal of Environmental Psychology, 20*: 335–342.

Evans, G. and Saegert, S. (2000) "Residential Crowding in the Context of Inner-City Poverty" in Wapner, S., Demick, J., Minami, H. and Yamamoto, T. (eds.) *Theoretical Perspectives in Environment Behavior Research* (pp. 247–267). New York: Plenum.

Fagot, B. (1977) "Variations in Density: Effect on Task and Social Behaviors of Preschool Children", *Developmental Psychology, 13*: 166–167.

Freud, A. and Burlingham, D. (1943) *War and Children.* New York: Ernest Willard.

Fuller, T., Edwards, J. N., Vorakitphokatorn, S. and Sermsri, S. (1993) "Household Crowding and Family Relations in Bangkok", *Social Problems, 40*: 410–430.

— (1996) "Chronic Stress and Psychological Well-being: Evidence from Thailand on Household Crowding", *Social Science Medicine, 42*: 265–280.

Garbarino, J. and Kostelny, K. (1996) "The Effects of Political Violence on Palestinian Children's Behavior Problems", *Child Development, 67*: 33–45.

Gillis, A., Richard, M. and Hagan, J. (1986) "Ethnic Susceptibility to Crowding", *Environment and Behavior, 18*: 683–706.

Glenn, L., Nerbonne, G. and Tolhurst, G. (1978) "Environmental Noise in a Residential Institution for Mentally Retarded Persons", *American Journal of Mental Deficiency, 82*: 594–597.

Goduka, I., Poole, D. and Aotaki-Phenice, L. (1992) "A Comparative Study of Black South African Children from Three Different Contexts", *Child Development, 63*: 509–525.

Gottfried, A. and Gottfried, A. (1984) "Home Environment and Cognitive Development in Young Children of Middle Socio-economic Status Families" in Gottfried A. (ed.) *Home Environment and Early Cognitive Development* (pp. 57–116). Orlando: Academic Press.

Gove, W. and Hughes, M. (1983) *Overcrowding in the Household*. New York, NY: Academic Press.

Gove, W., Hughes, M. and Galle, O. (1979) "Overcrowding in the Home", *American Sociological Review, 44*: 59–80.

Grantham-McGregor, S., Chang, S., Walker, S. and Powell, C. (1998) "School Feeding Studies in Jamaica" in *Pan-American Health Organization Scientific Monograph #566: Nutrition, Health and Human Development*. Washington, DC: Pan-American Health Organization.

Haines, M., Stansfeld, S., Job, R., Berglund, B. and Head, J. (2001) "Chronic Aircraft Noise, Stress Responses, Mental Health and Cognitive Performance in School Children", *Psychological Medicine, 31*: 265–277.

Hambrick-Dixon, P. (1986) "Effects of Experimentally Imposed Noise on Task Performance of Black Children Attending Daycare Centers near Elevated Subway Trains", *Developmental Psychology, 22*: 259–264.

— (1988) "The Effect of Elevated Subway Train Noise over Time on Black Children's Visual Vigilance Performance", *Journal of Environmental Psychology, 8*: 299–314.

Hannan, K. and Luster, T. (1990) "Influence of Child Parent and Contextual Factors on Quality of Home Environment", paper presented at the Seventh International Conference on Infant Studies. Montreal (April).

Heft, H. (1979) "Background and Focal Environmental Conditions of the Home and Attention in Young Children", *Journal of Applied Social Psychology, 9*: 47–69.

Hwang, K. (1979) "Coping with Residential Crowding in a Chinese Urban Society", *Acta Psychologica Taiwanica, 21*: 117–133.

Ilyas, Q. S. (1990) "Determinants of Perceived Role Conflict Among Women in Bangladesh", *Sex Roles, 22*: 237–248.

Insel, P. M. and Lindgren, H. C. (1978) *Too Close for Comfort: The Psychology of Crowding*. Englewood Cliffs, NJ: Prentice Hall Inc.

Jain, U. (1987) *The Psychological Consequences of Crowding*. New Delhi: Sage.

Johnston-Brooks, C., Lewis, M., Evans, G. and Whalen, C. (1998) "Chronic Stress and Illness in Children", *Psychosomatic Medicine, 60*: 597–603.

Jones, C. and Adamson, L. (1987) "Language Use in Mother-Child and Mother-Child-Sibling Interactions", *Child Development, 58*: 356–366,

Kağitçibaşi, Ç. (1988) "Diversity of Socialization and Social Change" in Dasen, P., Berry, J. and Sartorius, N. (eds.) *Health and Cross-Cultural Psychology* (pp. 25–47). Newbury Park: Sage.

— (1996) *Family and Human Development Across Cultures*. Hillsdale: Erlbaum.

Klingman, A., Sagi, A. and Raviv, A. (1993) "The Effect of War on Israeli Children" in Leavitt, L. A. and Fox, N. A. (eds.) *The Psychological Effects of War and Violence on Children* (pp. 75–92). New Jersey: Lawrence Erlbaum Associates.

Konner, M. (1977) "Infancy among the Kalahari Desert San" in Leiderman, P. H., Tulkin, S. R. and Rosenfeld, A. (eds.) *Culture and Infancy: Variations in the Human Experience* (pp. 287–328). New York: Academic Press.

Ladd, G. and Cairns, E. (1996) "Introduction-Children: Ethnic and Political Violence", *Child Development*, *67*: 14–18.

Langmeier, J. and Matejeck, Z. (1975) *Psychological Deprivation in Childhood*. New York: Wiley.

Leff, H. (1978) *Experience, Environment and Human Potential*. New York: Oxford University Press.

Lepore, S., Evans, G. and Schneider, M. (1991) "Dynamic Role of Social Support in the Link Between Chronic Stress and Psychological Distress", *Journal of Personality and Social Psychology*, *61*: 899–909.

Lepore, S. J., Evans, G. and Palsane, M. N. (1991) "Social Hassles and Psychological Health in the Context of Chronic Crowding", *Journal of Health and Social Behavior*, *32*: 357–367.

Lewis, M. and Feiring, C. (1998) "The Child and Its Family" in Lewis, M. and Feiring, C. (eds.) *Families, Risk and Competence* (pp. 5–30). Hillsdale: Erlbaum.

Liddell, C. (1994) "South African Children in the Year Before School", *International Journal of Psychology*, *29*: 409–430.

Liddel, C. and Kruger, P. (1987) "Activity and Social Behavior in a South African Township Nursery", *Merrill-Palmer Quarterly*, *33*: 195–211.

— (1989) "Activity Level and Social Behavior in a Crowded South African Township Nursery: A Follow-up Study on the Effects of Crowding at Home", *Merrill-Palmer Quarterly*, *35*: 209–226.

Lindsey, E. W. (1998) "The Impact of Homelessness and Shelter Life on Family Relationships", *Family Relations*, *47*: 243–252.

Loo, C. (1978) "Behavior Problem Indices: The Differential Effects of Spatial Density on Low and High Scorers", *Environment and Behavior*, *10*: 489–510.

Macksoud, M. S. and Aber, J. L. (1996) "The War Experiences and Psychosocial Development of Children in Lebanon", *Developmental Psychology*, *67*: 70–88.

Matheny, A. (1986) "Injuries Among Toddlers", *Journal of Pediatric Psychology*, *11*: 161–176.

Matheny, A. and Phillips, K. (2001) "Temperament and Context: Correlates of Home Environment with Temperament Continuity and Change, Newborn to 30 Months" in Wachs, T. D. and Kohnstamm, G. A. (eds.) *Temperament in Context* (pp. 81–101) Mahwah, NJ: Lawrence Erlbaum Associates.

Matheny, A., Wachs, T. D., Ludwig, J. and Phillips, K. (1995) "Bringing Order out of Chaos: Psychometric Characteristics of the Louisville Chaos Scale", *Journal of Applied Developmental Psychology*, *16*: 429–444.

Matheny, A., Wilson, R. and Thoben, A. (1987) "Home and Mother: Relations with Infant Temperament", *Developmental Psychology*, *23*: 323–331.

Maxwell, L. (1996) "Multiple Effects of Home and Daycare Crowding", *Environment and Behavior*, *28*: 494–511.

Maxwell, L. and Evans, G. (2000) "The Effects of Noise on Pre-School Children's Pre-reading Skills", *Journal of Environmental Psychology*, *20*: 91–97.

Merry, S. (1987) "Crowding, Conflict and Neighborhood Regulation" in Altman, I. and Wandersman, A. (eds.) *Neighborhood and Community Environments* (pp. 35–68). New York: Plenum.

Minturn, L. and Lambert, W. W. (1964) *Mothers of Six Cultures: Antecedents of Child Rearing.* New York: John Wiley & Sons Inc.

Mitchell, R. E. (1971) "Some Social Implications of High-Density Housing", *American Sociological Review*, *36*: 18–29.

Morelli, G. and Tronick, E. (1991) "Parenting and Child Development in the Efe Foragers and Lese Farmers of Zaire" in Bornstein, M. (ed.) *Cultural Approaches to Parenting* (pp. 91–114). Hillsdale: Erlbaum.

Munroe, R. H. and Munroe, R. L. (1971) "Household Density and Infant Care in an East African Society", *Journal of Social Psychology, 83*: 3–13.

— (1980) "Household Structure and Socialization Practices", *Journal of Social Psychology, 111*: 293–294.

Nober, L. and Nober, E. (1975) "Auditory Discrimination of Learning Disabled Children in Quiet and in Classroom Noise", *Journal of Learning Disabilities, 8*: 57–60.

Oglivy, C. (1990) "Family Type and Children's Cognition in Two Ethnic Groups", *Journal of Cross-Cultural Psychology, 21*: 319–334.

Papousek, H. and Papousek, M. (1991) "Innate and Cultural Guidance of Infant's Integrative Competencies" in Bornstein, M. (ed.) *Cultural Approaches to Parenting* (pp. 23–44). Hillsdale: Erlbaum.

Pearce, F. (1996) "Crowded Beds Spread Childhood Plague", *New Scientist, 2034*: 10.

Rahmanifar, A., Kirksey, A., Wachs, T. D., McCabe, G., Bishry, Z., Galal, O., Harrison, G. and Jerome, N. (1993) "Diet During Lactation Associated with Infant Behavior and Caregiver Infant Interaction in a Semirural Egyptian Village", *Journal of Nutrition, 123*: 164–175.

Regeni, R (2000) "Living in Urban Environment and Leading Toward External Locus of Control Orientation", *Journal of the Indian Academy of Applied Psychology, 26*: 129–133.

Repetti, R. (1994) "Short-term and Long-term Processes Linking Job Stressors to Father–Child Interaction", *Social Development, 3*: 1–15.

Repetti, R. and Wood, J. (1997) "Effects of Daily Stress at Work on Mothers' Interactions with Preschoolers", *Journal of Family Psychology, 11*: 97–108.

Ricciuti, H. and Thomas, M. (1990) "Early Maternal and Environmental Correlates of Quality of Infant Care and 18-month Bayley Performance", paper presented to the Seventh International Conference on Infant Studies, Montreal (April).

Rogoff, B., Mistry, J., Goncu, A. and Mosier, C. (1991) "Cultural Variation in the Role Relations of Toddlers and Their Families" in Bornstein, M. (ed.) *Cultural Approaches to Parenting* (pp. 173–184) Hillsdale: Erlbaum.

Roopnarine, J., Talukder, E., Jain, D., Joshi, P. and Srivastav, P. (1992) "Personal Well-being, Kinship Tie, and Mother–Infant and Father–Infant Interactions in Single-Wage and Dual-Wage Families in New Delhi, India", *Journal of Marriage and the Family, 54*: 293–301.

Ruback, R. B. and Pandey, J. (1991) "Crowding, Perceived Control, and Relative Power: An Analysis of Households in India", *Journal of Applied Social Psychology, 21*: 315–344.

Ruback, R. B., Pandey, J. and Begum, H. A. (1997) "Urban Stressors in South Asia: Impact on Male and Female Pedestrians in Delhi and Dhaka", *Journal of Cross-Cultural Psychology, 28*: 23–43.

Saegert, S. (1982) "Environment and Children's Mental Health in Baum, A. and Sanger, J. (eds.) *Handbook of Psychology and Health, vol. 2* (pp. 247–271). Hillsdale: Erlbaum.

Saito, K., Iwata, N., Hosokawa, T. and Ohi, G. (1993) "Housing Factors and Perceived Health Status Among Japanese Women Living in Aggregated Dwelling Units", *International Journal of Health Services, 23*: 541–554.

Samuels, H. (1980) "The Effect of an Older Sibling on Infant Locomotor Exploration of a New Environment", *Child Development, 51*: 607–609.

Schaeffer, M., Baum, A., Paulus, P. and Gaes, G. (1988) "Architecturally Mediated Effects of Social Density in Prison", *Environment & Behavior, 20*: 3–19.

Shapiro, A. H. (1974) "Effects of Family Density and Mothers' Education on Preschoolers' Motor Skills", *Perceptual and Motor Skills, 38*: 79–86.

Sinha, D. (1988) "The Family Scenario in a Developing Country and its Implications for Mental Health" in Dasen, P., Berry, J. and Sartorius, N. (eds.) *Health and Cross-Cultural Psychology* (pp. 48–70). Newbury Park: Sage.

Sinha, S. P. and Nayyar, P. (2000) "Crowding Effects of Density and Personal Space Requirements among Older People: The Impact of Self-control and Social Support", *The Journal of Social Psychology, 140*: 721–728.

Steinberg, L., Dornbusch, S. and Brown, B. (1992) "Ethnic Differences in Adolescent Achievement", *American Psychologist, 47*: 723–729.

Stevenson, H. and Lee, S. (1990) "Contexts of Achievement", *Monographs of the Society for Research in Child Development, 55*, Serial # 221.

Stokols, D. (1978) "In Defense of the Crowding Construct" in Baum, A., Singer, J. and Valins, S. (eds.) *Advances in Environmental Psychology, vol. 1*. Hillsdale: Erlbaum.

Straker, G., Mendelsohn, M., Moosa, F. and Tudin, P. (1996) "Violent Political Contexts and the Emotional Concerns of Township Youth", *Developmental Psychology, 67*: 46–54.

Super, C. and Harkness, S. (1999) "The Environment as Culture in Developmental Research" in Friedman, S. and Wachs, T. D. (eds.) *Measuring Environment Across the Life-Span* (pp. 279–326). Washington, DC: American Psychological Association.

Sutton-Smith, B. (1986). "Play Interactions and Developmental Processes" in Gottfried, A. and Brown, C. (eds.) *Play Interactions* (pp. 313–321). Lexington, MA: Lexington Books.

Valsiner, J. (1989) *Human Development and Culture*. Lexington: Lexington Books.

Vandell, D. and Wilson, K. (1987) "Infants' Interactions with Mother, Sibling and Peer", *Child Development, 58*: 176–186.

VanVliet, W. and Wohlwill, J. (1985) "Habitats for Children: The State of the Evidence" in Wohlwill, J. and VanVliet, W. (eds.) *Habitats for Children* (pp. 201–229). Hillsdale: Erlbaum.

Von der Lippe, A. L. (1999) "The Impact of Maternal Schooling and Occupation on Child-Rearing Attitudes and Behaviors in Low-Income Neighborhoods in Cairo, Egypt", *International Journal of Behavior Development, 23*: 703–729.

Wachs, T. D. (1979) "Proximal Experience and Early Cognitive-Intellectual Development: The Physical Environment", *Merrill Palmer Quarterly, 25*: 3–41.

— (1986) "Models of Physical Environmental Action: Implications for the Study of Play Materials and Parent–Child Interaction" in Gottfried, A. (ed.) *Play Interactions: The Contribution of Play Materials and Parent Involvement to Child Development*. New York: Lexington.

— (1987) "Specificity of Environmental Action as Manifest in Environmental Correlates of Infant's Mastery Motivation", *Developmental Psychology, 23*: 782–790.

— (1988) "Relevance of Physical Environment Influence for Toddler Temperament", *Infant Behavior and Development, 11*: 431–445.

— (1989) "The Nature of the Physical Micro-Environment: An Expanded Classification System", *Merrill-Palmer Quarterly, 35*: 399–420.

— (1992) *The Nature of Nurture*. Newbury Park: Sage.

— (1993) "Nature of Relations Between the Physical and Social Microenvironment of the Two-Year-Old Child", *Early Development and Parenting, 2*: 81–87.

— (1996) "Environment and Intelligence: Present Status, Future Directions" in Detterman, D. (ed.) *Current Topics in Human Intelligence, vol. 5: The Environment*, (pp. 69–86). Norwood: Ablex.

— (1999) "Celebrating Complexity: Conceptualization and Assessment of the Environment" in Friedman, S. and Wachs, T. D. (eds.) *Measuring the Environment Across the Life Span* (pp. 357–392). Washington, DC: American Psychological Association.

— (2000) *"Necessary But Not Sufficient: The Respective Roles of Single and Multiple Influences on Individual Development"*, Washington, DC: American Psychological Association.

Wachs, T. D., Bishry, Z., Sobhy, A., McCabe, G., Sheehan, F. and Galal, O. (1993) "Relation of Rearing Environment to Adaptive Behavior of Egyptian Toddlers", *Child Development, 64*: 586–604.

Wachs, T. D. and Camli, O. (1991) "Do Ecological or Individual Characteristics Mediate the Influence of the Physical Environment upon Mother–Infant Transactions?", *Journal of Environmental Psychology, 11*: 249–264.

Wachs, T. D. and Chan, A. (1986) "Specificity of Environmental Action as Seen in Physical and Social Environment Correlates of Three Aspects of Twelve-Month Infants' Communication Performance", *Child Development, 57*: 1464–1475.

Wachs, T. D. and Desai, S. (1993) "Parent Report Measures of Toddler Temperament and Attachment: Their Relation to Each Other and to the Social Microenvironment", *Infant Behavior and Development, 16*: 391–396.

Wachs, T. D. and Gandour, M. J. (1983) "Temperament, Environment and 6-Month Cognitive-Intellectual Development: A Test of the Organismic Specificity Hypothesis", *International Journal of Behavioral Development, 6*: 135-152.

Wachs, T. D., Užgiris, I. Č. and Hunt, J. M. (1971) "Cognitive Development in Infants of Different Age Levels and Different Environmental Backgrounds: An Exploratory Study", *Merrill-Palmer Quarterly, 17*: 283–317.

Watson-Gegeo, K. A. and Gegeo, D. W. (1989) "The Role of Sibling Interaction in Child Socialization" in Goldring-Zukow, P. (ed.) Sibling Interaction Across Cultures (pp. 54–72). New York: Springer.

Whiting, B. and Edwards, C. (1988) *Children of Different Worlds*. Cambridge: Harvard University Press.

Whiting, J. (1977) "A Model for Psychocultural Research" in Leiderman, P. H., Tulkin, S. R. and Rosenfeld, A. (eds.) *Culture and Infancy: Variations in the Human Experience* (pp. 29–48). New York: Academic Press.

Wohlwill, J. and Heft, H. (1987) "The Physical Environment and the Development of the Child" in Altman, I. and Stokols, D. (eds.) *Handbook of Environmental Psychology* (pp. 281–328). New York: Wiley

Woodson, R. and da Costa-Woodson, E. (1984) "Social Organization, Physical Environment, and Infant–Caretaker Interaction", *Developmental Psychology, 20*: 473–476.

Youssef, R. M., Salah-El-Din-Attia, M. and Kamel, M. I. (1998) "Children Experiencing Violence: Parental Use of Corporal Punishment", *Child Abuse and Neglect, 22*, 959–973.

Zukow-Goldring, P. (1989) "Siblings as Effective Socializing Agents: Evidence from Central Mexico" in Goldring-Zukow, P. (ed.) *Sibling Interaction Across Cultures* (pp. 79–96). New York: Springer.

— (1995) "Sibling Caregiving" in Bornstein, M. H. (ed.) *Handbook of Parenting* (pp. 177–208). New Jersey: Lawrence Erlbaum.

4 Play as a context for the socialization of interpersonal relationships

M. Cristina Ramirez

Introduction

Cultural meaning is embedded in interpersonal interactions. In every society, individuals interact according to their understanding of the ways in which these interactions should be carried out in various activities such as play, work or instruction. This understanding of interpersonal interactions is intimately related to the cultural understanding of specific activities and the roles that participants believe appropriate to assume in them (Geertz 1973).

Children begin to participate in interactions and activities with more mature members of their societies from the moment of their births. In the process of these interactions, children are socialized into appropriate ways of relating in their culture. Parent–child play is a context in which such socialization occurs. There is a vast number of studies on parent–child play that have examined the significance of play in the development of communication (e.g. Garvey 1977, Stern 1974, Užgiris and Raeff 1995). These studies offer detailed accounts of how children begin to construct meaning during interactions with their caregivers. Cross-cultural studies further demonstrate that the patterns of interactions by middle-class American parents and their children are not necessarily the norm for other cultures (Bornstein 1991, Field, Sostek, Vietze and Leiderman 1981, LeVine, Miller and Maxwell West 1988). Different levels of meaning, including cultural understandings about how relationships are organized and experienced, shape these interactions.

The structure of parent–child play can be expected to vary based on different parental and cultural conceptions of interpersonal relationships. Play, in turn, may serve as a means of fostering children's understanding of these relationships. The focus in the current chapter is on how play, viewed as communication, can be an important context for socializing children into culturally appropriate ways of interacting and relating to others. Play involves different levels of communication between parent and child. One level of this communication involves the relationship between the speakers (Bateson 1972). By eighteen months of age children have participated in multiple play routines with their parents, and already have some expectations as to what constitutes play interactions with parents. It is also a time in which they are somewhat skilled in interacting with more than one person (Adamson and Bakeman 1985), making it possible to study interaction patterns within a wider family setting, beyond the parent–child dyad. On the other hand, because toddlers are just beginning to develop their relational skills, their contributions to the interaction may be smaller, thus allowing parents' beliefs and values to become more evident during play with their children. Thus, we can expect that parents and children will interact during play according to their respective understandings of parent–child relationships, as sanctioned by their cultures.

We can also suggest that the roles that children assume while interacting during play with their parents becomes an opportunity for them to further construct and practice ways of interacting that are appropriate to their culture. These experiences are basic for children to construct an understanding of their physical and social reality, which they can carry over to other interactions with varied members of their communities (e.g. interactions with daycare teachers). A focus on the joint activities that occur between parents and children during play can provide important information as to how children are socialized into interpersonal relationships in this social context. Further, when interacting with children, parents do so in particular ways based on varied assumptions, including assumptions concerning the capacities of young children, the nature of the parental role, and the behaviors expected of parents (McGillicuddy-DeLisi 1985, Sameroff and Feil 1985). The meaning that adults see in their children's behavior derives from the adults' own cultural beliefs, expectations, and values. What adults accept as meaningful or appropriate behavior, and therefore what the child may construe as meaningful, depends in part on those culturally based expectations. Thus one can expect cross-cultural variation in terms of the ways in which parents and children engage during play, and in the meaning that those activities have for the members involved.

Overview

Research on parent–toddler interaction during play in the middle-class American culture will be compared with such interaction in the middle-class Colombian culture to explore ways in which children may be socialized through a common activity such as play. These cultures were chosen because they offer a contrast along several dimensions that characterize interpersonal relationships. Focusing on particular dimensions of interpersonal relationships is a means of understanding the variations in meaning that certain activities have for participants in the interaction. In particular, play activities can be understood in terms of the hierarchy embedded in the relationship and the structural features of the interaction.

The degree of hierarchy in social interaction may be represented along the dimensions of symmetry or asymmetry. In the American middle class, value is placed on establishing equality in relationships including relationships between parents and children (Martinez 1981, Sampson 1988). This tendency for equality in the interaction can be termed symmetrical in the sense that the interacting members can exchange the roles of leader and follower in the activity that is being shared. As a contrast, in groups that emphasize the hierarchic nature of parent–child interaction, the interacting members take on more differentiated roles. Such interactions are termed asymmetrical in that the adult typically assumes the role of leading the activity, while expecting the child to assume the role of follower. Hence one could expect greater interchangeability in the roles assumed by the participants during play in cultures where more egalitarian relationships are favored compared to those where hierarchical relationships are the norm.

A second important dimension of play involves structural features of the interaction, such as how relationships are structured in terms of the number of participants involved. That is, does play occur mostly in dyadic or in group interactions? In dyadic interactions, members of the dyad are focused on each other, allowing for one-to-one interactions in which individual goals may be more easily satisfied. In group interactions, there is a greater need to identify a common goal in order for the interaction to run smoothly. Both modes of relating are important in every society, but there may be cultural ideals as to the preferred mode of interaction (Greenfield 1994). These cultural ideals may become particularly evident in situations in which members of the culture are asked by a researcher to interact in ways that are typical of them as a family. In cultures such as the United States, individuals may sometimes be less willing to subordinate their personal goals to those of the group. In contrast, there is greater acceptance of subordination of personal goals to the group goals in some Latin-American cultures. Parents may want to instill these values when interacting with their children in play. Thus, the way in which the interaction is structured among family members may reveal cultural meanings related to dyadic and group contexts. We now turn to a consideration of middle-class American and middle-class Colombian values about relationships and how play interactions are expected to vary in terms of these two dimensions.

Play among American middle-class parents and their children

There are reports in the literature of the dyadic nature of parent–child interaction and the characteristics of face-to-face play in which parents engage (Schaffer 1984, Stern 1974, Parke 1981). For example, Parke (1981) has reported that parents show sensitivity to the infant's tempo and that the interaction appears to follow a "dialogue like" pattern. Descriptions of parents' speech in *en face* interactions also suggest that they address their infants as if they were communicating partners (Kruper and Užgiris 1987).

Most of the developmental descriptions of parent–child play have focused on mothers. Descriptions of middle-class American mothers and their children during play appear to indicate that there is a gradual progression toward symmetry in the interaction between them because the mother adjusts her actions to the child's level of development (Bruner and Sherwood 1976, Užgiris 1981, 1989). Mothers show sensitivity to their children's increasing skills as indicated by their ability to introduce complexity into the games that they play with their children (Bruner and Sherwood 1976, Miller and Garvey 1984), as well as by relinquishing dominance over those games (Dunn and Dale 1984, Ross and Kay 1980). In these activities the child becomes the agent of the activity and the mother moves to a role of expanding or facilitating the child's activity.

The way that American middle-class parents engage their children during play appears to be connected to several values pertinent to how social interactions occur in this culture. Martinez (1981), in comparing mother–child play between European-Americans and Mexicans, has discussed cultural differences in relation to the value that is placed on equality. Ochs and Schieffelin (1984) have used the term "child raising" to note the strategies that adult American middle-class caregivers use to reduce the competence gap between adult and child. This finding indicates that American mothers see their role in the interaction as that of facilitating their children's active participation and promoting their interaction on a one-on-one basis.

Values of equality, individual rights and individual autonomy have been connected to the middle-class American culture (Bellah, Madsen, Sullivan, Swidler and Tipton 1985). Parents' attempts to promote children's participation on a one-on-one basis may respond to the value of promoting separateness and self-reliance connected to ideas about equality, individual autonomy and rights. This mode of relating has been contrasted with cultures where the ideals focus on social obligation and prescribed roles (Triandis *et al.* 1986, 1988, Raeff, Greenfield, Quiroz 2000).

Play in Colombia and other Latin American cultures

Colombia and other Latin American countries share a history of invasion by the Spanish conquistadors who imposed, to some extent, their traditions on the native Indian culture in each country (Alba 1969, Pendle 1965). The Spanish legacy is particularly apparent in the hierarchical structure of interpersonal relationships and the strong influence of Catholicism. In Colombia, the importance of authority in parent–child relationships has been documented (Gutierrrez de Pineda 1975), but more recent publications have begun to discuss changes in the Colombian family (Ardila 1986, Gutierrez de Pineda 1983). With shifts in women's roles, changes are being noted in terms of a more egalitarian status within the couple and between parents and children. However, the extent to which these changes are now a part of family relationships is still an empirical question. Family relationships in Colombia and other Latin American countries also involve strong ties and responsibilities within the immediate family and with members of the extended family.

Given the limited literature on Colombian parent–child relationships, we will review some research in several Latin American cultures to explore similarities and variations in parent–child relationships and in play interactions in particular. In a cross-cultural study that included Colombia, the United States, and Japan, Posada, Gao, Wu, Posada, Tascon, Schoelmerich, Sagri, Kondo-Ikemura,

Haaland and Synnevaag (1995) compared mothers' ideals about secure base behavior in children and actual secure base behavior in their children. In a Q-sort task, mothers across cultures selected similar responses about ideal secure base behavior in children, as well as similar responses of actual secure base behavior in their own children. Differences were found, as Colombian mothers showed a preference for "having children return to mother, check her location, and go back to her when upset, bored or in need of help" (Posada et al. 1995: 46). In contrast, mothers from the United States and Japan emphasized their child's readiness to interact with the mother and his or her positive emotional tone in those interactions. It is important to note that in all cultures there were similarities in views of secure base behavior by children. There were differences, however, in mothers' preferences regarding the child's adaptive use of the mother as a secure base.

In the Mayan culture in Guatemala, Rogoff, Mistry, Goncu and Mosier (1991) reported that some Mayan mothers laughed with embarrassment at the idea of playing with their children. In this culture, the role of player is given to other children and occasionally to grandparents. Rogoff et al. (1991) also noted that the interaction between these mothers and their toddlers was characterized by attending simultaneously to other ongoing social activities while engaged with each other. Although these interactions were not play interactions, they suggest that there may be variations in the structure of play interactions across cultures.

In other studies, Martinez (1981) compared mother–child conversations to child–child conversations within a working-class Mexican community. Mexican mothers' interaction in toy-mediated play with their two- to three-year-old children can be analyzed in terms of the roles played by the members of the dyad. Mexican mothers used more nonverbal and directive strategies, whereas, children, on the other hand, assumed a more subordinate role in interaction with their mothers. This subordinate role was evidenced by the lower proportion of questions directed to their mothers, in comparison to the proportion of responses to their mothers' questions. In contrast, their interaction with peers involved more turn-taking in asking and responding to questions. Thus, the value of a more hierarchical relationship appears to be reflected in the interactions between mother and child in this culture. Mexican mothers appear to see their roles in the interaction as that of providing direction, an expected role within their culture. Hence their actions include more directive strategies. Children, in turn, may experience themselves as passive and in need of looking up to the adult for direction.

These studies suggest that by comparing the social interaction of parents and children in varied cultures, we can identify differences as well as similarities in their interactions that may be based on their cultural conceptions of interpersonal relationships. It is recognized that in every culture there are variations among individuals in terms of the meaning they attribute to activities and relationships. With regard to the current study, it is expected that the value placed by some Colombian families on the hierarchical organization of parent–child relationships will be evident in the structure of play. That is, Colombian parents view themselves not as partners in the interaction but as asymmetrical directors of the child's activity. Another value that is important for some Colombian families and which can influence the structure of play is the expectation of mutual obligation among family members. An example of this expectation is the view that just as parents take care of children, so should grown-up children take care of parents when the parents get old. Thus, families who cherish these values may interact in such a way as to foster group cohesiveness because it is an important aspect of family relationships. In contrast, American families may show interaction patterns that reflect the value of one-on-one interactions in which individual points of view can be expressed within the family unit. One can expect that such conceptions may permeate parent–child play through symmetrical and dyadic interactions.

In summary, the goal of this study is to identify the structure of play in the middle-class Colombian culture and to compare it with that of the middle-class American culture. It is expected that more symmetry will be found in the interactions among the American families, while greater asymmetry in roles will characterize the Colombian families. In addition, middle-class American families are expected to engage in more dyadic interactions while Colombian families will engage in more group interactions.

Method

Participants

Thirty-two families (sixteen from each culture) with a toddler between eighteen and twenty months of age participated in the study. The subjects were divided equally between middle-class Colombian and middle-class American families, and the toddlers were divided equally by gender (eight boys and eight girls per culture). In all the families there was at least one older sibling participating in the study, and the maximum number of older siblings participating was three. The age of the older siblings ranged from two years eight months to eleven years of age. American fathers ranged in age from thirty to forty ($M = 35.2$), and for American mothers from twenty-eight to thirty-eight ($M = 33.6$). The ages for the Colombian fathers ranged from thirty to forty-eight ($M = 37.1$), and for mothers from twenty-one to forty-three ($M = 31.1$). Table 4.1 provides more details of the demographic characteristics of the samples.

Procedure to recruit families

The procedure to solicit participation varied in each culture. For the American sample, the families were recruited by letters and follow-up telephone calls. Possible participants were identified from the birth announcements in local newspapers, and they were sent a letter describing the nature of the study and its general procedures. The investigator then called each family to inquire about the family's willingness to participate in the study, and to ascertain that they meet the

Table 4.1 Demographic characteristics of the sample

	Colombia	United States
Number of families in sample	16	16
Mean age of toddlers	1.6 yrs	1.6 yrs
Number of siblings		
% of toddlers with 1 sibling	75	62.5
% of toddlers with 2 sibs	25	31.3
% of toddlers with 3 sibs	0	6.3
Mean ages of parents		
Fathers	37.1 yrs	35.2 yrs
Mothers	31.1 yrs	33.6 yrs
Highest education of parents		
% with graduate/professional training	9.4	15.6
% with college degree	25.0	28.1
% with some college or specialized training	21.9	43.8
% with high school degree	31.3	9.4
% with tenth to twelfth grade	12.5	3.1
Social strata		
% of parents in major businesses or professional	25.0	31.3
% of parents in medium businesses, minor professional or technical	43.8	37.5
% of parents in skilled, or clerical work	25.0	18.6
% of parents in semiskilled work	6.3	12.5

requirements for participation (e.g. have an older child). Once the family agreed to participate, a meeting was arranged at a time when all the family members would be present.

For the Colombian sample, a listing of daycare centers located in the city of Cali, Colombia was obtained through people in contact with some of the day care centers. The investigator met with the directors of these centers to inform them about the study and to ask them to facilitate contact with the families whom they identified as qualified for the study. These parents were contacted and engaged by the director of the day care center to participate in the study. Some families were also recruited by word of mouth. As with the American families, once the Colombian families agreed to participate in the study, the investigator scheduled the home visit at a time when all family members would be present.

Demographic characteristics of the sample

For classification of social status, Hollingshead's (1975) criteria were used as a guide to establish a basis for a cultural comparison of the two countries. Table 4.1 shows various demographic characteristics of the sample. The families participating were representative of the wide span of what is considered middle-class. Parental occupation was used as the main marker of middle-class socioeconomic status. For both cultures, 69% of the families fell into the first two categories of major business/professional, or medium business and minor professional or technical. The remaining 31% were distributed among the categories of skilled/clerical work, or semiskilled work. In both cultures there was a wide range in educational level. Percentages for each educational level were obtained by adding the number of parents (mothers and fathers) in a specific category of education and dividing it by 32 (the total number of parents per culture). In the United States most parents had some specialized training or higher education (87.5%), and the majority of Colombian parents (56.3%) also had some specialized training. The remaining American and Colombian participants had a high school degree or less.

Procedure

Family interactions were videotaped, and parents were asked to spend time as they typically do when they are together as a family and have some free time to interact or play with their children. Twenty minutes of family interaction were videotaped.

Transcribing and coding

For the purpose of the current analysis, only play interaction episodes in which the focal child was involved were coded from videotape. A unit of interaction was considered to start when any of the three following events occurred: first, when the toddler engaged or was engaged in play by another family member; second, when the composition of the group changed by either one family member joining or leaving the group in which the toddler was participating; or third, when a shift in activity occurred. An interaction was considered to end when either of the following occurred: the toddler or family member was no longer engaged with another, or a new unit started in accordance with the second or third type of event outlined above. The interactions taking place were coded continuously.

Based on our earlier discussion of interaction structure as a dimension of social interaction, the structure of the play interaction was coded as follows.

Dyadic interaction

The toddler is engaged in mutual looking, verbal exchanges and/or reciprocal actions with one member of the family. The specific family member engaged in interaction with the toddler was noted. These interactions were distinguished from periods when the parent or sibling was watching the child's activity, or set up the toys for the child, but did not actively engage in the activity.

Semi-group interaction

The parent or sibling was watching the child play with another family member, but did not actively engage in the activity. The specific family member engaged in observing was noted.

Group interaction

Two or more family members were engaged in interaction with the toddler. In order to be considered a group interaction, the members had to be in contact either verbally or through a common activity.

Also, based on our earlier discussion, the relative hierarchy of the roles assumed by interaction partners is another key dimension of social interaction. For the current discussion, the analytic focus is on the symmetry and asymmetry of roles during dyadic interaction. Role symmetry and asymmetry were classified as follows.

Symmetrical roles

The roles between parent and child were interchangeable according to one of the following criteria: either one parent or older sibling initiated the activity, but the toddler was given the choice of participating; or, alternatively, the parent or sibling joined the activity in which the child was engaged. The member initiating and the member ending the activity were recorded.

Asymmetrical roles

The roles between parent and toddler were distinct according to either of the following criteria: one parent or older sibling initiated and insisted on the activity without asking the toddler for explicit consent; or, alternatively, the parent or sibling maintained a specific agenda as to the activity taking place. The person directing the activity was recorded. The member initiating and the member ending the activity were also recorded.

Each unit of interaction, measured in seconds, was coded in terms of the structure and roles occurring in the interaction. The number of seconds spent in each of the coded categories was added across the twenty-minute segment of family interaction. The total number of seconds for each category was then converted into a percentage by dividing that number by the total play time for this segment. Statistical analyses were based on the percentages obtained for each coding category.

Results

All of the videotapes were coded by the investigator. Two bilingual independent judges coded two Colombian families' tapes, and two other English-speaking independent judges coded two of the American families' tapes. All judges were unaware of the expectations of the study. Reliability was calculated by adding the number of agreements between the two coders for each category across the four tapes for each culture and then dividing the results by the total number of judgements made (agreements plus disagreements). These results were then converted into percentages. The percentages of agreement for the different categories coded ranged from 85.4% to 98.0%, indicating that reliability had been demonstrated for coding the categories of interest. Table 4.2 provides more detailed reliability information about the categories per culture.

The data from this study were organized so as to treat culture as an independent variable for the purpose of examining its effects on various dimensions of play activities. For the first analysis, an analysis of variance (ANOVA) was conducted to examine the effects of culture on the structure of interactions and roles families engaged in during play. The data were tested for normality using the Kolmogorov–Smirnov (K–S) test, and the data were also tested for homogeneity of variance with a one-way ANOVA. The data were found to fulfill these requirements.

Culture and roles in play

In dyadic interaction, the roles assumed by each member were classified as symmetrical or asymmetrical. The time during which each member (mother, father and sibling) assumed symmetrical roles was summed to construct the category of symmetrical interactions. The same procedure was followed for constructing the category of asymmetrical interactions. The number of seconds in interaction was converted into a percentage by dividing it by the total amount of family play in order to identify the preferred roles assumed in dyadic play by members of each culture.

The data were subjected to a two-way ANOVA examining the effects of culture on symmetrical and asymmetrical interactions. As expected, there was a main effect of culture ($F(1,28) = 14.03$, $p < .05$). The mean percentage of time that American families engaged in symmetrical play was 66.1%, while Colombian families spent 39.9% of their time in symmetrical play. In contrast, asymmetrical interactions were significantly higher in the Colombian culture ($F(1,28) = 20.89$, $p < .05$). American families spent 5.2% of their time in asymmetrical play, while Colombian families spent 21.4% of their time in asymmetrical play. It is important to point out that even though the Colombian families spent significantly more time in asymmetrical play than did the Americans, the Colombian families still spent more time in symmetrical play than they did in asymmetrical play.

Table 4.2 Percentages of agreement by coding category

	American	*Colombian*
Symmetry	93.8	89.7
Asymmetry	85.4	92.0
Dyad	96.6	98.0
Semi-group	94.3	94.7
Group	95.7	95.1

Culture and structure of the interaction

As previously described, the structure of interactions was classified into dyadic, semi-group, or group interactions depending on the number of family members interacting with the child. For each interaction structure category, these play interactions were added across all family members (mother, father and sibling). The number of seconds in interaction was converted into a percentage of the total amount of family play in order to identify the preferred types of interaction. A multivariate analysis of variance (MANOVA) was conducted on these three variables to examine the effects of culture.

As expected, the results indicate that dyadic interactions were significantly more frequent in the American culture than the Colombian culture ($F(1,28) = 6.10$, $p < .05$). The mean percentage of time that American families engaged in dyadic interactions was 55.3%, while Colombian families spent a mean of 33.8% of their time in dyadic play. In contrast, Colombian families spent significantly more time with one or two members observing than American families ($F(1,28) = 4.55$, $p < .05$). The mean percentage of time in semi-group play for American families was 17.1%, while Colombian families had one to two observers present a mean of 28.8% of the time.

The statistical analysis on group interactions indicated no differences by culture ($F(1,28) = 1.95$, $p < .05$). The mean percentage of time that American families spent in group play was 27.6, while Colombian families spent 37.5% of their time in group play.

Discussion

The present study compared parent toddler play interaction in the middle-class American culture and the middle-class Colombian culture to explore how children's understandings of culturally appropriate interpersonal relationships are shaped by cultural values. The results of the study indicate differences in parent–child play interaction, which can be understood in the context of cultural conceptions of parent–child relationships, and relationships in general.

Cultural values and social roles in parent–toddler play

As expected, the interactive play episodes showed that American parents were more likely to engage in symmetrical interactions with their children, while Colombian parents engaged in asymmetrical play. There was, however, greater variability in the interactions during play by Colombian families. They engaged in both symmetrical and asymmetrical interactions with their children during play. Asymmetry was observed in that Colombian parents chose the activity for play and geared their efforts towards engaging the child in the activity. Symmetry was observed in that they also joined their child in his/her activity. There was less variability in American parents' interactions during play, as few instances were observed of asymmetry in their interactions with their children. American parents allowed their children to choose the play activity and then followed the child's lead in the activity chosen. These results can be seen as examples of expressions of cultural conceptions for interpersonal relationships valued by each culture.

As has been described by several authors (Sampson 1988, Triandis *et al.* 1988), cultural values in the American middle class include those of independence, personal responsibility and achievement in self–other relationships. Sampson (1988) argues that part of the American belief system is that early independence training produces persons high in achievement. He also contends that related to the value placed on personal freedom is the belief that personal responsibility only occurs when individuals believe themselves to have personal efficacy as causal agents. However, Raeff (2000) suggests two points that are important to consider when focusing on parent–child relationships. One point is that it is likely that all cultures will focus on dimensions of self-reliance and independence as well as interdependence. The second point is that these dimensions may be more pronounced in certain specific social contexts. In her study on European-American parents' ideas about independence and interdependence, she found that parents are concerned with fostering aspects of interdependence as well as independence in relationships. Parents focused on values of interdependence when talking about their children's interaction with others. In that context, they emphasized the importance of being actively prosocial in interaction with others. In the context of parents' interaction with their children, they focused on treating the child as an independent person with individual preferences and goals.

The current study also shows examples of two kinds of specific social contexts. Values of independence were expressed in that American parents requested the toddler's explicit consent to participate in an activity by asking the child directly. Thus, the child was singled out and offered a choice. What gets communicated to the child is that "this social activity is for you, so you get to choose." In other instances, this value was communicated indirectly through the parent's participation in an activity already chosen by the young child. The interaction between a mother and her daughter – whom we will call Rose – illustrates this point.

> Mother remained available to Rose through most of the segment. She became directly involved in her daughter's activity in two instances: first, to comment when Rose kissed a dinosaur; and second, to expand on Rose's world of make-believe by joining in the pretense that the dinosaur bit her. Father joined the interaction in a facilitator role.

In this context, Rose was the agent of the activity by directing her own imaginary play. Her parents joined to expand her agenda in play.

The importance of being actively prosocial in interaction with others was observed in instances where rules for interaction were violated. For example, in one tape, the toddler was moving a doll down a slide. His brother attempted several times to get a turn at sliding the doll, meeting each time with resistance from the toddler. Their mother came into the room and intervened on behalf of the sibling; and their father then stated "for the sake of fairness." Thus, parents' actions were directed at regulating the children's behavior according to cultural norms of taking turns, sharing and being fair.

The results of greater variability in the Colombian families' parent–child play suggest within culture variability in parental views of parent–child relationships. Within group comparisons showed that the Colombian parents engaged in more symmetrical interactions than asymmetrical interactions. This finding may confirm Ardila's (1986) report of changes toward a more egalitarian status in parent–child relationships in the Colombian family. The specific social context of play may also elicit this type of symmetry, as the activity was organized with the toddler as the focus.

On the other hand, the tendency for asymmetry in parent–child play is also consistent with the cultural value of hierarchy in parent–child relationships (Gutierrez de Pineda 1975), and the high value placed on the family as a social unit. Hui and Triandis (1986) in a study characterizing cultures on dimensions based on self–other relationships classified Colombia toward the end of the collectivist spectrum. This sense of the collective has been described by these authors as involving the "subordination of personal goals to the goals of a collective, and a sense of harmony, interdependence, and concern for others" (p. 245). Subordination to a common goal implies that group members need to defer to some level of authority or guidance in order to reach that common goal (Triandis *et al.* 1988). It also seems to imply that, in some instances, this common goal might be determined by the person of higher status, and assumed to be the goal of its members. In the family unit, this role of authority falls on the parents, or on one of them, according to the family's hierarchical organization.

Thus, values of hierarchy and of presenting the family as a cohesive group seem to fit together to account for the results of asymmetry in the Colombian families. In many instances, Colombian children were participants in activities set up by others, and the families assumed that the toddlers would be interested in engagement. An activity was set up by the adult or older sibling and continued unless the toddler protested. In instances where the child was unclear as to the expectations that the adult had, the parents' actions were directed at demonstrating what to do, or at telling the child what they wanted. Thus, toddlers were presented with a situation in which to respond to requests from others, and which required an understanding of others' expectations. The child was in the position of responding to the goals of the group. When the young child did not engage in expected interactions, adults' and siblings' actions were directed at 'convincing' the toddler to engage in the activity.

Fabio's example is illustrative of these values. He is riding his tricycle. His father introduces a doll, assuming that Fabio wants it. Then he directs his son to take the doll for a ride, and repeats this idea several times when Fabio does not respond immediately. Finally, Fabio complies with his father's request. However, the scene that follows is illustrative of greater symmetry in the father's interaction with his son. This time Fabio has shown interest in a doll his sister has. Father then intervenes on behalf of Fabio to get the doll from the sister. In this case, the father followed the child's interest and intervened on his behalf to join with his request.

In conclusion, Colombian families presented patterns of both symmetry and asymmetry in their interactions with their toddler during play. Some Colombian families appeared to set up a situation as described by Heath (1983), in which children "come to know the way of doing things," in contrast to the negotiation described to characterize interactions by mainstream American parents (Heath 1983, Ochs and Schieffelin 1984). In other cases, they joined their child in the activity similar to patterns by middle-class American parents. These findings reveal that play is yet another context in which the structure of relationships in general is fostered.

Cultural values and the structure of interactions

In both cultures, parents' interactions involved both dyadic and group interactions. As expected, however, parent–child interactions for the American middle-class were significantly more dyadic in comparison to the Colombian parent–child interaction. In dyadic interactions, each member of the dyad is the focus, allowing for one-on-one interactions in which individual goals can be negotiated and satisfied more readily. Ochs and Schieffelin (1984) suggest that the process of being social takes place predominantly through dyadic interactions in the American middle class. Thus, social competence itself is measured in terms of the young child's capacity to participate in such interactions. Parents provide their children with ample opportunities to interact in this socially valued way, through interactive give and take (e.g. Bruner and Sherwood 1976, Parke 1981, Kruper and Užgiris 1987, Schaffer 1984).

The dyadic and turn-taking nature of parent–child play seems to occur because the parent treats the child as a partner, reflecting the value of equality, which is important in the middle-class American culture. Children's privacy, independence, and personal responsibility in dealing with their physical and interpersonal environment may be fostered through such interactions from very early on (Triandis *et al.* 1988).

On the other hand, the expectation that the Colombian families would engage in group interaction was not completely supported. No differences were found between the two cultures with respect to this category. It is believed that this result may be related to the fact that group interactions were not differentiated by number of participants. In both cultures it was common for one parent to engage in play with the two children, i.e. the focal toddler and the older sibling. It is also possible that this study may have elicited expectations in both cultures of group interactions because the study required all family members to be present. It is noted that the Colombian families had a higher percentage of group play than the American families. However, it still remains a question whether group interactions in which all family members are involved were similar or different in the two cultures.

The fact that semi-group interaction was significantly higher among the Colombian families suggests a preference for group interaction. The pattern of at least two family members focused on the child, although one of them might be an observer, suggests that family members were working on the idea that this activity was for the toddler and their efforts should be geared toward that goal.

The Colombian parents' engagement in both semi-group and group activities when presented with the task of "being together as a family," reflects the value placed on the family as a unit, and in presenting a united front when interacting in the presence of an outsider, such as the investigator. In particular, since the investigator was seen by the Colombian families as a professional and an observer of their interaction, it is possible that family members were responding to values related to the family unit by engaging in interaction in ways that demonstrated the closeness and solidarity among them. Ochs (1988) made similar observations of her presence as an investigator in eliciting formal speech when studying language socialization in the Samoan culture.

Goffman (1959) addresses this issue in a more general way by stating that an individual's definition of the situation, when in the presence of others, will mobilize his or her activity so that it will convey an impression on others that is in the person's interest to convey. As with the Colombian families, the context of the study also elicited particular modes of relating for the American middle class which involved more dyadic interaction. This is particularly striking as the study did require the presence of all family members in the room. This issue points to how cultural meaning creates activity (Geertz 1973) for the symbolic status of the investigator as an outsider seems to have elicited processes of interaction valued by each culture. For the American families, this involved one to one interactions. For the Colombian families, the task appeared to have accessed the values of presenting a united family front.

To summarize, the overall results of this study do suggest that in each cultural context children experience different levels of guidance by adults and are given opportunities to interact in ways appropriate to their culture. In parent–child play, the roles that children assume in each culture may be one way in which they practice ways of interacting appropriate to relations with adults in their culture.

The significance of play

Play as an interpersonal activity requires from the child a gradual understanding of the meaning of the activities he/she is participating in. At a structural level of play, processes of socialization between parent and child pertain to how play is to be carried out, what aspects of the interpersonal relationship are to be highlighted and what qualifies as play in these interactions. The differences in the structure and roles in play in the two cultures highlight this issue. An example from an interaction by a Colombian family may illustrate this point. In this case it was difficult at times for the toddler to understand the communication as play.

Father, in this instance, threw a ball at the older sister. Mother engages Lola (focal child) into taking the ball from them. Father throws the ball to the sister even higher, despite the child's attempts to grab it. Mother continues to encourage Lola to take the ball from them. Lola is very excited and everyone is laughing. When the ball falls to the floor, both sister and Lola run to grab it. Sister grabs it and bumps into Lola. Lola begins to cry. At this moment Father gives the ball to Lola and comforts her.

In this sequence, the mother engages Lola in a challenge by asking her to grab the ball from the father–sibling dyad. The father responds to the mother's challenge by making it more difficult for the child to take the ball from them, despite the problem this creates for the child. Mother's coaching is required, because it is difficult for the child to understand the meaning of this situation, as indicated by Lola's frustration at the end. Father, then, comforts her by giving the ball to her. Thus, in this situation, the child may be learning about teasing exchanges, beginning with the role of being teased, and that this mode of interaction is considered play. The level of sophistication of the communication, however, requires the guidance of an adult partner who can facilitate the child's participation in the activity.

The role of play in the development of communication and in fostering symbolic activity is pertinent here (Bateson 1972, Bruner, Jolly and Sylva 1976, Stern 1974). Children are embedded in meaning frames implicitly communicated in the interaction through actions (e.g. setting up toys and engaging the child in an activity) and explicitly through language (e.g. telling children what to play as opposed to asking children what they want to play). Families in each culture focused on the play activity in ways that seemed "natural" for them. Such "naturalness," however, is better understood in light of cultural conceptions for interpersonal interaction.

In the context in which this study was conducted, families were required to identify strategies to engage the toddler in play. For each cultural group, this elicited different strategies of engagement. For the American families, it involved asking the toddler or joining in his/her activity. For the Colombian families, the family unit became very important to obtain the child's interest and engagement. All family members directed their interactions at promoting the play activity, and engaging the child in play.

In these contexts, children assume specific roles while interacting in play with others, which may be a way in which they practice and gradually construct an understanding of the symbols and meanings involved in interpersonal interactions (e.g. status of self and other in defining who leads the activity). This is consistent with Mead's (1962) proposition that children construct the meaning of their social worlds by taking on certain roles while playing with others. However, it differs in that language is not seen as the only vehicle for children to construct these meanings. Children may construct these meanings as Piaget (1962, 1981) claims through their own organizing activities (e.g. imitation, pretend play, assuming agency in the activity).

Future directions

This study suggests many areas of research as it provides evidence for the fruitfulness of a model which views children's development in a cultural setting. It corroborates reports in the current literature of different patterns of interactions by parents in other cultures (Field *et al.* 1981, Lamb, LeVine *et al.* 1988). In addition, this study indicates that including cultural meaning (Geertz 1973) in an understanding of patterns of parent–child interaction provides important information as to how children are socialized in ways appropriate to their culture.

This study has demonstrated that focusing on interpersonal dimensions of the play activity reveals that cultural meaning is involved and constructed in the interaction. This issue needs to be explored further with other methods, such as showing the families the videotape of their own interactions and asking them to select out play activities. Further inquiry would offer a better understanding of how closely the recorded interactions correspond with their everyday activities, the importance they attach to play, and the meaning of specific activities in which they engaged.

Studies differentiating play from other activities such as mealtime could also offer some insight into the significance of this activity. Play sets out a very particular context for parents to interact with their children, for it is an activity that is "naturally" considered children's territory. Whether it may be conceived of as being for their own entertainment or as an activity in which children learn, it requires from parents some adjustments to the child's interests and focus (i.e. you cannot force children to play; you either join them, or "convince" them to play). Other contexts such as feeding, dressing, or putting the child to sleep are more explicitly conventionalized, leaving parents and children with a clearer idea of their role in the interaction. This study leaves open the question of the role of play in the context of other activities in which parents and children engage. An exploration of cultural meaning in other contexts, and of how play may permeate these other contexts, would also provide a better understanding of what part play has in the child's life and in parent–child relations.

References

Adamson, L. B. and Bakeman, R. (1985) "Affect and Attention: Infants Observed with Mothers and Peers", *Child Development*, 56: 582–593.

Alba, V. (1969) *The Latin Americans*. New York: Frederick A. Praeger, Inc.

Ardila, R. (1986) *Psicologia del Hombre Colombiano*. Colombia: Planeta Colombiana Editorial S. A.

Bateson, G. (1972) *Steps to an Ecology of Mind*. New York: Ballantine Books.

Bellah, R. N., Madsen, R., Sullivan, W. M., Swidler, A. and Tipton, S. M. (1985) *Habits of the Heart: Individualism and Commitment in American Life*. New York: Harper & Row.

Bornstein, M. H. (1991) *Cultural Approaches to Parenting*. Hillsdale, NJ: Lawrence Erlbaum Associates.

Bruner, J. S., Jolly, A. and Sylva, K. (1976) "Introduction" in Bruner, J. S., Jolly, A. and Sylva, K. (eds.) *Play – Its Role in Development and Evolution.* New York: Basic Books Inc.

Bruner, J. S. and Sherwood, V. (1976) "Peekaboo and the Learning of Rule Structures" in Bruner, J. S., Jolly, A. and Sylva, K. (eds.) *Play – Its Role in Development and Evolution.* New York: Basic Books Inc.

Dunn, J. and Dale, N. (1984) "I a Daddy: 2-Year-Olds' Collaboration in Joint Pretend with Sibling and with Mother" in Bretherton, I. (ed.) *Symbolic Play.* Orlando, Florida: Academic Press Inc.

Field, T. M., Sostek, A. M., Vietze, P. and Leiderman, P. H. (eds.) (1981) *Culture and Early Interactions.* Hillsdale, NJ: Lawrence Erlbaum Associates.

Garvey, C. (1977) *Play.* Cambridge, MA: Harvard University Press.

Geertz, C. (1973) *The Interpretation of Culture.* New York: Basic Books.

Goffman, E. (1959) *The Presentation of Self in Everyday Life.* Garden City, New York: Doubleday Anchor Books.

Greenfield, P. M. (1994) "Independence and Interdependence as Developmental Scripts: Implications for Theory, Research, and Practice" in Greenfield, P. M. and Cocking, R. R. (eds.) *Cross-Cultural Roots of Minority Child Development.* Hillsdale, NJ: Lawrence Erlbaum Associates.

Gutierrez de Pineda, V. (1975) *Estructura, funcion y cambio de la familia en Colombia, vol. I.* Bogota, Colombia: Asociación Colombiana de Facultades de Medicina.

—— (1983) "Avances y perspectivas en los estudios de familia" in *Avances y perspectivas en los estudios sociales de la familia en Colombia.* Medellín, Colombia: Editorial Presencia Ltda.

Heath, S. B. (1983) *Ways with Words: Language, Life and Work in Communities and Classrooms.* New York: Cambridge University Press.

Hollingshead, A. B. (1975) "Four Factor Index of Social Status", unpublished manuscript, Yale University.

Hui, C. H. and Triandis, H. C. (1986) "Individualism–Collectivism: A Study of Cross-cultural Researchers", *Journal of Cross-Cultural Psychology, vol. 17, no. 2:* 225–248.

Kruper, J. C. and Užgiris, I. Č. (1987) "Fathers' and mothers' speech to young infants", *Journal of Psycholinguistic Research, vol. 16, no. 6:* 597–614.

LeVine, R. A., Miller, P. M. and Maxwell West, M. (eds.) (1988) *New Directions for Child Development no. 40: Parental Behavior in Diverse Societies.* San Francisco: Jossey-Bass Inc.

Martinez, M. A. (1981) "Conversational Asymmetry between Mexican Mother and Children", *Hispanic Journal of Behavioral Sciences, vol. 3, no. 4:* 329–346.

McGillicuddy-DeLisi, A. V. (1985) "The Relationship between Parental Beliefs and Children's Cognitive Level" in Sigel, I. E. (ed.) *Parental Belief Systems: The Psychological Consequences for Children.* Hillsdale, N.J.: Lawrence Erlbaum Associates.

Mead, G. H. (1962) *Mind, Self and Society.* Morris, C. W. (ed.) Chicago: University of Chicago Press.

Miller, P. and Garvey, C. (1984) "Mother-Baby Role Play: Its Origins in Social Support" in Bretherton, I. (ed.) *Symbolic Play.* Orlando, Florida: Academic Press Inc.

Ochs, E. (1988) *Culture and Language Development: Language Acquisition and Language Socialization in a Samoan Village.* New York: Cambridge University Press.

Ochs, E. and Schieffelin, B. B. (1984) "Language Acquisition and Socialization: Three Developmental Stories and Their Implications" in Shweder, R. A. and LeVine, R. A. (eds.) *Culture Theory: Essays on Mind, Self and Emotion.* Cambridge, England: Cambridge University Press.

Parke, R. D. (1981) *Fathers.* Cambridge, MA: Harvard University Press.

Pendle, G. (1965) *A History of Latin America.* Baltimore, MD: Penguin Books.

Piaget, J. (1962) *Play, Dreams and Imitation in Childhood.* New York: W. W. Norton & Company.

— (1981) *The Psychology of Intelligence.* New Jersey: Littlefield, Adams & Co.

Posada, G., Gao, Y., Wu, F., Posada, R., Tascon, M., Schoelmerich, A., Sagri, A., Kondo-Ikemura, K., Haaland,W. and Synnevaag, B. (1995) "The Secure-Base Phenomenon across Cultures: Children's Behavior, Mother's Preferences, and Experts' Concepts" in Waters, E., Vaughn, B., Posada, G. and Kondo-Ikemura, K. (eds.) *Caregiving, Cultural and Cognitive Perspectives on Secure-Base Behavior and Working Models. New Growing Points of Attachment Theory and Research. Monographs of the Society for Research in Child Development nos. 2–3*: 27–48.

Raeff, C. (1997) "Individuals in Relationships: Cultural Values, Children's Social Interactions, and the Development of an American Individualistic Self", *Developmental Review, 17*: 205–238.

— (2000) "European-American Parents' Ideas about Their Toddlers' Independence and Interdependence", *Journal of Applied Developmental Psychology, 21*: 183–205.

Raeff, C., Greenfield, P. M. and Quiroz, B. (2000) "Conceptualizing Interpersonal Relationships in the Cultural Context of Individualism and Collectivism", *New Directions for Child Development, no. 87t.* San Francisco: Jossey-Bass.

Rogoff, B., Mistry, J., Goncu, A. and Mosier, C. (1991) "Cultural Variations in Role Relations of Toddlers and Their Families" in Bornstein, M. H. (ed.) *Cultural Approaches to Parenting.* Hillsdale, NJ: Lawrence Erlbaum Associates.

Ross, H. S. and Kay, D. A. (1980) "The Origins of Social Games" in Rubin, K. H. (ed.) *New Directions for Child Development no. 9: Children's Play.* San Francisco: Jossey-Bass Inc.

Sameroff, A. J. and Feil, L. A. (1985) "Parental Concepts of Development" in Sigel, I. E. (ed.) *Parental Belief Systems: The Psychological Consequences for Children.* Hillsdale, N.J.: Lawrence Erlbaum Associates.

Sampson, E. E. (1988) "The Debate on Individualism: Indigenous Psychologies of the Individual and Their Role in Personal and Societal Functioning", *American Psychologist, vol. 43, no. 1*: 15–22.

Schaffer, H. R. (1984) *The Child's Entry into a Social World.* London: Academic Press.

Stern, D. N. (1974) "Mother and Infant at Play: The Dyadic Interaction Involving Facial, Vocal and Gaze Behaviors" in Lewis, M. and Rosenblum, L. A., *The Effect of the Infant on its Caregiver.* New York: John Wiley & Sons.

Triandis, H. C., Bontempo, R., Betancourt, R., Bond, M., Leung, K., Brenes, A., Georgas, J., Hui, C. H., Marin, G., Setiadi, B., Sinha, J. B. P., Verma, J, Spangenberg, J., Touzard, H. and Montmollin, G. (1986) "The Measurement of the Etic Aspects of Individualism and Collectivism Across Cultures", *Australian Journal of Psychology vol. 38, no. 3*: 245–256.

Triandis, H. C., Bontempo, R., Villareal, M. J., Asai, M. and Lucca, N. (1988) "Individualism and Collectivism: Cross-Cultural Perspectives on Self-Ingroup Relationships", *Journal of Personality and Social Psychology, vol. 54, no.2*: 323–338.

Užgiris, I. Č. (1981) "Experience in the Social Context: Imitation and Play" in Schiefelbusch, P. L. and Bricker, D. D. (eds.) *Early Language Acquisition and Intervention.* Baltimore: University Park Press.

— (1989) "Infants in Relation: Performers, Pupils and Partners" in Damon, W. (ed.) *Child Development Today and Tomorrow.* San Francisco: Jossey-Bass.

Užgiris, I. Č. and Raeff, C. (1995) "Play in Parent–Child Interactions" in Bornstein, M. (ed.) *Handbook of Parenting, vol. 4.* Mahwah, NJ: Lawrence Erlbaum Associates.

5 Context and the dynamic construal of meaning in early childhood

Nancy Budwig

Although for many developmental psychologists, it has become a truism that the study of human development is inseparable from the study of sociocultural context, one of the greatest challenges has been to specify how cultural meanings become internalized or come to be meaningful to specific individuals over time. While theorists and researchers have increasingly stressed the importance of communication for understanding how cultural meanings form the fabric of individual experience, what is less clear is what methods can be employed to fruitfully study this relation. A central figure providing a rich account of the dynamic construal of meaning during early childhood was Ina Užgiris (Užgiris 1989, 1996, 1999). In her own research, Ina Užgiris struggled to clarify the relationship connecting personal meaning, sociocultural context and human development, especially during infancy.

In this chapter I show that answers to a problem Užgiris identified (but was unable to resolve), namely how to highlight the dynamic unfolding of meaning-making, could be aided by considering how the construct "context" is currently used in neighboring disciplines. That is, I will argue that although context has become quite central to many discussions within developmental psychology, such discussions stop short of work going on in fields such as cognitive linguistics and linguistic anthropology. After outlining an alternative view of context, I will consider how such a view dovetails with questions laid out by Užgiris and other developmentalists interested in the cultural construction of meaning over developmental time. I then illustrate this more dynamic view of context by drawing on two examples from my own research. I conclude by suggesting how more dynamic views of context stemming from frameworks developing in neighboring disciplines can help us better rethink the intricate and dynamic relationship among personal and cultural meaning systems and human development.

Dynamic approaches to meaning and context

Over the last few decades, theories of meaning have elaborated a notion of context that is increasingly dynamic. Central to such discussions has been the idea that symbolic forms themselves play a central role in the contextualization of meaning. Rather than studying human action *in* context, where context is equated with a priori situational or institutional and environmental factors, analysis switches to the way semiotic means are pivotal in the social construction of context. To this extent, context is not something "out there" to be tacked onto analysis but rather is viewed as a negotiated process that involves very subtle interpretations, interpretations that draw in part on symbolic forms that are constructed as part of culture-specific practices (see Gumperz and Levinson 1996).

One of the central stumbling blocks for developmental psychologists interested in context has been an adherence to an approach to meaning that views language primarily as a representational symbolic system. While developmental psychologists have clung to a more static view of language, over the last few decades there has been a resurgence of interest in multifunctional views of language in other disciplines (see Budwig, Wertsch and Užgiris 2000, for review). Discussion of the idea that meaning does not rest in language forms alone, and rather that meaning is dynamically constructed in social practices, has cropped up in several different fields (see Duranti and Goodwin 1992, Gumperz and Levinson 1996, Hanks 1996, Ochs, Schegloff and Thompson 1996, for excellent reviews). While it might appear that current interest has stemmed from recent discussions in anthropology, linguistics, philosophy, and sociology, the idea is new neither to psychology in general nor to developmental psychology in particular.

Precursors to dynamic accounts of meaning and context: the example of Karl Bühler

To take but one example, we can consider the work of Karl Bühler (1934–1990), a German psychologist who has been a central figure in the psychology of language. While psychologists have primarily drawn upon Bühler's multifunctional theory of language, his discussion of the connection between language and thought as found in his symbolic field theory, as well as his treatment of deixis can all be linked to recent developments in viewing context as emergent.

Bühler has been noted for explicating a view of language as multifunctional. According to Bühler, language is more than a representational system. He argued that language, in addition to being designational, or pointing to things in the world, also serves the functions of appeal and expression. For instance, one can use language or other symbolic means to request an object or to express internal states (see Budwig 1998, Bühler 1934–1990 for elaboration). As Taylor (1985) noted, viewing language as multifunctional paves the way for viewing it as doing more than expressing reality. Multifunctional views highlight the role of language in constructing reality to the extent that language can be used as a form of social action. Similarly, because of its expressive function, language allows for expression in a public sense to others and therefore allows for the intersubjective sharing of experiences.

Although Bühler has primarily been known for his multifunctional theory of language functioning within psychology, it is actually his "field-theoretic approach" that has played a major role in setting the stage for theorists in disciplines outside of psychology to understand the specific role of language in understanding human experience. A central claim of Bühler's field-theoretic approach is the idea that linguistic forms, viewed in conjunction with symbolic fields, help structure the nature of human experience. Bühler argued that sentences carry with them a level of meaning distinct from the individual words contained in them. It is through the complex alignment of sign and symbolic field that language plays a significant mediating role in the construction of reality. Put differently, Bühler draws an analogy with the act of painting. He writes: "But just as the painter's colours require a painting surface, so too do language symbols require a surrounding field in which they can be arranged. We call this the symbolic field of language" (Bühler 1934, 1990: 171). Between the actual acoustic sounds and the world there exists a set of mediators that can be viewed as sentence level gestalts that contribute to the understanding of meaning relationships between the particular lexical items. For Bühler then, languages, via their semantic fields, provide us with formula-like schemata that help in interpreting meaning relations. One example Bühler discusses at length is the development of case markers. He suggests that case markers derived from a syntactic schema involving the use of action words (i.e. a subclass of verbs) and only later were case markers systematically extended to non-action verbs. This syntactic schema required completion of two empty slots – one the *nominative* and the other the *accusative* (for instance, *He* kicked *him*). Bühler claimed that case markers are best viewed as related to the formula-like schemata based on conceptual units that begin as general meaning fields and only later come to take on purely grammatical roles. An implication of this view that links case markers to syntactic schemata is that the meaning of larger constructions involves more than the simple addition of meanings built up in word combinations. As has been noted by cognitive linguists (see Goldberg 1995), novel verbs can be inserted into the slot, and even without having a sense of the particular meaning of the novel word, a sense of the meaning is conveyed at the level of the construction itself, as for instance in the example *He dacked him*. The formula-like schemata provide larger meaning units speakers draw upon when communicating worldview.

Another central contribution of Bühler concerns his discussion of deixis. Deictic forms are those language forms – such as personal pronouns – whose meanings are relative to the specific utterances in which they appear and whose meanings must be determined in relation to the event of speaking. Consider, for instance, the use of first- and second-person pronouns; the meanings of these forms depend on speech roles like speaker and listener and therefore are dynamically produced in the process of speaking. Bühler argued that deictic forms such as pronouns play a fundamental role in guiding the communicative partner's perceptual activity and therefore function much like gestures in that they provide clues that help a listener orient among the details of a given communicative situation.[1]

Bühler contributed significantly to the development of dynamic approaches to context in that his theory of language touched on several relevant parts necessary for ultimately developing emergent views of context. These included emphasis on the multifunctional nature of language, units of meaning at the level beyond words and at the level of constructions, and his treatment of deixis to the extent that he discussed how speakers use particular linguistic forms to point to relevant aspects of the perceptual field. As we will see in the next section, these separate ideas of Bühler's, when linked together, result in an emergent notion of context.

Dynamic approaches to meaning and context: recent discussions

The emphasis on a view of language as more than designational was all but lost after the early part of the 1900s even though important exceptions can be found (see, for instance, Werner and Kaplan 1963, 1984). Although such work lost favor to behaviorism and subsequently to more nativist interpretations of language, over the last few decades there has been a growing interest in exploring the consequences of adopting a multifunctional approach to language both in psychology and neighboring disciplines (see Budwig, in press, Shweder *et al.* 1997, Tomasello 1998). Four major traditions that adopt a more dynamic sense of meaning include: cognitive linguistics, activity theory/dialogicality, conversation analysis, and functional linguistics embedded within a linguistic anthropological approach (referred to here simply as linguistic anthropology). Each of these views will be briefly reviewed in order to point out what they contribute to an understanding of meaning and the dynamic unfolding of context.

Cognitive linguists have suggested that meaning be viewed in relation to viewpoint, speaker perspective, and idealized cognitive models (see Lakoff 1987, Lakoff and Johnson 1980, Langacker 1987). For cognitive linguists, as was the case for Bühler, the use of particular linguistic constructions plays a central role in the structuring of experience. That is, speakers through the deployment of certain linguistic constructions (i.e. passives versus actives) call up particular vantage points or habitual ways of viewing reality. For instance, a speaker can select different representations of scenes, selecting for instance a vantage point that highlights an intentional act of agency or a scene that downplays that agency by switching between active and passive constructions (*John spilled the juice* versus *The juice was spilled*). To this extent, speakers when interacting with one another are not so much representing their understanding of an 'objective reality' but rather sharing perspectives that involve linguistically highlighting and backgrounding aspects of situations otherwise open to interpretation.

While cognitive linguists have tended to focus on the universal and experientially based aspects of meaning making, those adopting dialogic, conversational analytic, and linguistic anthropological views have emphasized the social situatedness of meaning construction. For instance, dialogic accounts, with their focus on utterances, suggest that utterances are always multivoiced in that they not only include the voice of the speaker, but also adopt the view that built into language forms are histories of usage. This sort of voice has been explored by what Bakhtin (1981, 1986) has called "speech genres and social languages" (see Wertsch 1991, 2000, for further discussion). Again, this sort of approach highlights that the use of language is not so much involved in representing reality as much as constructing versions, here versions that are socially situated.

With an emphasis on the local determination of meaning, those adopting a conversation-analytic perspective focus on how group members themselves interpret interactional sequences they are engaged in. Emerging from a rich tradition of American sociology, conversation analysts view meaning as best being examined through an analysis of the sequential organization of talk. Here focus shifts from the level of the organization of elements within the sentence or individual utterance to larger stretches of discourse and how meaning emerges across these sequentially organized units. The central idea of such work is the demonstration that conversational episodes are cooperative ventures that involve much social organizational work on the part of participants to coordinate their turn-taking with one another (see Sacks, Schegloff and Jefferson 1974). Like those working within a dialogic tradition, context is not taken as a given but rather something that is interactively achieved in the process of participating in social activities.

Linguistic anthropologists view speaking as a continual process of contextualization. The regular use of particular linguistic devices (whether they are individual words, morphological markers, or syntactic constructions) comes to index broader cultural notions. Focus is placed not only on the regular patterning of isolated forms and conditions of their use but also in particular on how subtle variations in forms come to be associated over time with shifts in meaning. A good example of the way forms come to index larger wholes can be found in an examination of the use of formal versus informal pronominal devices in languages that include them. In many languages the decision to refer to a conversational partner with the pronominal form "you" involves making a distinction based on social status or familiarity. For instance, some languages distinguish a formal and informal marker of second-person pronominal reference. (In French, this distinction is marked in the contrast *tu* versus *vous*.) While there are clear examples in which this sort of relationship is determined by institutional contexts, there exist many instances where the selection of one or another of these forms comes to index a broader interpretation of the way the relationship is construed by one or the other communicative partner. According to this view, language is not reduced to social activity, nor is social interaction taken to be a by-product of language forms. This allows for a more dynamic view of meaning that is open to the interpretive efforts of specific individuals interacting in novel ways, thereby suggesting a theory of meaning construction that is locally constructed (see Clark 1996, Gumperz 1982, Gumperz and Levinson 1996, Shore 1991). Such local constructions draw not only on culturally sanctioned mediational means, but also on the role of embodiment in contributing to an account of culturally accepted symbolic means (see Hanks 1996, Johnson 1987, Lakoff and Johnson 1980, Polanyi 1966).

These more recent views taking into account the dynamic nature of meaning have had rather limited treatment within developmental psychology. Not surprisingly, the few developmental psychologists who adopt the view of language as multifunctional are exactly the ones who have argued for more dynamic approaches to meaning-making. Some researchers interested in the interface among language, mind and culture have shed light on dynamic aspects of the meaning-making process (Bruner 1990, Budwig, Užgiris and Wertsch 2000, Nelson 1989, 1996, Shweder *et al.* 1997, Tomasello 1999). Central here has been the claim that meaning comes about through praxis – in the everyday interactions between the child and significant others. This is not so much the claim that the child needs to be studied *in* context, but rather involves the idea that the "entry into meaning" takes place as the child acquires symbolic means. Language in general (and for some others the ability to produce and comprehend narratives) plays a significant role in meaning formation (see Bruner 1990, Nelson 1989, 1996, Tomasello 1999). For instance, Bruner (1990) suggests that narrative provides the child with a means to both construct cultural meaning and understand cultural experience, while for Tomasello (1999: 107) the importance of language lies in its perspectival nature:

> The perspectival nature of linguistic symbols multiplies indefinitely the specificity with which they may be used to manipulate the attention of others, and this fact has profound implications for the nature of cognitive representations.

Regardless of particular differences in view, these developmentalists share the view that meaning is actively produced by interactants as they negotiate with symbols how they render experience within the ongoing flow of interaction. Most of this work has been carried out in connection with sociocultural theories of human development working within a dialogic framework. Nevertheless, such work has yet to significantly draw upon recent developments in cognitive linguistics and linguistic anthropology as a means to provide a better understanding of the role of context in the development of personal and cultural meaning systems in a developmental framework.

The notion of context in early child development research

The relevance of the notion of context has received increasing focus in discussions of human development. Since the 1970s several researchers have attempted to argue for perspectives that take into greater account contextual and, in particular, interpersonal relations in the role of early child development. We turn now to outline the view of context that has developed in early child development research and to explicitly compare it to the view of context that has developed within the more dynamic approaches to meaning outlined above. The aim of this consideration is to better understand the affordances of the more emergent views of context for understanding issues of human development.

Infancy researchers have debated the role of interpersonal relations in early childhood, and such debates have impacted on the importance granted to the role of context in development. One dominant view of early childhood emphasizes the distinction between the child's biological and social worlds. According to this view, it is commonly assumed that the child develops first as a biological organism and only gradually enters interpersonal relations (see Užgiris 1996, for review). The implicit idea here is that the individual must first construct certain capacities such that interpersonal relations are a product of individual developments. In contrast to this view, recently a more social view of the unfolding of development has been discussed, one that holds development to be jointly constructed by participants in and through communication (see Užgiris 1989, 1996).

The first view, labeled "infant as biological organism" downplays the notion of context. In contrast to a largely biological view of early child development, several researchers have argued for an alternative view that examines development *in* context. Here context is defined as the interactive setting, focusing in particular on the role of Other and Self in coordinating the social and cognitive development *within* the arena of dyadic interactions. The most extensive qualification of this position, quoted at length below, comes from Užgiris' discussion of the centrality of communication in human development (see Užgiris 1996: 23).

> Considerable research has provided a rich description of the facial expressions, vocal patternings, bodily movements and postures that serve as meaning guides to the coordination of action with an Other (e.g. Stern 1985). This is fundamentally important to my case. I am presuming not only that an adult is able to understand the infant's expression and to impute meaning to them, thereby helping the infant to construct socially meaningful signals out of originally noncommunicative acts, but that the infant at the outset finds certain aspects of the other's actions meaningful when they are carried out together with the infant. This does not imply that the infant interprets the Other's actions with the full range of meanings apprehended by adults in that culture. Nor does this imply that the infant's actions have a transparent meaning for the Other. Both the infant and the Other construct meaning out of the conjoining of acts, in which the acts of Other and of self define each other in the immediate context. This communication with the other is deemed important not only for constructing interpersonal relations, but for the development of knowledge overall, because all the infant's activities take place in an interpersonally constructed field of action.

In this extended quote, Užgiris highlights several key features of her position. Like others who adopt an interactionist view, she argues that the child does not first come to a sense of self and only later apply this knowledge in interaction, but rather from the earliest moments of life uses the communicative arena to build up meaning. In addition, Užgiris emphasizes that the child, in tandem with more experienced others, co-constructs meaning. What distinguishes her view – and makes it unique in comparison to others adopting an interpersonal view – is her adoption of certain features that suggest a more dynamic view of sense-making. In arguing for the active role of both expert and novice, Užgiris highlights the idea that meaning is not transparent and that infants and caregivers need not share an identical interpretation of one another's actions for context to play a role in development.

Užgiris' view of the dynamic process of constructing meaning has much in common with a view of meaning reviewed in the prior section, though, as will be argued below, it differs to the extent that the view of context is not viewed as an emergent property of the interaction. Rather, the idea of context being equated with situational and interpersonal setting is common to both Užgiris' views and other interpersonal perspectives of infancy. This becomes especially clear when considering Užgiris' discussion of the child's alone time. Here Užgiris suggests that an important aspect of development comes from the child's "alone time" where s/he has the opportunity, apart from interactions with others, to sort out aspects first worked on in the context of communications with others:

> My idea is that during the time of acting alone, the child sets goals and attempts to achieve them on her own, but not necessarily out of relation with the Other. This might be considered the time for integration, for the consolidation of structures of knowledge.
>
> (Užgiris 1996: 34)

The child's activity in alone time, "although not carried out without reference to the attitudes of the Other" (Užgiris 1996: 34) nevertheless distinguishes such activities from interactions carried out *in* the context of others.

Užgiris' view of the relation among cultural practices, communication, self/other systems, and fields of action comes quite close to Bruner (1990) and Nelson (1989, 1996), two other developmentalists who also have worked to bring to the foreground the dynamics of meaning-making in the early verbal routines of young children. While she sets the stage for the need for a dynamic view of meaning construction, and in particular a new unit of analysis that highlights the dynamics of this process, the problem remains how this can actually be executed. Užgiris' view comes close to that of both Bruner and Nelson to the extent that all three go beyond the sort of "interpersonal view" of development by looking at the dynamic construction of meaning in early communicative routines. Bruner and Nelson, though, by focusing on the development of verbal systems, consider the specific affordance of language as a symbolic tool central to meaning-making, rather than Užgiris' focus on interaction as simply a context for development. This focus allows them to get a step closer to the work on context discussed below by linguistic anthropologists.

Towards a more emergent view of context

As one shifts away from the designational views of meaning, towards more dynamic views such as the four reviewed briefly above, one finds a simultaneous shift in views about context. Central here is the idea that language involves more than the use of words that map onto a given reality. Furthermore, all these views entertain the idea that the use of the symbolic forms contribute in significant ways to the structuring of reality. Though the ways in which this takes place can be noted to differ, what is central here is the idea that language is viewed as a form of action and as such plays a role in the construction of reality. And all these views argue that it is not enough to situate the study of language *in context*, but rather that the very study of various aspects of language and other symbolic forms play a central role in defining context. Take, for example, the instance of a person who, after a long period of addressing a colleague with the formal pronominal form, shifts to the informal form, thereby redefining the context as a working relationship marked by greater intimacy. We will turn now to consider how the more dynamic approaches of meaning reviewed above view context and then shift to the consequences of such a view for issues of development.

Context as constitutive

What becomes apparent when examining recent approaches to meaning stemming from cognitive linguistics, activity theory, conversation analysis, and linguistic anthropology is that the notion of context takes on a more emergent role than in most current developmental theorizing. Rather than studying human action *in* context, where context is equated with a priori situational or institutional and environmental factors, analysis switches to the way semiotic means play a central role in the social construction of context. To this extent, context is not something "out there" to be tacked on to analysis but is rather viewed as a negotiated process that involves very subtle interpretations that are constructed as part of culture-specific practices (see Gumperz and Levinson 1996). More specifically, language is not examined *in* context in order to better understand social interaction, but rather it is argued that semiotic forms themselves play a central role in the very construction of contexts.

This dynamic view of context can be distinguished from more static views of context that played a role in the study of language as action up through the 70s and 80s in the social sciences. Here the point has been made, for instance by Austin (1962) and Searle (1969), that to use and understand language one must always connect speech with context. Notice, though, that context is not viewed as an interactional achievement here, but rather as a backdrop against which individual acts of speaking are produced and interpreted. The claim here is that the same sort of shift – from decontextualized studies to studies situated in context – that was part of the study of meaning in the 1970s and 1980s in linguistic circles is currently taking place in early child development research. Nevertheless over the last two decades an even more dynamic view of context has since been adopted in many other social sciences. We turn now to examine such views and will then consider how such a consideration might be beneficial to developmental psychologists interested in context.

Work by cognitive linguists such as Lakoff (1987) and Langacker (1987), and new work in the area of construction grammar (see Fillmore, Kay and O'Connor 1988, Goldberg 1995) is consistent with Bühler's discussion of the symbolic field of language. The overriding similarity lies in the questioning of more traditional views of language, opting instead for a closer linkage between language structure and worldview. This sort of view does not on its own embrace a particularly dynamic view of context and instead rests on the assumption that meaning is built up off of either universal image schemata (see, for instance, Lakoff 1987, Talmy 2000) or language typology (see Slobin 1997).

A feel for the more emergent nature of context can be found in the work of linguistic anthropologists who combine Bühler's focus on symbolic fields, with the discussion of deixis. Gumperz (1982, 1996), a linguistic anthropologist, has put forward precisely this sort of dynamic view of context in his discussion of contextualization cues. Gumperz defines contextualization cues as means through which speaker and listener in conversational activities negotiate the answer to the question "What is going on?", Gumperz (1996: 379) argues: "A contextualization cue is one of a cluster of indexical signs (. . .) produced in the act of speaking that jointly index, that is invoke, a frame of interpretation for the rest of the linguistic content of the utterance."

These cues exist at various levels of language including lexical and paralinguistic (e.g. prosody, pitch, tempo) aspects of structure and are used tacitly by speakers, often with little recognition of their central role in organizing the ongoing negotiation of meaning. Similar to Gumperz's notion of contextualization cues is Ochs's discussion of the indexicality principle (see Ochs 1996). Ochs (1996: 411) states:

> A linguistic index is usually a structure (e.g. sentential voice, emphatic stress, diminutive affix) that is used variably from one situation to another and becomes conventionally associated with particular situational dimensions such that when that structure is used, the form invokes those situational dimensions.

According to Ochs, it is through the use of such indexicals that participants slowly build up definitions of situational context over the course of an ongoing interaction. Gumperz's (1982) research on crosstalk, in which he examined the ongoing dialogues taking place between members of distinct ethnic groups highlighted the potential for miscommunication, in that members of the different communities took for granted the meaning of subtle shifts in prosody or gaze, often in ways that were unintended. Gumperz's work indicated ways the members of these distinct groups employed similar resources for distinct purposes and drew attention to the point that failure to recognize differences in interpretation leads to break downs in communication.

This view of context highlights the extent to which meaning is best viewed as the fusion between form and social setting. Symbolic forms do not "have meanings" apart from context that then get revised "in" context but, rather as Hanks (1996: 232) suggests, "linguistic meanings are inherently *underspecified* with respect to the propositions that people build up from them." Naturally, this sort of view makes more complex any view of how children come to make use of linguistic meanings in ways that are culturally sanctioned if a direct meaning linkage cannot be observed. We turn now to consider the issue of context and development.

Context and socialization

The claim has been made that language plays a fundamental role in the constitution of context, and the idea that context is negotiated and emerges within social interaction has been put forth. This not only paves the way for a new way of viewing context in human development, but also provides a new mechanism for understanding socialization of key cultural meanings. Naturally such a view of context is not without additional problems, because if context is emergent the question arises of exactly how young speakers come to apprehend meanings as they acquire symbolic means. Some answers are beginning to emerge from recent ethnographic work (see Budwig 2001, 2002, Shweder *et al.* 1997, for review)

Although Sapir (1933, 1970) has claimed that language plays a tremendous role in socialization, it has not been until more recently, as a more dynamic view of context has emerged, that theorists have begun to flesh out the particulars of this process. Ochs and Schieffelin (1984: 277) have developed a framework, now referred to as language socialization, that is based on the following two interrelated claims:

1   The process of acquiring language is deeply affected by the process of becoming a competent member of a society.
2   The process of becoming a competent member of society is realized to a large extent through language, by acquiring knowledge of its functions, social distribution, and interpretations in and across socially defined situations (i.e. through exchanges of language in particular social situations).

More specific to developmental processes, Cook-Gumperz (1986: 55–56) suggests:

> It is this interpretive process which guides children's acquisition of language within the conversational context, and which gives them the basis for the situated understanding of social processes. For it is by such means that interactional histories are developed on which children draw their background social knowledge.

Linking back to the discussion of contextual cues or indices, the claim of language socialization researchers is that the habitual use of particular linguistic symbols lends itself to tacitly constructed framings of experience. To this extent, language and the interactional routines of one's culture do not so much determine but rather "invite" children to construct culturally sanctioned meaning systems. In this sense, children construct context, as they come to interpret the patterned use of symbols in their everyday interactions with others.

Although language socialization research can be distinguished in a number of ways, such work nevertheless can be united in terms of a few overarching principles (see Budwig, in press, for more extensive discussion). First, language socialization researchers emphasize a view of language that focuses on situated use or praxis. Second, for language socialization researchers, language is viewed not only in terms of structure but also in terms of language function. A third tenet shared by language socialization researchers is the notion that children are actively involved in the dynamic construction of meaning. That is, meaning construction is a bidirectional process and children are not simply internalizing prior, established meaning systems (see Budwig 2001, in press, for a review of current language socialization research).

Interim summary

In this section, I have reviewed a variety of perspectives on the notion of meaning that have been discussed in the social sciences, all of which support the claim that as linguists, sociologists, and anthropologists altered the dominant ways of viewing language, a more dynamic view of context emerged. More specifically, adopting a view of language as more than designational opens the possibility that language can best be viewed as a form of social action. After a phase of viewing this as an individual achievement, more recently researchers, especially those working within an ethnographic framework, have begun to highlight the dynamic ways in which meaning is co-constructed in acts of participation. Communication is viewed as a multi-modal activity in which speech and other symbolic resources (gesture, body) are used to co-construct meaningful interpretations of reality. To this extent, speaking has come to be viewed as part of larger activities. As Duranti (1997: 21) summarizes:

> Participation assumes cognition to manage the retrieval of information and the prediction of others' action necessary for problem-solving. It also assumes a corporeal component, a live body that interacts with the environment not only physically (. . .) but also meaningfully. To be a human being means to be engaged in a continuous process of interpretation of our spatial and temporal relations to the world around us (*Umwelt*). Such a world includes material objects – tools and artifacts – as well as other live bodies. . .

Social activities are viewed as culturally organized and culturally interpreted. Accordingly, indexicality has been noted to play an important role in this process. The habitual and patterned use of symbolic forms with a cluster of notions aids the online construction of meaning. To this extent, context is negotiated in large part in and through the use of indexical forms. Language socialization researchers have taken this one step further by extending the notions of participation and indexicality to account for the processes by which novices come to be full members of a community. Symbolic means have been noted to play a fundamental role in the co-construction of meaning in early interactional routines within the family.

To this extent, the material reviewed here distinguishes itself from the majority of research in development psychology that also discusses the role of context in human functioning, to the extent that it views communication as a more fluid and dynamic activity. That is, developmental psychologists on the whole have continued to view language primarily in terms of its designational or representational function, and continue to view meaning-making as the process of information transfer from one individual (a speaker) to another (a listener). Such a view has received ample criticism (see, for instance, Budwig, Wertsch and Užgiris 2000, Duranti 1997, Gumperz and Levinson 1996, Hanks 1996, Reddy 1979). Užgiris' work is unique in developmental psychology in that she has picked up on the dynamic nature of meaning-making and has highlighted how participation is central in part because meaning must be viewed as co-constructed by both novice and expert. Nevertheless, the notion of indexicality has largely been ignored in such work, in part because of the referential view of language and because context has been taken as more static than in other related disciplines such as sociology and anthropology. We will turn now to consider the affordances of importing the notion of indexicality, as well as a more dynamic notion of context, into the field of developmental psychology.

Two illustrations of a dynamic approach to context in early child development

In this section I briefly illustrate how a dynamic approach to context, with a focus on language as indexical, can shed light on the ontogenetic unfolding of meaning-making capacities in young children. In doing so I will examine two related domains, namely the construction of personhood and mind. Following the language socialization approach outlined above, the aim will be to suggest that habitual use of specific linguistic markers of person and mind play a significant role in children's construction of such notions. At the same time, it will be emphasized that children are actively interpreting sign systems and in so doing are part of a process involving the use of contextual cues.

The construction of context is part of a dynamic sense-making process in which children play an active interpretive role. To anticipate slightly the direction of the argument, it will be argued that at one level the children studied who are growing up in different linguistic and cultural communities all appear to be doing quite similar things when engaging in dyadic play. That is, the children and caregivers studied played with objects, and all engaged in goal-directed behavior with these objects in ways that continually built up meaningful ways to construct self, other and mind. But what the brief discussion of such work aims to highlight is that the particular ways self, other and mind are constructed differed both in terms of speaker (caregiver versus child) and community (American versus German).

Here it will be suggested that the habitual use of language provided a sort of contextual cue or index to the children about how to view such interactions and, as such, the language-based interactions contributed to providing a dynamic or emergent view of context. In learning language, the children were not simply learning how to label their world, but rather were being guided into socially appropriate ways of being in the world. As we will see, the children were also actively involved in their use of the symbolic resources, and were not merely adopting, in any simple way, the worldviews expressed in their caregivers' talk. To this extent, the build up of interpretive frames, and thus context, was negotiated and emergent in the ongoing interactions taking place over developmental time. We turn now first to a brief discussion of the construction of personhood that will involve an analysis of the use of self reference forms, and next we will turn to the construction of mind by reviewing an analysis of the use of mental state verbs.

The construction of personhood: the use of self-reference forms

Over the last two decades I have investigated ways in which young children and their caregivers living in America, Germany and India make use of self and other reference forms. Originally my focus was on some creative errors that young American children made en route to adult-like patterning of personal pronouns. I had conducted a longitudinal study of six children, ranging between eighteen and thirty months of age at the onset of the four-month-long longitudinal study, while the children interacted once a month with caregivers and once a month with a playmate at a day-care cooperative they regularly attended. The participants were videotaped as they engaged in play in naturalistic situations. The pattern I had originally noticed highlighted the fact that before the children regularly referred to others they employed a variety of self-reference forms – often in ways that deviated from adult English usage. For instance, three of the children, those in the early phases of word combinations, were known to say *I want that*, *My maked French toast* and *Me jump*. The error-like productions were nothing unique to this group and had been noticed by several researchers in the past. At the time I suspected that the children were using distinct forms to differentiate a variety of ways to situate self, using distinct forms to mark various degrees of agency. A developmental–functional analysis lent support for this idea. For instance, the children used *My* in subject position to refer to self as agent acting to bring about change, *Me* to refer to self as affected agent, and they reserved the use of *I* primarily for a scene involving the portrayal of self as experiencer (see Budwig 1989, 1995 for details).

After completing the original analysis, I was curious as to whether the finding was part of children's attempts to mark salient notions, such as agency, universally or whether children, for instance in cultures that were less focused on agency, would build different systems of self-reference. For this reason I selected to work with German children growing up in East Berlin because, while German offered a case system that shared certain typological features with English, the culture was not as focused on individual agency as American culture.

Further analysis of a matched sample of German children growing up in the former East Germany shortly after reunification revealed that the German children also used a variety of self-reference forms to situate self in relation to ongoing events, yet the specific contrasts they focused on were distinct. Most notable was the lack of the use of the first-person pronominal form *Ich* (I) in the early sessions. In addition, these children did not linguistically mark the notion of prototypical agency as the American children did with the form "My". The German children did use a related form *meine* (mine!) to claim objects – usually when they were be taken away by others. But although the American children extended the possessive form "My" to subject position to mark their own intentional acts to bring about change, the German children never extended this form in a similar way. Finally, the German children relied on a form of self-reference not found in the American data set. That is, the German children often made use of the German form *man* (one) to adopt an impersonal perspective on a scene. Note that the issue here is not one of correctly labeling self in relation to an event. Both the German and American children talked about self in relation to events – for instance, building block towers. Rather, the point is that the children adopted distinct stances on personhood. The American children were likely to index self as prototypical agent, saying things like "My build the tower" while their German counterparts were more likely to adopt a more impersonal perspective for what appeared to be a similar event uttering *"Man kann so einz bauen"* ("One can build something like this"). The relevant point to notice is how the American children have focused in on their own role in the building, while the German children have adopted a stance linking their doings with ways any other might have acted in a similar situation (see Budwig 2000a).

As these findings became apparent the natural question became why? Why do we find these differences? Were the sorts of distinctions the children made modeled in the input? The answer to this would seem to be obvious in that American caregivers do not typically use forms like "I", "My", and "Me" interchangeably in subject position as was noted for the American children. A more careful analysis, though, revealed some intriguing patterns that were not anticipated but which made good sense after further reflection. While the children were not specifically modeling contrasts of the caregivers, the caregivers' talk was consistent with what the children created. For instance, analysis of the American caregivers' input has shown that the caregivers most frequently used *I* with mental state verbs and verbs that ranked low in agentivity (i.e. "I like your little teapot, I think they don't want you to touch that"). Furthermore the caregivers often gave their children credit for carrying out actions that the caregivers themselves did alone, or that the dyad did together. For instance, upon completing a large block structure alone, the caregiver turned to her child and said, "Look, you built a nice tower!" Thus, the children's linkage of *I* with verbs ranking low in agency was similar to a pattern provided in the caregivers' input.

A flavor of how personhood is marked by the American caregivers and children is illustrated in Example 1. Note in particular how even when the mother does refer to herself in combination with an action verb, low agency is implied to the extent that she is asking the child for permission to act in that way. Otherwise, in this example much of the discussion focuses on the child's agentive potential.

Example 1 American mother (*AMO*) and her child (*ACH*) are building with blocks
and playing with a plastic helicopter:

ACH: My play with the helicopter and you play with the blocks.
AMO: Okay. What should I build?
ACH: A tower.
AMO: A tower, okay.
         [Both build independently.]
AMO: How about ... should we build a little something for the helicopter?
         (Mother is already putting the blocks in place.)
ACH: No! (whining) This not working (trying to adjust his own block
         structure).
AMO: Where would you like to build it? Can you get it? That's it. Okay. You
         gonna make a big tall house.
ACH: No, I want to (implied negative through intonation)

In contrast, the German caregivers' discourse was limited in the number of
markers of individual agency attributed to their children. When the caregivers
did talk about agency often it was to link together, via the use of their own name
and their child's name in tandem, their independent contributions to joint events.
In addition, the German caregivers, in comparison to the caregivers from
America, made use of many more forms marking generic agency and normative
behavior including the use of the *man* construction, as well as frequent use of
modal markers like *sollen* (should) and *können* ("can"). Often the German
conversations included a lot of spatial descriptions, while lacking extensive
marking of persons. Example 2 illustrates the more generic focus of the German
mother–child dialogues and the frequent absence of person markers. It involves a
similar situation as in Example 1 in that the mother and child are discussing
building a block tower as they play with blocks.

Example 2 German mother (*GMO*) and child (*GCH*) are playing with blocks
negotiating how to jointly construct a block tower.

GCH: Noch einen Turm.
         Another one tower.
GMO: Na, komm wir machen zusammen einen ganz hohen.
         Okay, come we (will) make together a very big (one).
GCH: (begins to build) Das.
         This.
GMO: Ja hier.
         Yes, here.
GCH: Das nicht, nein? (showing a triangle block)
         This not, no?
GMO: Doch, das kann man auch nehmen.
         Yes, one can also take that.

GCH: Das noch.
         This also.
GMO: Ja. Jetzt kann man so was machen.
         Yes. Now one can make something like this.
GCH: Kann man hier wieder eins drauf?
         Can one again (place) one here?

In the German dialogues the issue of personal agency seems backgrounded to procedural ways of getting things done (see Budwig 2000a).

In sum, we find that the American and German caregivers and their children all ground self in relation to other, though they do so in ways that differ from one another. In particular, we have noted that the American caregivers and children linguistically focus on the children's budding autonomy, while the German caregivers and children emphasize ways in which the children's behavior relates to others in a normative sense.

Relating these findings to the issue of context, here the claim is made that the interactants are jointly negotiating the context. To a large part, at this age, the children turn to the caregivers for guidance. The caregivers' use of particular linguistic symbols (for instance the heavy use of or, in contrast, the paucity of self or other references) comes to tacitly contribute to the framing of experience. Over time then, the linguistic forms become a short form and act as contextual cues for how meaning is understood. The children too enter into this creative process, as we saw most dramatically in the American children's systems as they went beyond the input received when building a special way to mark independent agency with the form "My", as in "My build the tower". To this extent, then, context is something that emerges between the participants as they negotiate their understandings of the world, rather than something that is more statically tacked on to the analysis in terms of noting location of talk (such as home versus school context).

The construction of mind: the example of desire talk

We turn now to a second illustration of the potency of language in the dynamic construction of context. Here we turn to consider children's and caregivers' talk about the mind. The issue here again is not whether children "have" desires or beliefs, or whether children's talk about desires or beliefs can be taken as an indication of children having developed underlying mental state categories that subsequently get mapped onto language forms. Rather, of interest has been whether particular social interaction patterns, and in particular, differences in the way desire is construed by speakers of different language communities, can be taken to contribute to children's construction of desire and more broadly their construction of mental experience. If caregivers regularly use particular ways to index mind, in so doing they could be providing children with contextual cues for how to construct or frame experience about the mind. The children too could be entering into this negotiation by making use of forms in unique ways and to this extent both partners, both the caregiver and the child, could be viewed as centrally involved in the emergent process of constructing context.

Although there has been quite a lot of experimental work highlighting a universal unfolding of mental-state understanding, other recent work has suggested that particular aspects of social interactions and discourse impact children's attention to thoughts, feelings, and desires (see Dunn 1991, Vinden 1996, Wootton 1997, among others). Thinking about this in light of my prior work on personhood, raises the question of whether there might not be differences in how self and others are positioned in discourse about mental experience. Several more particular questions can be raised. Are there differences in the range of forms the American and German participants in this study used when talking about desires? Whose desires get indexed by the different speakers in the two language communities? And finally we examined the functions of desire talk for caregivers and their toddlers.[2] All of this was part of a broader interest in the interplay between conceptual universals and cultural variations in mental-state talk among American and German caregivers and their young children when interacting with one another (see Budwig, Moissinac and Smith 2000, Budwig, Smith, Moissinac and Pinet, in progress, Moissinac and Budwig 2000 for more details).

Before briefly outlining some central findings of this work, I will summarize key features of our method. Based on the same six dyads of American and German caregivers and their toddlers, we isolated all caregiver and child discourse about desire. These utterances were further coded in terms of form of desire talk (that is the specific lexical item), the semantics of whose desires were indexed in such utterances, and the communicative function of such talk. Our analysis was based on more than a thousand utterances containing desire verbs.

Our analysis of form of desire talk revealed many stable patterns. Although caregivers were more likely to talk about desire than their children, all speakers were most likely to use one primary form when talking about desire, namely [want].[3] When examining speakers' usage of the most frequent lexical form of desire talk in terms of whose desires get indexed, a common pattern was found. That is, regardless of community (American or German) or speaker (caregiver or child) everyone preferred talking about the children's desires. One might even want to say this is part of a broader cultural universal of parenting, given that a primary goal of parents is to comfort and attend to their young, barely verbal children.

Nevertheless, looking more closely at the speech patterns it becomes clear that there are some community differences between the two groups worth noting. For instance, although the American speakers – both children and their caregivers – almost exclusively spoke about the children's desires (87% of all desire talk for American caregivers, 90% for their children), German speakers also tended to talk about others' desires and joint desires. That is, although the children's desires were what was most frequently talked about by the German caregivers, they did so only about half the time (49% of all desire talk) and spent 22% of their desire talk commenting on their own desires and another 28% of the time talking about joint desires. Similarly, the German children spent only about 58% of their desire talk utterances talking about their own desires while they often talked about their caregivers' desires 32% of the time and spoke of joint desires 9% of the time.

When we turn to language functioning and how desire talk is used in the ongoing negotiation of social interaction we find certain community (American versus German) as well as speaker (caregiver versus child) differences. For instance, although all caregivers and children made use of a variety of speech functions when engaging in desire talk, caregivers in the two communities differed in the proportions with which they made use of these functions. For instance, more than half of American caregivers' desire talk occurred when asking children questions (inquiry) and seeking permission to act in particular ways. In contrast, although inquiries were the second most frequent kind of speech function found with desire talk for the German caregivers, they showed a preference to embed desire talk in invitation bids to their children to act in particular ways. Children, although sensitive to the patterning of their caregivers (e.g. German children were more likely to invite and American children were more likely to use desire talk to gain permission) nevertheless preferred to link desire forms with functions that matched their own communicative needs. That is, both the American and German children tended to use desire talk in the context of making assertions. These differences are illustrated in Examples 3 and 4:

Example 3 American mother (*AMO*) and her daughter (*ACH*) are playing teaparty with assorted cups, plates, muffin papers and nuts.

AMO:	Mmm. It's very good.
ACH:	Chocolate.
AMO:	It's chocolate tea?
ACH:	Yeah.
ACH:	I xxx xxx some more.
AMO:	**You want** me to pour some? (Pragmatic function is inquiry)
ACH:	Yeah # in my cup.
AMO:	Mmm.
ACH:	**I want** some. (Pragmatic function is assertion)
ACH:	# Pour some in my cup (Mom then pours.)

Example 4 German mom (*GMO*) and her daughter (*GCH*) are playing teaparty with plastic cups, plates, nuts, etc.

GMO:	# Und das sind Paranüsse. Die kann man ganz schwer knacken.
	And these are Brazil nuts. They are hard for one to crack.
GCH:	(Continues to cook with cookware)
GMO:	**Willst *du*** die mal alle hier in den feinen Korb einsammeln oder hier wieder in die Kiste? (pragmatic function is invitation)
	Would you like to collect them all here in the nice basket or here again in the box?

GCH: Nee!
       No!
GMO: Nein, wo denn?
       No, then where?
GCH: Nee.
       No.
GMO: **Wollen *wir*** die mal einsammeln? (Pragmatic function is invitation.)
       Do we want to collect them?
GMO: # beide? #nein?
       Both? No?
GCH: # **wollen *wir*** mal kosten? (Pragmatic function is invitation.)
       Do we want to taste?
GMO: na, denn koste mal.
       Well then, taste.

Example 3 illustrates how the American mothers used desire talk primarily to inquire whether their child wanted the mother to act in particular ways. In contrast, we see how the German mother and child focused the discussion around invitations, which, like queries, are "other"-centered. The caregivers' invitations for instance, while focusing on the children's desires, nevertheless use as their starting point the mother's planned course of action and thereby grant more agency to the speaker. The difference is subtle and depends in part on the ongoing interactional flow. Example 3 also highlights a developmental trend that was found. Early on, when the American children often misused pronominal forms saying things like "My want that," the mothers were likely to respond with a clarification query. As the children were able to express their desires in more adult-like ways, there is a simultaneous change in the function of the American caregivers' desire talk (see Budwig 2002). In sum, the American dyads appear to be more child-focused in their use of desire talk. The German caregivers also focus on their children's desires, but Example 4 nicely shows that they also made use of reference to joint desires. As the German caregivers and their children negotiated with one another their joint desires, they talked less about an individualistic conception of desire than their American counterparts.

Pulling all this together, the point to be illustrated here is that regular and habitual use of particular forms of desire talk to refer to particular experiencers in conjunction with particular communicative functions provides a potent index of how desire is to be understood. Our work highlights that the story to be told is indeed complex. Caregivers from distinct speech communities showed both similarities and differences in their use of desire verbs. The children followed many of the patterns of their caregivers, especially with regard to the range of forms and the semantics of whose desires got talked about, but the children in both communities put desire talk to use in their own ways. This highlights the active role of the children in linking forms and functions as they negotiate a dynamic sense of desire.

It should be stressed that the issue is not one of comparing whether children and caregivers in different cultures refer to underlying desires. It is clear that all the participants from the outset of the study had a rich vocabulary for talking about desires. The issue of particular interest here is how speakers make use of desire talk to index culturally sanctioned ways of experiencing the world. The claim here is that the subtle differences in marking whose desires, linked with the particular communicative functions of such talk, provide interpretive frames for how the context is to be construed, as participants negotiate meaning in their ongoing interactions. In this sense, context unfolds dynamically within the arena of communicative interactions taking place between the caregivers and children.

Concluding comments: the role of context in early child development revisited

In this chapter I have argued that a shift in many disciplines to return to a multifunctional view of language, one grounded in the belief that language is best viewed in terms of social activity, has led to more dynamic theories of meaning. Rather than viewing the understanding of meaning as unfolding through the transfer of underlying cognitions from one speaker to another in the form of packaged messages (see Reddy 1979 for further discussion of the conduit metaphor), as is often the case with psychologists and psycholinguists, other social science disciplines have revised their understanding of meaning-making in light of the idea of language as social activity. Two notions that have been found to become central to such discussions include participation and indexicality. The idea that participation is central stems from the belief that participation emphasizes the moment-by-moment coordination involved in the continual build-up of meaning based on participants' individual and shared interpretations of both verbal and nonverbal actions. Indexicality provides a tool for understanding the apprehension and (re)construction of meaning to the extent that habitual use of particular verbal or nonverbal forms can call up larger socially agreed-upon meaning packages, packages which nevertheless are not fixed and are always open to further negotiation. Such a view of meaning allows for a more emergent notion of context, one which has been used not only to understand the ongoing sense-making activities of members of diverse cultures (see Gumperz 1982 discussion of crosstalk). In addition, this more dynamic view has also played a central role in understanding the co-construction of meaning by novices and experts in language socialization research.

Although the notion of context has been creeping into discussions of human development, I have argued that developmental psychology on the whole has picked up neither on the dynamics of meaning nor on the emergent sense of context described as dominant in neighboring disciplines within the social sciences. In part this can be attributed to the fact that developmental psychologists also lag behind in maintaining a more restricted view of language, one which emphasizes the referential or designational function. It would seem that the renewed interest in meaning-making, combined with the resurgence of interest in incorporating a notion of context into discussions of human development, sets the stage for considering how such developmental discussions might profit from both a more dynamic notion of meaning and a more fluid notion of context.

In this chapter, I have suggested that Užgiris' work has been pioneering in beginning such a discussion. First, she has been among the minority of developmental psychologists to focus on the importance of studying practices rather than behaviors, as well as the cultural embeddedness of notions such as imitation that had previously been considered primarily from the standpoint of individual development (see Užgiris 1999). Furthermore, I have suggested that her emphasis on the co-construction of meaning already draws important linkages with work situated in anthropology and sociology reviewed above highlighting the importance of participation. Nevertheless, consistent with an implicit view of language as solely representational – a view shared by most developmental psychologists – such work has not examined the contribution of a notion of indexicality in further understanding the ontogenetic unfolding of sense-making activities. Such a move allows developmental psychologists a way to move beyond an artificial distinction between individual and social worlds or a view that at best places individuals *in* a social world, and rather incorporates a more holistic view of the unfolding of individual and cultural meaning systems.

The research reviewed above on the talk about self and desires represents a starting point for how one might go about developing a more dynamic account of meaning and context in early child development research. In my work on personhood, I have attempted to illustrate how subtle variations in pronominal forms, when interpreted in light of other verbal and nonverbal practices, come to play a fundamental role in children's budding attempts to construct categories of personhood. The illustrations given above begin to show how caregivers and children living in different communities use subtle variations in the patterning of verbal forms which, when consistent with a variety of other practices, help contribute to encouraging a particular slant on experiencing reality. At the same time, the patterning of the children's pronouns showed some unique contributions, and in general highlighted the bidirectional nature of the unfolding of interpretations of personhood by caregivers and children alike. It is important to emphasize that, as was noted above for anthropologists working with notions of indexicality, the claim is *not* that the meanings are fixed in any way. Their interpretation is guided in part by other related verbal, nonverbal and material practices. For instance, it is not unrelated that the American dyads emphasized a more individualistic perspective on personhood and a more child-centered interpretation of desire talk, while the German dyads emphasized a more generic sense of persons and a simultaneous interest in the joint and intersubjective experience of desires as located within the dyad. Furthermore, nonverbal routines and material artifacts (for instance whether the children are given their own beds or own rooms for sleeping in or their own cutlery for eating) contribute as well in ways that as yet have received insufficient discussion (see Ochs 1988: 218–221 for an intriguing discussion of the issue of vectors of indexicality).

Future avenues for research

It seems important to close with some suggestions for where future work should be directed if one were to adopt a more dynamic view of meaning and context in developmental theorizing. While we can turn to related disciplines for input on how to revise notions of meaning and context, as I have argued elsewhere (Budwig 2000b, 2001), such frameworks remain non-developmental unless developmental psychologists modify them so as to best understand ontogenetic issues. To this end, Užgiris provides valuable insight about how to proceed. In one of her last articles (Užgiris 1999: 186–187) she writes:

> A developmental perspective considers both continuities and transformations, claiming that a fuller understanding is gained by locating specific functioning within a developmental trajectory. The directionality indicates which aspects of (...) activity are important to note and to examine.

One important direction for future work in this area is to situate discussions of indexicality within a developmental framework (see Budwig 2002, Kyratzis 2001, Richner and Nicolopoulou 2001 for some initial attempts). Central here is the role prior interactive histories play in the ongoing interpretation and buildup of meaning and context.

A second avenue of future investigation ought to be a better understanding of what Užgiris refers to as "time alone." Užgiris (1996: 38) has emphasized that although communication with others is central in early human development, what is less clear is how the child benefits from time alone – a time Užgiris describes as allowing for both integration and consolidation.

> My idea is that during the time of acting alone, the child sets goals and attempts to achieve them on her own, but not necessarily out of relation with the Other. This might be considered the time for integration, for the consolidation of structures of knowledge.

This point is illustrated by several others as well (see Karmiloff-Smith 1979, Nelson 1989, Piaget 1936, 1952, Preyer 1893, 1982, Weir 1962). For instance, as Užgiris (1996) and Bruner (1990) have noted, researchers such as Nelson and colleagues and Weir have documented that some toddlers rehearse language patterns in monologic activities taking place when they are alone in their beds either before falling asleep or upon waking up. Researchers adopting an indexical perspective would do well to perform similar analyses of alone time in efforts to better understand children's sense-making activities, not only understanding processes of integration and transformation, but also to better understand the unique patterning found in monologic and dialogic speech.

One last avenue to be mentioned here worthy of future research is one that was briefly mentioned above, namely the need to focus on the interplay between verbal and nonverbal indexicals in the ongoing co-construction of meaning and context. While sociologists and anthropologists have already made headway here (see for instance work by C. Goodwin 1994, 1996, M. Goodwin 1990, Goodwin and Goodwin 2000, Hanks 1990, Haviland 1996), little is known about the developmental unfolding of reliance and interconnection between verbal and nonverbal systems in early development. Užgiris (2000: 135) emphasizes the need for researchers to consider the interface between verbal and nonverbal systems across the life span:

> Consequently, in the course of development, one would expect that the relation of the verbal and nonverbal systems would change. A child's initial learning of verbal language might regulate the nonverbal system in a different way than when greater mastery of verbal language is attained.

The central point she makes – which has yet to be examined – is that the relation between verbal and nonverbal systems must continually be re-examined because as children's capacities and abilities change, so too would this interface.

In conclusion, it is a dynamic time for developmental psychology. One of the biggest challenges for those interested in culturally informed developmental psychology is a better understanding of how cultural meanings come to be meaningful to individual children in an array of situations over developmental time. Ina Užgiris has left us a rich legacy of starting points which, if combined with notions stemming from neighboring disciplines, could position us better to meet this challenge.

Notes

1   The idea that deictic forms contribute in important ways to the creation of context paves the way for more recent discussions by a number of cultural and linguistic anthropologists who have introduced terms such as "shifters" (Silverstein 1976), "frames" (Goffman 1974), "contextual cues" (Gumperz 1982), and "deictic fields" (Hanks 1996) All of these terms, despite subtle differences, emphasize ways that linkages between symbolic forms and functions contribute to the local unfolding of meaning.
2   The "we" refers to Luke Moissinac and Melissa Smith, two students who collaborated with me on this research.
3   The symbols [ ] are used with the English word reference to indicate the use by American speakers of the word listed and the use of a similar lexical term by German speakers. For instance, in this case the desire term under examination includes the English term *want* and the German terms *wollen* and *möchten*.

Acknowledgements

The ideas for this chapter were inspired in part by many discussions with Ina Užgiris in the context of our joint teaching at Clark University. I am grateful for the opportunity to have worked so closely with her on issues of meaning-making and human development. I would also like to thank the editors of this volume and anonymous reviewers for their feedback on an earlier version of the manuscript. The writing of this chapter was assisted by sabbatical support from the Max Planck Institute for Evolutionary Anthropology, Department for Developmental and Comparative Psychology, Leipzig, Germany.

References

Austin, J. L. (1962) *How to Do Things with Words*. Oxford: Oxford University Press.

Bakhtin, M. M. (1981) *The Dialogic Imagination: Four Essays by M. M. Bakhtin* (Holquist, M. (ed.) and Emerson, C. and Holquist, M. (trans.)). Austin, TX: University of Texas Press.

— (1986) *Speech Genres and Other Late Essays* (Emerson, C. and Holquist, M. (eds.) and McGee, V. W. (trans.)). Austin, TX: University of Texas Press.

Bruner, J. (1990) *Acts of Meaning*. Cambridge, MA: Harvard University Press.

Budwig, N. (1989) "The Linguistic Marking of Agentivity and Control in Child Language", *Journal of Child Language, 16*(2): 263–284.

— (1995) *A Developmental-Functionalist Approach to Child Language*. Mahwah, NJ: Lawrence Erlbaum Press.

— (1998) "Bühler's Legacy: Full Circle and Ahead", *From Past to Future, 1*: 36–48.

— (2000a) "Language, Practice, and the Construction of Personhood", *Theory and Psychology, 10*(6): 769–786.

— (2000b) "Language and the Construction of Self: Linking Forms and Functions across Development" in Budwig, N., Užgiris, I. Č. and Wertsch, J. (eds.) *Communication: An Arena of Development* (pp. 195–214). Stamford, CT: Ablex.

— (Vol. ed.) (2001, July) "Language Socialization and Children's Entry into Schooling" [Special issue]. *Early Education and Development, 12*(3).

— (2002) "A Developmental-Functionalist Approach to Mental State Talk" in Amsel, E. and Byrnes, J. (eds.) *Language, Literacy, and Cognitive Development* (pp. 59–86). Mahwah, NJ: Lawrence Erlbaum Press.

— (2003) "The Role of Language in Human Development" in Connolly, K. and Valsiner, J. (eds.) *Handbook of Developmental Psychology* (pp. 217–237). London: Sage Publications.

Budwig, N., Moissinac, L. and Smith, M. (2000, June) *"How Literal is Desire Talk in Two-Year-Olds' Interactions with Their Caregivers? A Comparative Analysis of German and American Dyads"*, paper presented at Seventh International Pragmatics Conference, Budapest, Hungary.

Budwig, N., Smith, M., Moissinac, L. and Pinet, M. (in progress) *A Comparative Analysis of Mental State Talk in American and German Caregiver–Child Dyads*.

Budwig, N., Užgiris, I. Č and Wertsch, J. V. (eds.) (2000) *Communication: An Arena of Development*. Stamford, CT: Ablex Publishing.

Budwig, N., Wertsch, J. and Užgiris, I. Č. (2000) "Communication, Meaning, and Development" in Budwig, N., Užgiris, I. Č. and Wertsch, J. V. (eds.) *Communication: An Arena of Development* (pp. 195–214). Stamford, CT: Ablex.

Bühler, K. (1990) *Theory of Language: The Representational Function of Language* Goodwin, D. (trans.) Amsterdam: John Benjamins. (Original work published in 1934.)

Clark, H. (1996) "Communities, Commonalities, and Communication" in Gumperz, J. J. and Levinson, S. C. (eds.) *Rethinking Linguistic Relativity*. Cambridge: Cambridge University Press.

Cook-Gumperz, J. (1986) "Caught in the Web of Words: Some Considerations on Language Socialization and Language Acquisition" in Cook-Gumperz, J., Corsaro, W. and Streeck, J. (eds.) *Children's Worlds and Children's Language* (pp. 37–64). New York: Mouton de Gruyter.

Dunn, J. (1991) "Young Children's Understandings of Other People: Evidence from Observations Within the Family" in Frye, D. and Moore, C. (eds.) *Children's Theories of Mind* (pp. 97–114). Hillsdale, NJ: Lawrence Erlbaum.

Duranti, A. (1997) *Linguistic Anthropology.* Cambridge: Cambridge University Press.

Duranti, A. and Goodwin, C. (eds.) (1992) *Rethinking Context.* Cambridge: Cambridge University Press.

Fillmore, C., Kay, P. and O'Connor, M. C. (1988) "Regularity and Idiomaticity in Grammatical Constructions: The Case of Let Alone", *Language, 64*: 501–538.

Goffman, E. (1974) *Frame Analysis: An Essay on the Organization of Experience.* New York: Harper & Row.

Goldberg, A. (1995) *Constructions: A Construction Grammar Approach to Argument Structure.* Chicago, IL: Chicago University Press.

Goodwin, C. (1994) "Professional Vision", *American Anthropologist, 96*(3): 606–633.

— (1996) "Transparent Vision" in Ochs, E., Schegloff, E. A. and Thompson, S. (eds.) *Interaction and Grammar* (pp. 370–404). Cambridge: Cambridge University Press.

Goodwin, M. H. (1990) *He-Said-She-Said: Talk as Social Organization Among Black Children.* Bloomington, IN: Indiana University Press.

Goodwin, M. H. and Goodwin, C. (2000) "Emotion Within Situated Activity" in Budwig, N., Užgiris, I. Č. and Wertsch, J. V. (eds.) *Communication: An Arena of Development.* Stamford, CT: Ablex Publishing.

Gumperz, J. J. (1982) *Discourse Strategies.* Cambridge: Cambridge University Press.

— (1996) "The Linguistic and Cultural Relativity of Conversational Inference" in Gumperz, J. J. and Levinson, S. C. (eds.) *Rethinking Linguistic Relativity* (pp. 374–407). Cambridge: Cambridge University Press.

Gumperz, J. J. and Levinson, S. C. (eds.) (1996) *Rethinking Linguistic Relativity.* Cambridge: Cambridge University Press.

Hanks, W. F. (1990) *Referential Practice: Language and Lived Space Among the Maya.* Chicago, IL: University of Chicago Press.

— (1996) *Language and Communicative Practices.* Boulder, CO: Westview Press.

Haviland, J. B. (1996) "Projections, Transpositions and Relativity" in Gumperz, J. J. and Levinson, S. C. (eds.) *Rethinking Linguistic Relativity* (pp. 271–323). Cambridge: Cambridge University Press.

Johnson, M. (1987) *The Body in the Mind: The Bodily Basis of Meaning, Imagination, and Reason.* Chicago, IL: University of Chicago Press.

Karmiloff-Smith, A. (1979) *A Functional Approach to Child Language: A Study of Determiners and Reference.* Cambridge: Cambridge University Press.

Kyratzis, A. (2001, July) "Emotion Talk in Preschool Same-Sex Friendship Groups: Fluidity over Time and Context", *Early Education and Development, 12*(3): 359–392.

Lakoff, G. (1987) *Women, Fire, and Dangerous Things: What Categories Reveal about the Mind.* Chicago, IL: University of Chicago Press.

Lakoff, G. and Johnson, M. (1980) *Metaphors We Live by.* Chicago, IL: University of Chicago Press.

Langacker, R. (1987) *Foundations of Cognitive Grammar* (vol. 1). Stanford, CA: Stanford University Press.

Moissinac, L. and Budwig, N. (2000) "The Development of Desire Terms in Early Child German", *Psychology of Language and Communication, 4*(1).

Nelson, K. (ed.) (1989) *Narratives from the Crib.* Cambridge, MA: Harvard University Press.

Nelson, K. (1996) *Language in Cognitive Development: The Emergence of the Mediated Mind.* New York: Cambridge University Press.

Ochs, E. (1988) *Culture and Language Development*. Cambridge: Cambridge University Press.
— (1996) "Linguistic Resources for Socializing Humanity" in Gumperz, J. and Levinson, S. (eds.) *Rethinking Linguistic Relativity* (pp. 407–437). Cambridge: Cambridge University Press.

Ochs, E. and Schieffelin, B. (1984) "Language Acquisition and Socialization: Three Developmental Stories and Their Implications" in Shweder, R. and LeVine, R. (eds.) *Culture Theory: Essays on Mind, Self, and Emotion* (pp. 276–320). New York: Cambridge University Press.

Ochs, E., Schegloff, E. and Thompson, S. (eds.) (1996) *Interaction and Grammar*. Cambridge: Cambridge University Press.

Piaget, J. (1952) *The Origins of Intelligence* (Cook, M., trans.) New York: Norton. (Original work published 1936.)

Polanyi, M. (1966) *The Tacit Dimension*. Garden City, NY: Doubleday.

Preyer, W. (1982) *Mental Development in the Child* (Brown, H. W., trans.) New York: Appleton. (Original work published 1893.)

Reddy, M. (1979) "The Conduit Metaphor: A Case of Frame Conflict in Our Language about Language" in Ortony, A. (ed.) *Metaphor and Thought* (pp. 284–324). Cambridge: Cambridge University Press.

Richner, E. S. and Nicolopoulou, A. (2001, July) "The Narrative Construction of Differing Conceptions of the Person in the Development on Young Children's Social Understanding", *Early Education and Development*, *12*(3): 393–432.

Sacks, H., Schegloff, E. and Jefferson, G. (1974) "A Simplist Systematics for the Organization of Turn-Taking for Conversation", *Language*, *50*: 696–735.

Sapir, E. (1970) *Culture, Language and Personality: Selected Essays edited by D. Mandelbaum*. Berkeley, CA: University of California Press. (Original works published 1924, 1929, 1933.)

Searle, J. (1969) *Speech Acts: An Essay in the Philosophy of Language*. Cambridge: Cambridge University Press.

Shore, B. (1991) "Twice Born, Once Conceived: Meaning Construction and Cultural Cognition", *American Anthropologist*, *93*: 9–27.

Shweder, R. A., Goodnow, J., Hatano, G., LeVine, R. A., Markus, H. and Miller, P. (1997) "The Cultural Psychology of Development: One Mind, Many Mentalities", *Handbook of Child Psychology*, *1*: 865–937.

Silverstein, M. (1976) "Shifters, Linguistic Categories and Cultural Descriptions" in Basso, K. and Selby, H. (eds.) *Meaning in Anthropology* (pp. 11–56). Albuquerque, NM: New Mexico.

Slobin, D. (1997) "The Origins of Grammaticizable Notions: Beyond the Individual Mind" in Slobin, D. (ed.) *The Crosslinguistic Study of Language Acquisition. Volume 5: Expanding the Contexts*. Mahwah, NJ: Lawrence Erlbaum Press.

Stern, D. (1985) *The Interpersonal World of the Infant*. New York: Basic Books.

Talmy, L. (2000) *Towards a Cognitive Semantics*. Cambridge, MA: MIT Press.

Taylor, C. (1985) *Human Agency and Language: Philosophical Papers 1*. Cambridge: Cambridge University Press.

Tomasello, M. (1998) *The New Psychology of Language*. Mahwah, NJ: Lawrence Erlbaum Press.

— (1999) *The Cultural Origins of Human Cognition*. Cambridge, MA: Harvard University Press.

Užgiris, I. Č. (1989) "Infants in Relation" in Damon, W. (ed.) *Child Development Today and Tomorrow* (pp. 288–311). San Francisco, CA: Jossey-Bass.

— (1996) "Together and Apart: The Enactment of Values in Infancy" in Reed, E., Turiel, E. and Brown, T. (eds.) *Values and Knowledge*. Mahwah, NJ: Lawrence Erlbaum.

— (1999) "Imitation as Activity: Its Developmental Aspects" in Nadel, J. and Butterworth, G. (eds.) *Imitation in Infancy* (pp. 186–206). Cambridge: Cambridge University Press.

— (2000) "Words Don't Tell All: Some Thoughts on Early Communicative Development" in Budwig, N., Užgiris, I. Č. and Wertsch, J. V. (eds.) *Communication: An Arena of Development* (pp. 131–141). Stamford, CT: Ablex Publishing.

Vinden, P. (1996) "Junin Quechua Children's Understanding of Mind", *Child Development*, 67: 1707–1716.

Weir, R. (1962) *Language in the Crib*. The Hague: Mouton.

Werner, H. and Kaplan, B. (1984) *Symbol Formation*. Hillsdale, NJ: Lawrence Erlbaum Press. (Original work published 1963.)

Wertsch, J. V. (1991) *Voices of the Mind*. Cambridge, MA: Harvard University Press.

— (2000) "Intersubjectivity and Alterity in Human Communication" in Budwig, N., Užgiris, I. Č. and Wertsch, J. V. (eds.) *Communication: An Arena of Development* (pp. 17–31) Stamford, CT: Ablex Publishing.

Wootton, A. J. (1997) *Interaction and the Development of Mind*. Cambridge: Cambridge University Press.

6 The multiple agendas of intersubjectivity in children's group writing activity

Chikako Toma and James V. Wertsch

Over the past few decades investigators have used the notion of intersubjectivity from a variety of perspectives (e.g. Goncu 1993, Kujiraoka 1999, Matusov 1996, Rogoff 1990, Rommetveit 1979a–c, 1985, Smolka, De Goes and Pino 1995, Stern 1985, Toma 1994, Trevarthen 1977, Trevarthen and Hubley 1978, Wertsch 1985, 1998). Depending on the perspective employed and the topic involved, quite different accounts of this term have emerged. In this chapter we shall examine intersubjectivity from the perspective of two potentially competing demands that must be met when a group carries out a task: namely the demand to generate a good product on the one hand and to maintain a good relationship among the members on the other.

In philosophy, the origins of the term "intersubjectivity" can be traced to Husserl (1960). Somewhat unfortunately, however, the original notion is rarely discussed or even mentioned in the psychological literature using the term. The problematic that concerned Husserl in his original notion of intersubjectivity is often related to, but not necessarily identical with various ways in which the term has come to be used by investigators in psychology. Given the diverse use of the term intersubjectivity in the literature in psychology, we need to start by discussing the ways in which we use it here, after briefly touching upon how the term was used originally by Husserl. In order to avoid conceptual confusion, we will distinguish the original notion of intersubjectivity from others and shall use quotations when referring to the notion presented by Husserl.

"Intersubjectivity" became one of the central concepts in Husserl's later writings. In Husserl's work, the "problematique" of intersubjectivity was presented in the context of explaining how the objective world comes to be constituted by a subject without either slipping into the trap of solipsism or relying on metaphysical assumptions about the existence of an objective world independent of a subject. Husserl argued that the objective world has to be constituted when the intersubjective communality among subjects is projected toward objects. According to Husserl, "intersubjectivity" is concerned with "I's" conviction that "other minds" exist as subjectivity, as "I" do, and other minds must be convinced of the existence of the same and only world that the "I" is convinced exists. "Intersubjectivity" is treated as a crucial notion by which the "I" comes to accept the existence of the objective world as undoubted. The phenomenological meaning of the objective world is understood as "inter-subjectivity", which is the conviction that "I" and "others" may have different contents of subjectivity yet both belong to the same and only world.

The notion of intersubjectivity we use in this chapter is grounded in the use of the term found in writings by Rommetveit (1979a–d, 1985). This notion of intersubjectivity focuses on the dynamic process of communication. It is related to, but not identical with Husserl's "intersubjectivity." While "intersubjectivity" is concerned with explaining how a subject comes to see the existence of the objective world to be self-evident, the notion of intersubjectivity we use here deals with the communicative process that both presupposes and also may contribute to "intersubjectivity." (Further discussion about the relationship between "intersubjectivity" and intersubjectivity as we use it here would involve discussion by Merleau-Ponty and others who picked up and extended the problematic presented by "intersubjectivity." This, however, is beyond the scope of this chapter.)

We use the term intersubjectivity, then, when dealing with the process in which people generate, maintain and reorganize what Rommetveit calls "temporary shared worlds" through communication in a given activity. Rommetveit claims that communication "aims at transcendence of the 'private' worlds of the participants" and sets up what can be called "states of intersubjectivity" (1979a: 94). This notion of intersubjectivity focuses on the dynamic coordination between *what is said* and *what is taken for granted* in an ongoing process of communication. Here, intersubjectivity is not taken to be an all-or-nothing phenomenon. It involves multiple levels and requires constant generation, maintenance, and reorganization by interlocutors.

At the most basic level, any "normal" interaction needs to maintain what Rommetveit (1979a: 96) calls "mutual faith in the shared social world." In this regard Rommetveit notes:

> The full-fledged act of verbal communication is thus, under normal conditions, based upon a reciprocally endorsed and spontaneously fulfilled contract of complementarity: *Encoding* is tacitly assumed to involve *anticipatory decoding*. It is taken for granted that speech is continuously *listener oriented*. The speaker therefore monitors his speech in accordance with his assumptions about the extent of the social world and strategies of categorization which are shared by him and his listener. Conversely – and on precisely those premises – *decoding* is tacitly assumed to be *speaker oriented*, aiming at a reconstruction of what the speaker intends to make known.
>
> (1979a: 96, italics in original)

This feature of "normal" social interaction is so basic and pervasive that it typically remains inaccessible to conscious reflection. However, it is necessary for this basic level of intersubjectivity to be assumed in order for other levels to be achieved in social interaction. As Rommetveit puts it (1979a: 96): "Intersubjectivity has thus in some sense to be taken for granted in order to be achieved."

Beyond this basic level, various aspects of intersubjectivity are achieved when people engage in an activity. In his writings Rommetveit emphasizes the potential variability of the meaning of any sentence, word or phrase by using terms such as "message potential" and "draft of a contract." He then argues that we need to look into the process by which a common interpretation comes to be generated to produce a "temporary shared social world" in communication. One of the important processes of communication involves figuring out the variant premises for intersubjectivity that may vary according to the institution and situation. For example, Rommetveit points out that an utterance such as "I too was invited, I went to the ball ... and it rolled and rolled away..." may sound strange when it is made in the course of an ordinary conversation between two friends yet may sound perfectly fine when spoken as a part of a poem. Therefore "what is made known is dependent on what kind of meta-contract of communication has been tacitly and reciprocally endorsed in each particular case" (Rommetveit 1979a: 97–98). However, such premises are often unthinkingly taken for granted and established without explicit negotiation. The partly institutionalized and situated premises are of crucial importance for successful communication yet are brought to conscious/explicit negotiation only when the interlocutors discover problems in ongoing communication.

In this chapter we focus specifically on the dynamic communicative process involved in a group text-writing activity. In any activity where more than one person is involved, each participant needs to coordinate his/her actions with those of other participants in one way or another by generating, maintaining and reorganizing some level of common ground. This certainly does not mean a total overlap in understanding, opinions, and "worlds" among those involved in a given activity. Even in examples of interaction where participants engage in conversation based on a high level of agreement there are always certain aspects of each individual's "world" that do not perfectly coincide or overlap with others. Conversely, even in an interaction where the participants are in vehement disagreement, the participants are in a "temporarily shared social world", at least to the extent that they share the perspective that they are in dispute.

In any kind of group activity, there is always more than one agenda at stake. The list of agendas involved in a particular activity may vary a great deal from one case to another. In the type of activity we shall be examining, however, there are two principal agendas. One concerns producing a "good" product, and the other concerns maintaining sufficiently good relationships among group members for them to operate well as a team.

The importance of these two agendas has been recognized in the literature of group processes for some time. Bales (1950) claimed that any group working toward achieving a particular task goal engages not only in task-related processes but also in socio-emotional processes for maintaining interpersonal relationships among the group members. Various behaviors that group members employ have been identified as effective ways to accomplish the achievement of a task goal (e.g. Cartwright and Zander 1968) on the one hand, and the goal of group maintenance (McGrath and Altman 1966) on the other. A number of functional theories of leadership have also been formulated concerning task performance and the maintenance of interpersonal relationships (Blake and Mounton 1964, Hersey and Blanchard 1972, Misumi 1966).

In this chapter we shall examine how intersubjectivity is generated, maintained and reorganized with regard to these two potentially conflicting demands by examining how a group of children work on producing a single written text. The group we shall discuss comes from a fourth-grade classroom at a public elementary school in Japan. The group consists of two girls (Mari and Saeko) and two boys (Kenji and Taro) who are experienced at working together in a grouping called a *seikatsu-han* in their classroom. The four children in a *seikatsu-han* eat lunch together, carry out some daily chores together, such as cleaning the classroom and delivering lunch, and take responsibility for committee work in classroom activity. They also often perform academic tasks together.

The researcher told the children she was interested in collecting messages from elementary school children for a radio broadcast on the topic of environmental protection and asked them to produce a written message on the issue as a group. They were told they could produce the text in any way they wanted and take as long as they liked. The number of sheets of paper and pencils provided was larger than the number of the group members in order to ensure flexibility in the way the group could choose to develop the activity.

The group started out writing individually, then proceeded to read each other's drafts, and finally integrated them into a single text. The whole process took about thirty-five minutes and resulted in the following text:

On the Destruction of Nature – A Message –

   xx Elementary School, fourth grade, xx class, Group 7.

   What is happening to Nature around us now?
Greenery is diminishing and oxygen is diminishing, too.
If we don't take care of greenery, the earth will be left to grow barren.
Because of that, we are going to need to recycle.
Let's work together for greenery and for us all.
This is a wish from us.

The segment of the group activity that we shall use for our discussion is translated from Japanese to English, divided into three successive segments, and presented in Excerpts 1 to 3. Excerpt 1 begins at the time when the children start to compose a single draft as a group by putting together the drafts written by each member individually. Excerpt 3 ends at the point when the group came up with the first sentence of the message. It took about one and a half minutes from the beginning of Excerpt 1 to the end of Excerpt 3.

   The fact that the word order patterns of English and Japanese differ (i.e. English is a left-extending language and Japanese is a right-extending language) creates a challenge when trying to follow the English translation of the Japanese transcript. This reflects the fact that sentences in spoken dialogue emerged in an order that is unusual or even impossible in English. In order to aid the reader in following the transcript, we shall provide the first sentence of the text in Japanese below.

In Japanese:
ima,	*watashitachi*	no	*mawari*	no	*shizen*	wa	*doonatteirudesyoo*
(now	us		around		nature		what is happening)

English translation of the whole sentence:
   What is happening to Nature around us now?

In the excerpts, the oral production of text is enclosed by quotation marks.

Two agendas in harmony

During the interaction directly preceding Excerpt 1, the group spent about two minutes discussing how to go about putting together the drafts from each member. They decided to do it by asking Kenji to take the role of the writer for the group while everybody else worked on integrating the drafts. They also agreed that Mari would make a clean copy for submission once the integrated message of the group was produced. All the individual drafts were spread out on a table in front of the participants.

Excerpt 1
(@ indicates simultaneous utterances)

1 *Taro*: Everybody, *[looking around at the individual drafts]*
2 *Mari*: Hurry up! Put them together!
      @Whose should go in first?
3 *Taro*: @"Now." *[looking at everyone's drafts]*
      Everyone wrote down "Now", "Now", "Now", *[at the beginning of their drafts]*.
4 *Kenji*: I would like mine to be first. *[Responding to Mari]*
5 *Taro*: "now" *[Looking at Kenji]*
6 *Kenji*: What?
7 *Taro*: "now" *[Prompting Kenji to write down "now" by pointing on the paper in front of Kenji.]* 'Cause "now", "now", "now" *[Pointing to drafts one after another]*
      <<*Kenji starts writing down "now"*>>
8 *Kenji*: But I think "today" sounds cooler (than "now").
      <<*while writing down "now"*>>

In this interaction, the first word of the group message "now" was produced rather smoothly. This is mainly due to the fact that everybody in the group started out with this word. The first sentence in each of the various participants' drafts was:

Saeko: "In the world where we live, nature is disappearing *now.*"
Mari: "Nature is getting destroyed *now.*"

> *Taro*:   "We are discussing the destruction of nature *now*."
> *Kenji*: "We are discussing what is happening with regard to the destruction of nature *now*."

During the interaction represented in Excerpt 1, multiple aspects of intersubjectivity are at stake. Throughout all three excerpts, the children seem to share the understanding that Kenji is the writer for the group and they are working on coming up with a group text by integrating individual drafts. However, the concrete process for integrating individual drafts was not established in the group's "temporary shared social world" at the beginning of Excerpt 1. This is indicated by the simultaneous and separate attempts by Mari and Taro to move the activity in different directions. In turn 2, Mari attempts to move the activity by suggesting that they choose one draft from which the first sentence of the group text is to be generated. Simultaneously, Taro invites the group to pay attention to the fact that everybody started their drafts with "now" and announces it in turn 3.

Taro's move does not receive immediate attention from the other children. In turn 4, by responding to Mari's prompt, Kenji contributes to generating another aspect of intersubjectivity that is concerned with how to go about integrating drafts. Taro's utterance in turn 3 may or may not have been heard by others, but his proposal is not endorsed by other members explicitly as the direction in which the activity will move. Mari's proposal, on the other hand, is endorsed at least by Kenji, thus generating a potential common ground in terms of the ways in which the text can be put together. At this point there are at least two competing possibilities for how to come up with the first sentence of group text.

However, in turn 5, Taro turns to Kenji and tells him "now", suggesting that it should be the first word of the group's text. At this point, Kenji and Mari pay attention to Taro and Kenji asks Taro what he wants to say in turn 6. Taro repeats in turn 7 almost the same utterance he has just made in turn 3 but more loudly and also with pointing gestures toward the paper. This gets Kenji to write down "Now" as the first word for the group's text as other members watch over it without raising objections. At this point, the socially shared world among the children includes the first word for the group text as "now."

During the activity in Excerpt 1, the agendas of producing text and maintaining good relationships are not in conflict. This is not surprising, given that everybody started out their individual draft with "now." Thus children were in potential agreement about the first word before they started to generate the group's text.

Two agendas in conflict

In contrast to the rather smooth production of the first word of the group's text in Excerpt 1, the two agendas (i.e. task completion and maintenance of good relationships among members) were in conflict in the subsequent segment of interaction presented in Excerpt 2. In this segment serious disagreements arose about the use of a first-person pronoun. In Japanese, there are several first-person plural pronominal forms (i.e. for "we"). The most general form is *watashitachi*, and this can be used for both male and female referents. Another form of the pronoun is *bokutachi*, which is used almost exclusively to refer to male referents.

Excerpt 2
(@ indicates simultaneous utterances. @2 coincided with @2)

 9 *Saeko*: "Where we (*watashitachi*/general) live" [*Reading her own draft*]
10 *Taro*: "We" (*bokutachi*/masculine in Japanese) [*half jokingly, with a smile*]
11 *Mari*: Why "we" (*bokutachi*/masculine) ? [*protesting to Taro*]
12 *Kenji*: What's wrong with that? "We" (*bokutachi*/masculine) is just great, right? [*looking at Taro*]
13 *Mari*: "Now" ... I think "*the world*¹ (*yononaka* in Japanese)" is fine [*laughs slightly*], "*the world* (*yononaka*)".
    [*Taro smiles.*]
14 *Kenji*: Are you stupid? "*World* (*yononaka*)" is bad.
15 *Taro*: "The world (*sekai* in Japanese)" will do.
16 *Mari*: "The world (*sekai*)", "the world (*sekai*)", "the world (*sekai*)"!
17 *Taro*: "The world (*sekai*)", "the world (*sekai*)", "the world (*sekai*)". [*shaking Kenji's upper arm and suggesting to him to write down* "the world (*sekai*)"]
18 *Mari*: "Now, the world (*sekai*)".
19 *Taro*: "Now in the world (*sekai*)".
    [*Mari notices that Kenji is writing down "we" (bokutachi/masculine).*]
20 *Mari*: Why? ! [*in a loudly protesting tone toward Kenji*]. If you use "we (*bokutachi*/masculine)", it (the message) sounds like a wish from men (male).
21 *Taro*: Because you guys are women/. [*to Kenji*]
    [*Saeko plays with a pencil and drops it, then leaves her seat to pick it up.*]
22 *Mari*: Saeko (in the tone of meaning "What are you doing?")
23 *Kenji*: Then, "we (*watashitachi*/general)" is fine. "We (*watashitachi*/general)" includes both men and women "We (*watashitachi*/general)" will do, won't it? [*to Taro*]
24 *Mari*: No! "*the worl(d)* (*yonona*)" [*makes a slip of the tongue*]
    Write down "the world (*sekai*)" [*in a loud, insistent voice*]
25 *Kenji*: Why? [*angrily*]
    <<*Taro erases "we (bokutachi/masculine)" that Kenji wrote on the draft paper for the group* >>
26 *Taro*: Calm down, you guys. Don't fight. "The world (*sekai*)" is fine.
27 *Mari*: "We (*watashitachi*/general)" sounds funny.
28 *Taro*: Go with "the world (*sekai*)".
    <<*Kenji is writing down "us (watashitachi/general)".*>>
29 *Mari*: "The world (*sekai*)!" [*in forcefully protesting tone toward Kenji*]
30 *Saeko*: That's fine! [*to Mari*]
    Even boys can say "we (*watashitachi*/general)".

31 *Mari*:   Well, then I can switch it to "the world" when I write the final version.
32 *Saeko*:   I won't take the responsibility for that. *[objecting to Mari]*
33 *Kenji*:   You @ should take the responsibility for that. *[to Mari, holding an eraser.]*
34 *Taro*:   @Calm down! This is not a time to fight!
35 *Kenji*:   I say, you take the responsibility for it. *[to Mari]*
36 *Mari*:   "Now, in the world (*sekai*)". *[assertive tone]*
37 *Taro*:   It's okay, you go ahead and write it down and *[to Kenji]*, gosh, you say
           it. *[in a critical tone to Mari]*
38 *Saeko*:   "Now, in the world where we live". *[Reads aloud her own draft in a quiet
           voice and puts it in the center of the table toward Kenji.]*
39 *Mari*:   I was trying to think about the text. *[being upset]*.
           I won't work on it anymore.
40 *Taro*:   Then why are you saying "the world (*sekai*)"?
           <<*Kenji starts writing down "around"*>>
41 *Mari*:   I say @"the world" is better . . .
42 *Taro*:   @Hurry, be quiet.
43 *Mari*:   Then why @2 are you taking Kenji's side?
44 *Taro*:   @2 We won't have enough time.

This excerpt starts from the point when the children begin to work on coming up with the text following the word "now" produced in Excerpt 1. In turn 9, Saeko provides a candidate for such a text by reading aloud a part of the first sentence from her own individual draft. In this utterance, she uses the general form for the first-person plural pronoun *watashitachi*. In turn 10, Taro introduces a male form of the first-person plural pronoun, *bokutachi*, half-jokingly and with a smile on his face. Mari quickly objects to Taro's move in turn 11. In turn 12, Kenji puts forward the idea of using the male form *bokutachi*, making an explicit bid to form a coalition of boys with Taro by soliciting agreement from him both verbally and by an exaggerated gesture of looking into his face. Mari counteracts this by suggesting the alternative "the world (*yononaka*)" for the text.

However, *yononaka* does not work very well in this context (see Note 1 for further information on the usage of the word in Japanese). Mari's giggle while talking seems to indicate that she realizes the awkwardness of her choice of word. Kenji dismisses Mari's suggestion in turn 14, and in turn 15 Taro suggests a more appropriate word for referring to the world in this context, namely, *sekai*. In turn 16, Mari takes up Taro's suggestion and promotes it by repeating "the world (*sekai*)" three times.

Taro immediately enforces Mari's move by also repeating "the world (*sekai*)" three times as he prompts Kenji to write it down by shaking Kenji's upper arm (turn 17). At this point, both Mari and Taro seem to assume that Kenji will write down "the world (*sekai*)." They recite the words "now the world" as if "the world (*sekai*)" has been recognized as the second word of the sentence in the "socially shared world" of the group (turns 18 and 19). Up to this point, although there are differences in opinion regarding the choice of word, no serious conflict surfaced among children.

The tone of the activity alters dramatically when Mari notices that Kenji is writing down "we (*bokutachi*/masculine)" instead of "world (*sekai*)." It becomes clear that the aspect of "the social world" that Mari and Taro assumed to be shared has not been shared intersubjectively by the whole group. At this point, then, the intersubjectively shared world includes the understanding that they have *not* reached an agreement on the second word of the first sentence. In turn 20, Mari raises her voice and questions what Kenji is doing in a strong accusatory tone. She makes it clear that she has not endorsed the proposal to use "we (*bokutachi*/masculine)" as the second word for the first sentence. She explicitly provides a quite reasonable rationale behind her objection, namely that using "we (*bokutachi*/masculine)" makes it sound as if the message is coming from boys despite the fact that there are also girls in the group. In turn 23, Kenji responds to Mari's argument by proposing to use "we (*watashitachi*/general)" instead of "we (*bokutachi*/masculine)" and gives a good rationale for this counter-proposal [i.e. that "we (*watashitachi*/general)" includes both men and women].

In turn 24, instead of either agreeing with Kenji's proposal or providing an argument for other choices, Mari insists on "the world (*sekai*)" as the second word for the sentence. She even uses the imperative form and a loud forceful tone of voice to demand that Kenji write down "the world (*sekai*)." Kenji responds to Mari in a quite angry voice (turn 25). The emotional tension is getting quite high at this point. Mari and Kenji share the understanding that they disagree, but are not showing any move toward using this disagreement constructively. At this point, the agenda concerning the product (i.e. text) is threatening the goal of maintaining a good relationship among members.

At this point Taro jumps in and scolds Mari and Kenji for carrying the disagreement to such a level, while erasing the words [i.e. "we (*bokutachi*/masculine)"] that Kenji had written down without consent from the group. Neither Kenji nor Mari objects to what Taro does at this point. The heightened tension between them appears to be reduced at least to the level that both Kenji and Mari stop yelling at each other. Then Taro tells Kenji to go along with "the world (*sekai*)." Mari now gives her reason for not wanting to choose "we (*watashitachi*/general)" stating that it sounds funny to her (turn 27). This was not convincing to the others since "we (*watashitachi*/general)" could be a perfectly fine choice here. Taro prompts Kenji to write down "the world (*sekai*)" again in turn 28. However, Kenji starts writing down "we (*watashitachi*/general)" as the other children watch what Kenji writes. Mari sees what Kenji is writing down and insists in a forceful voice that he should be writing "the world (*sekai*)."

At this point (turn 30), Saeko, who has been rather quiet for a while, jumps in and objects to Mari for her insistence. In a rather accusatory tone of voice, she points out the fact that "we (*watashitachi*/general)" can include both men and women. By saying so Saeko implies that she thinks "we (*watashitachi*/general)" is a fine choice. The tension among the children is increasing again here to the level of threatening the goal of maintaining good relationships among the group members.

In the next turn (turn 31), Mari, who had lost ground for insisting on "the world (*sekai*)," resorts to an unfair means for promoting her idea. She asserts that she will take advantage of her role as a writer of the final clean copy and switch the second word of the sentence from "we (*watashitachi*/general)" to "the world (*sekai*)." Saeko becomes quite annoyed with Mari, telling her that she will not take responsibility for the choice of word if Mari changes anything without obtaining the consent of other group members. Kenji holds an eraser in his hand and gets ready to erase what he has written down [i.e. "we (*watashitachi*/general)"] as he aligns himself with Saeko by repeating in an angry tone of voice what she has just said (turn 33). Dissatisfaction and negative feelings are growing rapidly between Mari on the one hand and Kenji and Saeko on the other. At this point all the children shared the perspective that they were in disagreement over the choice of word for the group text and also that the disagreement had grown into an interpersonal conflict. In other words, the intersubjectively shared world among the children included not only disagreement on the content of the text but also dissatisfaction with the ways in which the disagreement had been handled.

In turn 34, an attempt is made to change the handling of the disagreement over the choice of the word, reshaping the intersubjectively shared world with respect to interpersonal relationships among the members so that conflict does not grow further. Once again, as soon as Taro hears Kenji's angry comment in turn 33, he jumps in and attempts to cool down the tension, telling them to calm down and not to fight. After Taro's intervention, Kenji again tells Mari to take the responsibility for changing the word but in a far less angry tone (turn 35). Mari puts her idea forward once more in turn 36, but in a much less aggressive tone of voice this time. The disagreement about the choice of word remains, but now the group seems to share the perspective that they cannot go on with escalating the negative emotional and interpersonal conflict. At least, it appears that a major rupture of group relationships was avoided.

Taro then tells Kenji to go ahead with writing and tells Mari that she needs to come up with a text, insinuating that if she is so insistent she should be ready to take the lead in coming up with the group's text. Mari protests at this move by Taro (turn 39). She justifies herself by stating that she is only doing what she is supposed to do, namely come up with the text. Mari gets upset and says she won't work on it. Taro does not let this pass, and pushes Mari by asking why she is so insistent on "the world (*sekai*)" if she is so ready to give up work on the text (turn 40). In turn 41, Mari again says she prefers "the world (*sekai*)", but Taro cuts her off in turn 42. In turn 43, Mari responds by accusing Taro of taking Kenji's side. Before Mari has finished her turn Taro interrupts her by bringing up his concern about taking too much time. However, contrary to what she has just said, the tone of Mari's voice has become mild and the tension that existed earlier is no longer in evidence. Meanwhile, Kenji has proceeded to write down "around" on the paper.

Two agendas in harmony once again

In Excerpt 3, which presents the segment of interaction immediately following Excerpt 2, Mari notices that Kenji has written down some more text on the paper but does not object to it this time. She talks to Kenji in a soft tone and Kenji responds likewise (turns 45 and 46). In turn 47, Taro recites a part of what has been written down so far, looking in the air as he does so, trying to come up with the next word. Mari does not bring up her preference for "the world (*sekai*)" again. Instead, she prompts Kenji to integrate ideas from individual drafts and aids him by spreading the individual drafts in front of him (turn 48). As Mari speaks, Kenji comes up with the full sentence that will be written down as the first item in the group's text (turn 49–50). [This sentence is going to be discussed among children right after turn 49 for about a minute before it is put down on paper.]

Excerpt 3
(@ indicates simultaneous utterances. @2 coincided with @2)

45 *Mari*: Whose words are you copying right now?
46 *Kenji*: Who knows. *[stops writing]*
47 *Taro*: "Nature around (us)".
48 *Mari*: Then put together from this one. *[Spreading the individual drafts in front of Kenji so that he can see them better.]*
          Okay? @Put them together.
          @2 Put them together quickly.
49 *Kenji*: @Should I write "around us (*watashitachi*/general)?"
50 *Kenji*: @2 "us (*watashitachi*/general)"
          Should I write "what is happening in the nature around us (*watashitachi*/general)"?

Conclusion: Multiple agendas of intersubjectivity

The three segments of interaction we have discussed demonstrate that children engage in quite complicated efforts to coordinate intersubjectivity when multiple agendas are involved. Even in the first minute and a half of their interaction, during which they produced the first sentence of their message, the dynamics were quite complex.

Throughout the interaction the group coordinated intersubjectivity at several different levels. At the most basic level, the group has maintained what Rommetveit (1979a: 96) calls "mutual faith in the shared social world". This is the feature of "normal" social interaction that needs to be assumed in order for other aspects to be achieved.

Beyond this basic level, the group also created, maintained and reorganized other sorts of intersubjectivity. For example, they manifested a shared perspective on the procedures for carrying out the task by the time Excerpt 1 started, and this was maintained throughout the rest of this interaction segment. That is, the socially shared world of the group included the arrangement that Kenji was the writer for the draft of the message and all members would work on generating the group's text.

However, other aspects of intersubjectivity underwent much more dynamic transformation as the children worked on the task. Creating intersubjectivity on rough procedures was not enough for the children to move on to actually producing a text. They needed to generate concrete ways of going about integrating ideas from each member of the group. In Excerpt 1, two ways for proceeding were proposed, not through explicit discussion but by patterns of action (i.e. one by Mari in turn 2 and another by Taro in turns 3, 5 and 7). Mari proposed to look at one individually written text at a time by asking, "Whose should go in first?" Taro proposed looking over all the individually written drafts to find the commonality among them by identifying "now" as a word used by everyone. Without explicitly discussing which way should be adopted, "the draft of a contract" provided by Taro's move became endorsed and the word "now" got written down as the first word of the group text.

In this process, intersubjectivity with respect to how to go about producing the first word of the text and what should be the first word was generated without conflicting with the agenda of maintaining interpersonal relationships. The initial differences in the proposals about how to integrate ideas momentarily dissolved. A similar pattern of intersubjectivity was maintained up to turn 19 in Excerpt 2. Different children proposed different ideas for the second word of the group message, but these differences did not turn into interpersonal conflict.

However, the organization of intersubjectivity changed dramatically after Mari found out that Kenji had gone ahead and written down his choice of word. At this point it became clear that Taro's and Mari's assumptions about the shared world differed from Kenji's. This gave rise to a challenge for the group to come up with a mutually acceptable way of deciding on what the next word of the text should be. Given the fact that they had produced only the first word and the sentence was capable of being developed in several different ways, there were no grounds for deciding that one word was better than another at that point. The first sentence could have been developed into either "What is happening to nature in *the world* now?" by choosing "world (*sekai*)" for the second word, as Mari insisted, or "What is happening to nature around *us* now?" by using "us (*watashitachi*/ general)", as Kenji insisted. However, the intersubjective frame of communication did not remain focused on what is good for the text. As Mari and Kenji each pushed forward their own ideas about the second word for the group's text, the communication came to be centered around the question of whose idea should be adopted. What started out as a dispute over word choice turned into an emotionally loaded interpersonal conflict among the group members.

The negative emotional tone of the group process grew as the interpersonal conflict escalated. If the conflict escalated further, it could have jeopardized the group activity itself. Indeed, Hilgers (1987) reported that in his study of group story-writing in fourth- and fifth-grade classrooms in a Hawaiian elementary school, some groups broke apart after experiencing conflict among the members. Hilgers observed that the children struggled for control of the group and of the common text. Such struggles often continued for extended periods, and some were never resolved. Five of the twelve groups in his study ended up submitting multiple stories in spite of the original request from the researcher to produce a single text from each group. Hilgers also reported that the typical group-generated text was either "dominated by the ideas of one group member or was a 'round-robin' product marked by a lack of coherence" (p. 114). He concludes that effective collaborative writing is likely to be the outgrowth not only of individual writing skills but also of successful interpersonal and group dynamics.

The group we have analyzed in this chapter did not disintegrate, however. When the interpersonal conflict became heated, Taro jumped in and reflected on the ways in which the interaction was moving. Taro's intervention in the conflict was accepted by other members and effectively rearranged the intersubjectivity in such a way that the group could bring the two agendas into harmony again. In the end, the group produced a coherent single message incorporating contributions from each member.

In the larger study of group text-writing activity from which the group discussed in this chapter is drawn, Toma (1994) reported that none of the forty-one groups (twenty-two fourth-grade groups and nineteen sixth-grade groups in two public elementary schools in Japan) disintegrated or failed to produce a text. All but three of these groups generated a text by integrating ideas of the members (the other three groups voted on texts produced individually). This may suggest that an aspect of the shared world among these groups in the Japanese elementary schools included the assumption that members should not insist on their own opinion to the point of jeopardizing the group activity. Apparently, this was not a part of the temporary shared world for many of the groups studied by Hilgers (1987).

This certainly does not mean that children in the Japanese elementary school reached or even worked toward total agreement. In the group discussed in this chapter, it is entirely possible that Mari never fully agreed with using the word "us (*watashitachi*/ general)." Indeed, later in the process when Mari was a writer of the clean copy of the final text, she asked the group again whether "us (*watashitachi*/ general)" would fit well or not. It is quite possible that she went along with group decision even though she did not feel comfortable with the nuance of this particular word.

The point we would like to make here is that the agendas of producing a text and maintaining interpersonal relationship are always at stake during the process of shaping and reshaping various aspects of intersubjectivity in a group activity, but these agendas may be differently coordinated in different institutional settings. It is likely that what was taken for granted in what Rommetveit called "partly institutionalized aspects of intersubjectivity" (1979a: 96) for the activity such as group text-writing was different for the Japanese elementary school groups studied by Toma (1994) than for those groups studied by Hilgers (1987) in Hawaii.

One of the questions that remains to be explored in the future is how the institutionalized aspects of intersubjectivity with regard to group writing activity are formed in different institutional settings. It may be tempting to relate the differences between the groups in Hawaii and in Japan to the individualistic versus sociocentric cultural values of the United States and Japan respectively. However, we would prefer to avoid rushing to this kind of judgment. We take the position that to employ such terms as "individualistic" or "sociocentric" in describing the culture of an entire nation is to show too little sensitivity to the considerable diversities that exist within any nation. This kind of terminology often has the effect of reinforcing unhelpful national stereotypes and lends support to the practice of creating and re-creating nations as "imagined communities" (Anderson 1991). It is worth questioning whether the nation can be taken as a useful unit for the discussion of "culture" and whether such notions as individualism and sociocentrism can rightly be judged as characterizing the members of any nation (see Shimizu 2000 and Toma 2000). We argue that in order to approach the above-mentioned question, we need to look at the histories of concrete practices of institutions and the nexus of practices related to institutions.

The analysis of interaction in this chapter demonstrates that children engage in quite complex and active processes of shaping and reshaping intersubjectivity as they coordinate the potentially competing demands of a group activity. They are required both to create a good product and to maintain good relations among themselves. This often involves asserting one's opinion on the one hand while knowing how to go along with group consensus on the other. In order to understand what is involved in the way children learn to carry out various tasks as a group, we need to look closely into the details of the process of interaction from the perspective of the multiple agendas of intersubjectivity involved in a given activity.

Note

1 There are two Japanese words, *yononaka* and *sekai*, for the English "world." *Yononaka* is used mainly to refer to the everyday world of ordinary people, that is the world of living human beings and their social relationships. In contrast, *sekai* covers a range of uses, such as the earth, all nations or the world within a particular academic or artistic field (e.g. the world of literature, the world of Picasso). *Sekai* also includes *yononaka*. In this transcript we used italic "world" for *yononaka* to distinguish it from *sekai*.

Acknowledgements

The writing of this chapter was assisted by a grant from the Japan Society for the Promotion of Science to the first author and one from the Spencer Foundation to the second. The statements made and the views expressed are solely the responsibility of the authors.

References

Anderson, B. (1991) *Imagined Communities*. London: Verso.

Bales, R. F. (1950) *Interaction Process Analysis: A Method for the Study of Small Groups.* Chicago: University of Chicago Press.

Blake, R. R. and Mounton, J. S. (1964) *The Managerial Grid: Key Orientations for Achieving Production through People.* Houston: Gulf Publishing Company.

Cartwright, D. and Zander, A. (eds.) (1968) *Group Dynamics.* 3rd ed. New York: Harper & Row.

Goncu, A. (1993) "Development of Intersubjectivity in Social Pretend Play", *Human Development, 36: 185–198.*

Hersey, P. and Blanchard, K. H. (1972) *Management of Organizational Behavior: Utilizing Human Resources.* Englewood Cliffs, NJ: Prentice Hall.

Hilgers, T. L. (1987) "Young Writers Facing a New Collaborative Writing Task", *Journal of Research in Childhood Education, 2, 2: 108–116.*

Husserl, E. (1960) *Cartesian Meditations: An Introduction to Phenomenology.* (Cairns, Dorion, trs.) Hague: Martinus Nijhoff.

Kujiraoka, S. (1999) *Kankei hattatsu ron no koochiku* [Construction of the Relational Theory of Development]. Kyoto: Mineruba-shoboo.

Matusov, E. (1996) "Intersubjectivity Without Agreement", *Mind Culture, and Activity, 3, 1: 25–45.*

McGrath, J. E. and Altman, I. (1966) *Small Group Research: A Synthesis and Critique of the Field.* New York: Holt, Rinehart & Winston.

Misumi, J. (1966) *Atarashii Leadership: Shuudann sidoo no koudougaku.* [New Leadership: A Behavioral Science of Leading Groups]. Tokyo: Daiamondo-sha.

Rogoff, B. (1990) *Apprenticeship in Thinking: Cognitive Development in Social Context.* New York: Oxford University Press.

Rommetveit, R. (1979a) "On the Architecture of Intersubjectivity" in Rommetveit, R. and Blakar, R. M. (eds.) *Studies of Language, Thought and Verbal Communication* (pp. 93–107). New York: Academic Press.

— (1979b) "Deep Structure of Sentences versus Message Structure" in Rommetveit, R. and Blakar, R. M. (eds.) *Studies of Language, Thought and Verbal Communication* (pp. 17–34). New York: Academic Press.

— (1979c) "On Negative Rationalism in Scholarly Studies of Verbal Communication and Dynamic Residuals in the Construction of Human Intersubjectivity" in Rommetveit, R. and Blakar, R. M. (eds.) *Studies of Language, Thought and Verbal Communication* (pp. 17–34). New York: Academic Press.

— (1985) "Language Acquisition as Increasing Linguistic Structuring of Experience and Symbolic Behavioral Control" in Wertsch, J. (ed.) *Culture, Communication, and Cognition: Vygotskyan Perspect* (pp. 183–204). New York: Cambridge University Press.

Shimizu, H. (2000) "Beyond Individualism and Sociocentrism: An Ontological Analysis of the Opposing Elements in Personal Experiences of Japanese Adolescents", *Human Development, 43: 195–211.*

Smolka, A. L., De Goes, M. C. and Pino, A. (1995) "The Constitution of the Subject: A Persistent Question" in Wertsch, J. V., del Rio, P. and Alvarez, A. (eds.) *Sociocultural Studies of Mind,* pp. 165–184. Cambridge: Cambridge University Press.

Toma, C. (1994) "The Development of Intersubjectivity in Group Text Writing Activity Among Japanese Elementary School Students", doctoral dissertation. Worcester, MA: Clark University.

— (2000) "Ontisch vs. Ontologisch Approaches to Individualistic/Sociocentric Distinction", *Human Development, 43: 227–229.*

Trevarthen, C. (1977) "Descriptive Analyses of Infant Communicative Behavior" in Schaffer, H. R. (ed.) *Studies in Mother–Infant Interaction.* London: Academic Press.

Trevarthen, C. and Hubley, P. (1978) "Secondary Intersubjectivity: Confidence, Confiding and Acts of Meaning in the First Year" in Loke, A. (ed.) *Action, Gesture and Symbol: The Emergence of Language* (pp. 183–229). London: Academic Press.

Wertsch, J. V. (1985) *Vygotsky and the Social Formation of Mind.* Cambridge, MA: Harvard University Press.

— (1998) *Mind As Action.* New York: Oxford University Press.

Part II

Developing through culturally shaped social interactions

7 Object manipulation in context

Jeffrey J. Lockman

Over the course of the first year, infants become more proficient in the ways in which they manipulate objects. More generally, this skill is believed by many to be foundational for a variety of cognitive and social achievements that occur across childhood. Consider, for instance, how object manipulation figures prominently in accounts of the development of such abilities as physical knowledge, mathematical understanding, play, imitation and social interaction (Piaget 1952, Rogoff 1990, Siegler 1996, Vygotsky 1978). In view of the centrality of object manipulation across developmental domains, how should the origins of object manipulation be best understood? The answer to this question is important for understanding not only object manipulation per se, but the various abilities for which object manipulation is considered a primary part. My thesis in this chapter is that the early development of object manipulation is most appropriately considered an ability that emerges across individual, social and cultural contexts. Although I will argue that the perception–action framework of the Gibsons (Gibson and Pick 2000, J. J. Gibson 1979) is well suited to accommodate this view, my thinking on this topic has also been influenced by the pioneering work of Ina Užgiris on experience and early development.

During her distinguished career, Ina Užgiris offered the field of psychology profound insights into the ways in which children shape and are shaped by their environments. Much of her work centered on the infancy period, but the lessons afforded by this work inform our understanding of the ontogenetic process, more generally. In her pioneering studies with Joseph McVicker Hunt (Užgiris and Hunt 1975), she provided researchers and practitioners with beautifully detailed scales of infant cognitive development. These scales, based largely on Piaget's (1952, 1954) proposals about sensorimotor development, represented a synthesis of sorts between a structural approach endorsed by Piaget and psychometric theory embraced by more quantitatively oriented psychologists. The scales are also notable for the way in which they conceptualized the sequencing of development as a joint product of organism and environment, a view which constituted a challenge to some strongly held maturational views at that time.

In her subsequent work, Ina Užgiris continued to address fundamental questions about the role of experience in early development. An exacting theoretician, she eloquently defended Piaget's proposals, but also recognized that some important aspects of Piaget's theory were not confirmed by the results of careful empirical studies. She also recognized that Piaget did not fully appreciate how the child's social environment or culture might influence the developmental process. So as she did in her earlier research, in which she sought to provide a solid empirical base for Piaget's infancy proposals, Užgiris considered the empirical implications of sociocultural theories for understanding early ontogenesis. Specifically, she used these theories to offer a new way at looking at the development of imitation, one that differed from but did not entirely disregard Piagetian theory. In Užgiris' contextually based view, infant imitation was to be understood by examining its adaptive function at the time that the infant was imitating. Imitation or matching might be serving a communicative or sharing function in one context and a learning function in another (Užgiris 1981, Užgiris, Benson, Kruper and Vasek 1989). This real-time functionalist perspective, while representing a departure from Piagetian theory, anticipated important theoretical developments in the child psychology field. Consider, for instance, the resurgence of interest and extension of Vygotskyan theory (e.g. Rogoff 1990), work on the development of joint attention (Moore and Dunham 1995) and the emergence of dynamic systems theory (Thelen and Smith 1994). Many of the themes that appear in these newer approaches were anticipated in one form or another in Užgiris' work. Theoretically loyal and independent at the same time, Ina Užgiris provided the field of developmental psychology with new ways of thinking about the contributions of experience to early development.

It is in this spirit that I would like to turn my attention to the development of a set of infant abilities that traditionally have been viewed from either a maturational perspective and/or from a perspective that has been largely devoid of contextual considerations. The abilities that I will consider are the motor skills that enable infants to manually engage their environments. These skills fall under a number of names including object manipulation, play, problem-solving and exploration. To one degree or another, however, they all require infants to relate their hands in an adaptive fashion to some property of the environment, whether that be an object, a surface or relations that may exist between objects or surfaces.

In this chapter, I will argue that the role of experience in the development of these types of manual behaviors has been largely ignored. Most often, the emergence of these types of manual ability has been attributed to maturation or normative development, independent of experience (Gesell and Amatruda 1941). Further, even when experiential contributions to manipulation development have been recognized, the types of experience that have been considered have been limited, primarily self-generated ones that infants produce on their own (Piaget 1952, 1954). In contrast, investigators have focused little attention on the role that caregivers may play in helping infants develop finer control of their manual actions. I will suggest that over a diverse range of tasks, various kinds of experience – especially opportunities provided by caregivers, play an important role in the early development of manual skill.

My focus will be on the development of object manipulation. By object manipulation I refer to the manual skills infants display which indicate that they are exploring and using objects adaptively or appropriately, based on the object's physical characteristics. I will argue that infants' abilities to manipulate objects appropriately are not simply a product of maturation but also perception–action learning. Further, I will argue that past treatments of object manipulation development have ignored experiential contributions in general, especially those from individuals in the infant's social world. To document the potential contribution of social figures to the development of object manipulation, I will review some of our research on how parents and siblings manipulate objects with their infants. I will contend that in such interchanges rich opportunities for learning about manipulation exist. In concluding, I will suggest that additional consideration of how infants learn through experience to engage objects and surfaces manually can lead to new insights about the development of skilled action more generally, including tool use.

Object manipulation

The development of object manipulation has been of considerable interest to investigators in a variety of psychological domains. For investigators of motor development, object manipulation has been viewed as an important index of manual skill and more broadly, adaptive behavior (Connolly 1970, Gesell and Amatruda 1941). For investigators of cognitive development, object manipulation has been seen as a basic marker of cognitive growth. In the cognitive literature, researchers have examined early object manipulation to gain insights into such areas as the development of symbolic thinking, play, self–environment differentiation, means–ends and problem-solving behaviors (Belsky and Most 1981, Fenson, Kagan, Kearsley and Zelazo 1976, Piaget 1952, Willatts 1990).

Perhaps most famously, Piaget considered the development of object manipulation as a window onto the course of infant thinking over the first two years of life. According to Piaget, during much of the first year, infants manipulate objects in an undiscriminating manner, performing the same actions on objects regardless of an object's specific features. For Piaget, such behavior signaled a more general cognitive deficiency: infants have not yet differentiated themselves from their surrounding environments. Based on observations of his own children, Piaget contended that such a fundamental egocentrism begins to wane in the latter part of the first year. Infants start to handle objects in a discriminative manner, signaling more generally that the process of self–environment differentiation has begun.

This account of object manipulation has been influential. In the play literature, researchers have formulated developmental scales of early play based largely on Piaget's proposals (e.g. see Belsky, Goode and Most 1980, Belsky and Most 1981, Fenson *et al.* 1976). According to such scales, infants' dealings with objects prior to the latter part of the first year are characterized as being undifferentiated. Infants are portrayed as performing the same actions on objects and, in particular, not using objects in a conventional manner. With the onset of representational functioning near the end of the first year, infants are said to handle and relate objects in ways that are not only more differentiated but culturally appropriate. For example, infants may no longer treat a spoon as an object just to be banged but as an eating utensil to be placed in a bowl or brought to the mouth. Further, such instances of spoon use may occur not only during times for feeding but in pretense contexts as well.

Mechanisms of object manipulation development

While there is little disagreement over the importance of object manipulation as a psychological achievement, the mechanisms by which infants become skilled in manipulating objects has been the subject of little direct empirical investigation. A dominant theoretical view in the motor development field has been that changes in hand function over most of the first year are largely under maturational control. This view underlies many popular scales of motor and adaptive development (Bayley 1969, Gesell and Amatruda 1941). Such normative scales are grounded in the view that regular changes in manual actions and capabilities over the first few years of life represent the unfolding of a biological program that is to a large degree impervious to normal variations in exogenous experience.

By the same token, in the cognitive development literatures associated with hand function, researchers have assigned only a limited role to experience in the development of adaptive manual behaviors. Although researchers have demonstrated that maternal input can influence the development of symbolic play in the second year of life (Belsky *et al.* 1980, Tamis-LeMonda and Bornstein 1989), advances in the sensorimotor aspects of object manipulation in the first year have been attributed to central nervous system development, enabling infants to gain greater voluntary control of their hands and fingers (Gesell and Amatruda 1941).

Even when investigators have acknowledged that experience plays a role in the development of object manipulation, the types of experience that are thought to be important have centered on the individual. Most notably, Piaget (1952) maintained that changes in infants' manual behaviors were the product of the complementary processes of assimilation and accommodation. Infants exercised their existing manual schemes, but when these schemes failed to meet environmental demands, change gradually resulted. Importantly, Piaget attributed such changes to experience, but the experience was largely of a self-generated kind. In short, Piaget considered infants to be the agents of their own change. Although a provocative proposal when originally put forth, it ignored other kinds of salient experience that might also influence the development of hand function.

The salient experiences I have in mind are those that caregivers provide when they play with or introduce objects and surfaces to their infants. Sociocultural theorists such as Vygotsky (1978) and more recently Bruner (1983), Rogoff (1990) and Tomasello (1999) have alerted us to the idea that children's activity is always embedded within the wider social milieu in which children develop. For Vygotsky, the role of the social context is pervasive. Caregivers instruct their children not only directly but also indirectly. Caregivers and the larger culture in which they reside are the source of the artifacts and tools that infants play with, even when infants are playing alone. In a related vein, Bruner (1982) has suggested that parents scaffold their children's activities during joint interaction, enabling children to engage in higher-level behaviors that the children ordinarily would not be able to perform on their own. Applied to the development of object manipulation, this perspective suggests that we pay closer attention to the ways in which caregivers and infants use objects together as well as the types of object that caregivers offer infants to explore. Object manipulation, on this view, is largely a socially mediated skill, which caregivers directly and indirectly (e.g. through the provision of cultural artifacts) promote in their infants.

Important as this type of sociocultural framework has been, particularly in terms of reminding us of the way in which the development of many, perhaps all, skills are embedded within a larger sociocultural context, it does not entirely explain the regularities in the development of object manipulation that researchers have documented. Cultural variation (Rogoff 1990), not to mention individual differences within cultures, might lead us to expect a good deal more variability in the development of infant object manipulation than actually exists. By the same token, in such sociocultural accounts, little theoretical guidance is provided for ways of determining how the different tools or objects across or within cultures may be functionally equivalent insofar as the development of object manipulation is concerned. The regularities in the development of different types of object manipulation skills across many studies (Bushnell and Boudreau 1993) suggest that to the extent that variation in objects and object usage across cultures exists, such variation does not deflect a universal developmental pattern.

Does this mean that we should accept maturational accounts as satisfactory explanations of object manipulation development and other related sensorimotor skills? Not necessarily. I would like to suggest another theoretical framework that might be used to consider the development of object manipulation and the contributions of caregivers and other social figures to the development of this skill. The framework that I have in mind is the ecological viewpoint of Eleanor and James J. Gibson for understanding perception–action development.

Gibsonian theory and object manipulation

In their ecological approach, the Gibsons make several proposals that are relevant for considering the development of object manipulation. First, they take the organism–environment relation as the appropriate unit of analysis for under-standing perception–action development (Gibson 1988, Gibson and Pick 2000). Second, they point out that organisms register environmental information that is geared to their physical characteristics and their action capabilities. J. J. Gibson (1979) coined the term "affordance" to denote this simultaneously objective and subjective relation. The same element in the environment may hold different affordances for an organism, depending on the organism's physical characteristics (e.g. weight) and/or action capabilities (e.g. prelocomotor or locomotor). Third, the Gibsons maintain that the environment is rich in information that specifies affordances. Organisms do not need to mentally construct meanings from impoverished environmental information that they register. Further, organisms are adapted to register and differentiate relevant information that specifies affordances by employing various perception–action routines.

This framework has important implications for considering the development of object manipulation. It suggests that object manipulation belongs to a larger class of exploratory or instrumental behaviors that infants use in order to gain information about their environments and act in it. Further, it suggests that objects, rather than being impoverished stimuli which infants use to construct notions about the world (Piaget 1952), are potentially rich sources of information about the environment. To gain this information, however, infants must learn to differentiate relevant from irrelevant information and learn to employ their arms, hands and fingers to accomplish this goal. Certain object properties may be perceived simply by looking at an object, but additional information may become available once infants manipulate the object, enabling more dynamic sources of information to be obtained.

Caregivers and object manipulation

The Gibsonian viewpoint thus directs us to consider some interesting ways in which to conceptualize the role of experience in the development of object manipulation. Active experience in manipulating objects is clearly implicated as an avenue through which infants hone their manual exploratory skills and differentiate relevant from irrelevant perceptual information for various object properties or affordances. But what about the role that caregivers and other social figures play in this process? As noted, this question, broadly construed, is certainly one that sociocultural theorists address in their accounts of skill development. The idea that caregivers contribute to the development of children's manipulation skills, however, is consistent with Gibsonian theory as well. Caregivers may demonstrate how to manipulate objects when they show infants what various objects can do or what objects afford for action. Moreover, demonstrations in which individuals highlight dynamic information may be an especially effective means of conveying an object's affordance to infants. Hodapp, Goldfield and Boyatzis (1984) suggested a related possibility when they described how mothers engage their infants in games like peekaboo or rolling a ball back and forth. During such games mothers scaffold infant activities and by doing so demonstrate the properties of the objects involved in the game – a cover in the case of peekaboo and a ball in the case of rolling. More generally, when caregivers engage their infants in games or object play, infants may be learning about objects' affordances. Likewise, during these types of interactions, infants may also be learning about efficient ways of apprehending this information.

Thus in my view, Gibsonian theory can incorporate the contributions of caregivers to the development of perception–action coupling, and particularly to the types of perception–action coupling entailed in object manipulation. Further, even though the Gibsons maintain that organisms have perception–action systems that have evolved to perceive affordances, such a viewpoint would not exclude a role for caregivers in the ontogenesis of object manipulation. From a developmental perspective, caregivers may aid infants in the process of perception–action coupling that is so critical to the emergence of skilled object manipulation (Gibson and Pick 2000).

Although I argue for a deeper consideration of a role for caregivers in the development of object manipulation, there are important differences to consider between Gibsonian and sociocultural treatments of this skill. In a sociocultural approach like Vygotsky's, object manipulation is viewed as a class of actions that cannot be divorced from the particular sociocultural context in which it emerges. Further, objects are not considered neutral or decontextualized stimuli. Caregivers and other skilled individuals in the culture help infants to construct the social meaning of objects. That meaning is embodied in the ways in which caregivers direct or show infants how to manipulate a given object. It is also embodied in the types of objects that caregivers and the larger culture endorse and provide to infants. Thus according to sociocultural views like Vygotsky's, the information to be gained from objects is – in an important sense – culturally mediated and often culturally specific. Objects do not exist apart from the culture that gives meaning to them. In short, objects, in and of themselves, are impoverished stimuli that need to be socially constructed.

In contrast, Gibsonian theory would take a different approach to the contribution of social figures to object manipulation development. Objects are not considered impoverished stimuli. By the same token, caregivers do not need to construct the meaning of the object for their infants. Instead, caregivers help infants to perfect ways of maximizing information gain from objects. In some instances, caregivers might provide infants with opportunities to practice perception–action routines that infants are already able to perform on their own. In other instances, caregivers might teach infants new ways of manipulating objects. An alternative but related view is that objects may offer multiple affordances, but caregivers, due to their cultural background and the culture in which the infant is being raised, may highlight certain affordances over others and the means by which to gain information about such affordances (Tomasello 1999).

In any case, such teaching may occur in a number of ways. Caregivers, for instance, may demonstrate new methods of object manipulation to infants, requiring infants to engage in a form of observational learning or imitation. Such demonstrations may occur either directly or indirectly, within the context of the everyday activity of the caregiver (Rogoff 1990). For such a mechanism to operate, however, infants would have to be capable of learning how to perform actions through imitation. In addition, for such a mechanism to be a powerful one, infants would also have to be capable of imitating or reproducing these actions after considerable delays. In fact, Meltzoff (1988) has reported that by nine months, infants will evidence deferred imitation of novel manual actions that they witnessed an adult model perform twenty-four hours previously. Impressively, the demonstrations by the adult model lasted only a few minutes.

If nine-month-olds are capable of deferred imitation with such limited prior exposure, it is certainly possible that they can learn about ways of manipulating objects from watching others under more naturalistic circumstances. In the home, for instance, caregivers are likely to show infants repeatedly how an object or class of objects may be manipulated. Further, such repeated demonstrations are not likely to be confined to one time period but distributed over a period of weeks. Additionally, there are likely to be commonalties in the ways in which different caregivers manipulate particular objects in front of infants. Surprisingly, we know little about the actions that individuals use when they show infants particular classes of objects. My hunch, however, is that the similarities far outweigh the differences. A squishy toy, for instance, is likely to be pressed and kneaded by a caregiver regardless of who that caregiver is. Taken together, these considerations suggest that the conditions under which infants are being shown actions on objects – repeated demonstrations of similar behaviors by different individuals over extended periods of time – are just those that are likely to promote and consolidate learning in infants.

Besides promoting observational learning in infants, caregivers may also engage in a more direct form of instruction for teaching infants how to manipulate objects. In particular, caregivers might actively move their infants' hands and fingers so that infants perform a desired action. In doing so, caregivers would guide infants through selective perception–action routines to maximize information gain from various objects. For example, a caregiver may show an infant how to shake an object by first placing the infant's hand over the object. The caregiver would then cover the infant's hand with his or her own hand and subsequently shake the object together. Or a caregiver might take the infants' fingers and gently drag them across the object's surface to explore the object's texture. As was the case with demonstrations, we have little information about how caregivers guide their infants' hands when caregivers manipulate objects with their infants.

If caregivers frequently, as I suggest, demonstrate object manipulation or guide their infants to perform these behaviors, how should we conceptualize the psychological contribution that caregivers are making? From a Gibsonian perspective, it is important to realize that caregivers would not be adding information to the object. Rather, caregivers, by virtue of their activities, would be helping infants to gather information that is already present in the environment. The task for infants in turn is to learn how to harness their motor skills to gather this information on their own. On this view, objects are not impoverished stimuli, as might be claimed in a sociocultural perspective. Objects, instead, are potentially rich sources of information, but the perceiving–acting organism must access this information through effective forms of exploration.

Caregivers assist infants in achieving this goal. They help infants to register environmental information in efficient, economical and targeted ways. Caregivers are thus enabling infants to engage in just the sorts of activities that characterize the ways in which mature perceivers function in their environments.

Is there empirical evidence for such a view? Some investigators have noted that during mother–child interaction, mothers will often attempt to capture infants' attention by using objects (Bakeman and Adamson 1984, Zukow-Goldring 1996). Although not typically considered in relation to the development of object manipulation, these attempts may be rich sources of information about objects and what can be done with them. Banging an object to gain an infant's attention, for instance, might convey to infants something about the hardness of the object and the surface being banged. Moving an object across the infant's field of vision so that the infant will take notice of an object (and perhaps shift his or her focus from another activity) might also convey to infants information about the object's shape, size, composition and so on. In this regard, it is known that in the first few months of life infants can use visual information about object motion to perceive whether an object is rigid or elastic (Gibson, Owsley, Walker and Megaw-Nyce 1979). Nevertheless, the precise attention-getting or focusing actions used by caregivers, especially in relation to the characteristics of the objects being shown, have not been well documented. And as a result, the potential consequences of these attention-focusing actions for infant manipulation development have been largely ignored.

Apart from caregivers' attention-focusing or shifting routines, other investigators have suggested that caregivers may teach infants various skills, including presumably object manipulation, through a process of collaborative interaction. In such exchanges, caregivers may scaffold or structure infants' actions in ways that promote skill development in infants (Bruner 1983, Kaye 1982). That is, while the caregiver and infant jointly explore an object, the caregiver might help the infant perform an action or support an activity that the infant would not be normally able to carry out completely on the infant's own. Of course, this type of scaffolding or structuring notion is related to Vygotsky's proposals about development occurring in a zone of proximal development in which more skilled individuals help children to develop the capacity to complete various psychological operations solely by themselves.

Applying this notion to the development of object manipulation, caregivers might support infants' attempts to manipulate objects until infants can manipulate objects skillfully on their own. In doing so, caregivers might help infants not only perform individual actions but structure more complex sequences of exploratory behaviors so that the object's properties are thoroughly apprehended. Some evidence in support of the idea that infants benefit from manipulating objects with caregivers is available. In a study with a small sample, Hofsten and Siddiqui (1993) reported that six- and twelve-month-old infants selectively imitated some manual behaviors that their caregivers demonstrated during periods of caregiver–infant interaction.

There is another reason to suspect that the role of experience in the development of object manipulation has been previously underestimated. The reason arises from recent work on the development of locomotion, a motor skill whose onset was long thought to be under maturational control (Gesell and Amatruda 1941). In this recent work, a number of investigators have gathered evidence to suggest that the role of experience in the development of locomotion is greater than previously believed (Adolph 1997, Benson 1993, Campos *et al.* 2000). Not surprisingly, in much of this more recent work, locomotion is conceptualized as a perception–action skill in which infants need to learn how to relate different forms of locomotion (crawling, walking) to various environmental demands. In this connection, Adolph and her colleagues have shown that infants' knowledge about whether a slope is risky or safe for ascent or descent does not immediately transfer from crawling to walking (Adolph 1997, Adolph, Eppler and Gibson 1993). Even though infants have gone through an extended process of learning which slopes are safe for crawling (i.e. the pitch of the slope will not result in the infant falling), infants go through a similar extended process of learning once they begin to walk (Adolph 1997). Related results have been obtained across other motor transitions. Adolph (2000) found that infants' knowledge about the gap size that was safe to cross did not generalize immediately from sitting to crawling, but instead needed to be learned anew with the onset of the new posture associated with crawling. In a related vein, Lockman (1984) reported that when infants begin to make detours around barriers, they do not immediately generalize this ability from reaching to crawling.

Taken together, these findings have interesting implications for the consideration of manipulation development. At the very least, they suggest that the role of experience in the development of many major infant motor skills, including manipulation, may have been previously underestimated. The findings also suggest that to the extent that experience plays a role in the development of an infant motor behavior, experience is likely to promote learning about perception–action relations within that skill context. Knowledge about such perception–action relations, in turn, enables infants to function adaptively in their environments. My major point is that caregivers are likely to contribute to this learning process as well.

Research on infant object manipulation in context

I now turn my attention to discussing some of our research on how caregivers may promote the development of object manipulation in infants. We have conducted a series of studies on how infants manipulate objects with their parents and their older siblings. The studies were largely motivated by the idea that object manipulation may be a skill whose origins can also be found in interchanges with caregivers and other social figures in infants' environments. At a theoretical level, our investigations were guided largely by Gibsonian theory, particularly how the proposals of the Gibsons might be applied to consider caregivers' contributions to perception–action development.

As outlined above, we view object manipulation as a skill employed by individuals to gain information about objects so that objects may be used adaptively. Caregivers and other social figures may help infants in learning how to explore objects by giving infants opportunities to practice perception–action routines that maximize information gain from objects and by teaching infants, either through demonstrations and/or active guidance, how to engage in these routines.

In our work, we have been careful to control the properties of the objects that caregivers and infants are given to explore. In much of the past research on infant manipulation and object play, objects have varied markedly within and across studies in terms of the object's properties or dimensions. As a consequence, it has been difficult to determine whether infants are manipulating or exploring objects in a discriminative manner (for an exception, however, see Palmer 1989). A related problem has occurred when the appropriateness of infant manual behaviors has been defined in terms of an object's conventional usage. As noted in research on play, investigators have described infant manual behaviors during much of the second half year as indiscriminate (Belsky and Most 1981, Fenson *et al.* 1976). Influential as this viewpoint has been, it ignores the possibility that some other measure or definition of appropriateness might lead to a different and more positive characterization of infant manipulation skills. If the definition of appropriateness were considered with reference to an object's physical dimensions (e.g. texture, rigidity, size), infants' manipulation skills might appear more discriminative than they are typically portrayed to be. Additionally, caregivers' contributions might also be viewed in a new light. Caregivers might be seen as helping infants manipulate objects selectively and appropriately, independent of the object's conventional or culturally specified usage.

To explore these possibilities, James P. McHale and I conducted a study to contrast how infants and their caregivers manipulate objects together and how infants manipulate objects on their own (Lockman and McHale 1989). In this investigation we tested seventy-two infants (twenty-four each at six, eight and ten months of age) with pairs of pyramid-shaped objects that were carefully constructed to vary along a given physical dimension. One pair varied along color (alternating sides of either red and green or blue and yellow), another along texture (alternating sides of Velcro or different grades of sandpaper) and another along sound potential (the pyramids containing either a bell or grains of rice).

At each age level, infants were assigned either to a Dyad or Alone condition. Infants in the Dyad condition initially explored one object from each pair with their caregiver (Phase 1) and then explored the remaining object from the pair by themselves (Phase 2). Thus each infant in the Dyad condition participated in six trials: three trials with the caregiver and three trials alone. All trials lasted one minute each. Infants in the Alone condition were also given one object from each pair during each Phase 1 trial and the remaining object from the pair during each Phase 2 trial. Thus infants in the Alone condition also received six trials, lasting one minute each. However, infants in the Alone condition explored the objects by themselves on both Phase 1 and Phase 2 trials.

This design enabled us to examine a number of important issues regarding caregivers' contributions to the development of object manipulation. First, we were interested in documenting the ways in which caregivers manipulate objects with their infants, particularly the extent to which caregivers highlight the properties of the object that they are examining with their infants. As suggested earlier, caregivers may evidence various infant-directed actions that might promote manipulation development in infants. Second, and in a related vein, we were interested in describing the strategies that caregivers use to promote object appropriate manipulation in infants. As noted, we hypothesized that caregivers might not only show infants how to manipulate objects but also physically guide their infants' arms and hands in this process. Third, our design enabled us to examine whether infants display higher levels of object appropriate manipulation in dyadic (i.e. with their caregivers) situations than they do in solitary contexts. Finally, we wished to know whether infants, after having manipulated objects with their caregivers, evidenced higher levels of object appropriate manipulation when now handling objects alone. Thus we were interested in the question of transfer from dyadic to solitary contexts. Collectively, examination of these issues begins to address the social origins of manipulation development in infancy.

Caregiver contributions: Infant-directed action

Did caregivers tailor their actions to the properties of the object that they were exploring with their infants? The answer is clearly yes. Consider first how caregivers demonstrated actions to infants. When we examined demonstration behaviors, we found that caregivers' manual behaviors were geared precisely to an object's physical characteristics. With the textured objects, mothers evidenced more fingering of the object's surfaces in front of their infants. With the objects with different colored sides, caregivers displayed more pointing and rotation – behaviors that clearly highlight the different visual characteristics of each side or surface. And with the sounding objects, caregivers demonstrated more shaking.

Caregivers' efforts to highlight the objects, however, were not restricted to demonstrations. For some of the object properties, caregivers physically contacted the baby and often actively guided their infants' hands to perform a desired action. Specifically, with the textured objects, caregivers more often placed the objects on their infants' skin, presumably so that infants would feel the textures. Additionally, caregivers more often gently dragged their infants' fingers over the sides of the textured objects. In contrast, with the sounding objects, caregivers often shook the object jointly with their infants, moving their infants' arms up and down so that their infants would perform the action as well. These types of joint behaviors – fingering and shaking – provide infants with basic information about the object's properties. Importantly, these joint behaviors also offer infants direct experience performing actions that can be used to apprehend information about an object's properties in efficient and targeted ways.

Effects of context

In our study, we directly considered the effects of context (social or individual) on infant object manipulation. One way to consider such effects is to contrast how infants in the Dyad condition manipulated objects relative to infants in the Alone condition. If infants are benefiting from manipulating objects with their caregivers, we might expect to see higher levels of appropriate (defined with reference to the object's physical characteristics) or discriminative manipulation by infants in the Dyad condition. We examined this possibility by first comparing how infants in the Dyad and Alone conditions manipulated objects during Phase 1 of the experiment. These results suggest that infants benefit from manipulating objects with their caregivers. In particular, infants in the Dyad condition held the objects more often while looking at the objects. In contrast, infants in the Alone condition were more likely to hold the objects without looking at them. Taken together, these findings suggest that Dyad infants' manual behaviors were more focused and more coordinated with respect to looking. In addition, eight- and ten-month-old infants in the Dyad condition evidenced more fingering of the textured object than infants in the Alone condition. Thus for at least some aspects of object manipulation, we found that infants evidenced more focused and selective exploration when infants were manipulating objects with their caregivers. Recall that Hofsten and Siddiqui (1993) obtained similar findings under related conditions of joint exploration.

What about the question of transfer from social to non-social contexts? To address this question, the most relevant comparison involves Phase 2 infants. (Recall that in Phase 2 both Dyad and Alone condition infants were now exploring objects on their own.) When we compared the manipulation behaviors of Dyad and Alone condition infants in Phase 2, we found little difference across the two groups. Thus the differences that we did observe between Dyad and Alone condition infants occurred only when the immediate social context differed – that is, when caregivers were exploring objects directly with their infants.

Taken together, these findings suggest that when caregivers explore an object jointly with their infants, caregivers show very appropriate forms of manipulation. These forms of manipulation are linked directly to the properties of the object. These findings are consistent with the reports of other investigators who have suggested that caregivers exaggerate object demonstrations to infants, which may help infants to parse and interpret complex sequences of actions in meaningful ways (Brand, Baldwin and Ashburn 2002). Our findings also indicate that under some circumstances, caregivers physically guide their infants' arms and hands so that infants will perform an appropriate manual behavior. We suggest that these forms of infant-directed action – demonstrations and active physical guidance – on the part of caregivers may help promote manipulation development in infants. We obtained some preliminary evidence in support for this idea. At least during the context of joint manipulation with their caregivers, infants showed higher levels of object appropriate manipulation than their infant counterparts who manipulated objects on their own. Nevertheless, these facilitating effects of social context did not immediately transfer to a situation in which infants subsequently manipulated similar objects alone. The failure to find transfer to individual contexts under the present conditions is perhaps not surprising. In the home environment, caregivers and their infants presumably manipulate objects repeatedly and for longer periods of time. Longer and repeated demonstrations, including instances of active physical guidance of infant manual behaviors by caregivers, might promote object appropriate manipulation by infants across dyadic and individual contexts.

Sibling contributions: Infant-directed action

The above findings prompted us to think about other social figures in infants' immediate environments and what role these might play in the development of object manipulation in infants. Specifically, we wondered whether older siblings contributed to the development of object manipulation in their younger infant siblings. Indeed, investigators have noted that in some cultures the social transmission of many skills may occur primarily through older children, especially via siblings (Rogoff 1990, Zukow 1989). Additionally, we know from research on language development that older children adjust their language when talking to younger children (Shatz and Gelman 1973). Although the matter of some debate (Gleitman, Newport and Gleitman 1984), investigators have suggested that this simplified or specialized input, along with similar forms of input from adult members of the culture, promotes language acquisition in young children.

Applying these ideas to the development of object manipulation, we might ask whether older siblings provide their infant siblings with opportunities to learn how to manipulate and gain information from objects. To address these issues, Laurie Olson and I (in preparation) examined how adult caregivers and their older children each manipulate objects with their infant family members. We considered two primary questions. First, when older children explore or play with objects with their infant siblings, how do the older children adjust their manual behaviors? And second, if the older children do make adjustments, are those adjustments comparable to those made by adult caregivers?

To investigate these issues, we studied a group of forty-eight families, all of whom were comprised of at least a primary caregiver and two children. In all the families, the younger sibling was an infant who ranged in age from six to twelve months; the older sibling ranged in age from three to five years. In this investigation, we directly compared the actions that caregivers and their older siblings used when they manipulated objects with their infant family member. Caregivers and infants played together on one pair of trials; during the other pair of trials, siblings and infants played together. Specifically, during one pair of trials, caregivers and their infants explored a textured object on one trial and a sounding object on the other trial. Likewise, during the other pair of trials, the older child and sibling explored a different textured object on one trial and a different textured object on the other trial. The order in which infants played with their caregiver or sibling was counterbalanced to control for potential carryover effects across the dyad groups.

What did the results of this study tell us about how caregivers and older siblings manipulate objects with an infant family member? First consider how adult caregivers explored the objects with their infants. Caregivers evidenced both demonstrations and active physical guidance of their infants' behaviors, results similar to those obtained in our previous study. Specifically, with the textured object caregivers demonstrated more fingering of the object's sides, and for the sounding object they demonstrated more shaking and banging. Caregivers also physically guided their infants' arms and hands to perform these behaviors. That is, caregivers gently pulled infants' fingers along the textured object's surfaces and jointly shook the sounding object with their infants.

When we considered the actions of the older siblings, a related but different pattern of findings emerged. First, older siblings also differentially handled the objects in front of the infants. Like their caregivers, the older siblings demonstrated more fingering of the textured object and more shaking and banging of the sounding object. As for physically guiding infants to perform these behaviors, however, older siblings rarely engaged in such mutual activities. The reason is clearly not due to the older siblings' inability to perform the joint actions. The older siblings demonstrated the relevant actions in front of their younger brother or sister. Why, then, did older siblings not evidence these joint behaviors? One reason may have to do with social conventions within our culture. The older siblings may have been observing a social prohibition against touching an infant sibling without direct caregiver supervision. But there may be a cognitive reason as well for the relative absence of joint actions in the sibling–infant dyads. Given the age range of the older siblings in our study, the failure of older siblings to guide infants' manual actions may indicate that the older siblings were not aware of the potential importance of direct practice for learning these motor skills. With subsequent development of cognitive and metacognitive abilities, particularly with increased understanding of other individuals' abilities and mental states, siblings beyond the preschool years may begin to actively guide infant action.

Despite the differences between caregiver and preschool children's teaching strategies, our results suggest that preschool children also provide infant siblings with demonstrations of how to manipulate objects in a discriminative manner. These actions are adapted to the properties of the object and thus maximize information gain. Whether preschool siblings have learned how to interact effectively with infants from watching their caregivers is an interesting question that merits investigation. But based on the results of the two studies that I have described, it appears that the social world is a rich source of information for infants as they learn to manipulate objects. Adults and older children show infants how objects may be manipulated and, in a related vein, what objects afford for action.

Conclusions

Infant object manipulation has been treated often as a skill that is largely under maturational control. In this chapter, I have suggested that experience may also contribute to the development of this skill. Experience may allow infants to practice and perfect various perception–action routines so that they may gain information from objects and use objects adaptively. However, the experience that I have in mind is not the kind that has been typically considered in prior discussions of object manipulation development. Indeed, when experiential contributions to object manipulation development have been acknowledged, the experiences that have been discussed are self-generated ones, produced by infants (Piaget 1952). Instead, I suggest that individuals who are part of infants' social world provide infants with important opportunities for mastering the skill of object manipulation. In particular, caregivers and older siblings show infants how to manipulate objects adaptively. These older family members highlight the information available in objects and demonstrate effective ways in which this information may be apprehended. Additionally, adult caregivers may also physically guide or direct infants to perform an appropriate action. In such instances, infants are not only learning or practicing a basic manual skill; they are also learning how to relate to the environment around them.

In Gibsonian terms, infants are engaging in a process of perceptual learning (Gibson and Pick 2000). They are learning about information that specifies various object affordances. They are learning to master the actions that enable them to detect these affordances. And at some level, they are learning about the reciprocal relation between perception and action, which enables them to function adaptively in their environments. Presumably, similar processes are involved in more microgenetic contexts that occur throughout the lifespan as individuals learn new motor skills. However, during infancy, when the task of coordinating perception and action with new emerging motor skills may be especially challenging due to the relative absence of prior experience in that or related skill domains, input from caregivers in terms of guidance and practice may be critical.

These types of considerations about the role of social figures in the development of infant manipulation skills also have implications for discussions about manual skill development in the preschool years. One of the most important manual skill advances during these years is the emergence of tool use. Recent treatments of tool use have suggested that instead of being considered solely a cognitive advance, tool use should also be viewed as an advance in perception–action development. According to this new view, tools change the properties of the effector organs, and children, through a process of perceptual learning, explore ways in which tools open up new affordances in the environment (Gibson and Pick 2000, Lockman 2000, Smitsman 1997). To this, however, I would add that caregivers and other figures in the child's social world help in this process of perceptual learning. In a related vein, Tomasello (1999) has suggested that caregivers and other social figures directly and indirectly help children to learn what he has termed the intentional affordances of objects. Tools afford many possible uses, but the actions of more skilled individuals in the culture largely determine the specific ways in which young children use particular tools. Surprisingly, we know very little about the social origins of tool use. That infants appear to learn from individuals in their social world about object manipulation suggests that the development of tool use may in part be mediated through a similar process. Additional consideration of the role of experience – both self-generated and socially mediated – in the development of infant object manipulation can serve as a window onto the development of manual skill more generally.

Let me end by quoting from an influential chapter that Ina Užgiris authored entitled "Plasticity and Structure: The Role of Experience in Infancy" (Užgiris 1977). In writing about psychological development in all its forms as a socially situated phenomenon, she stated:

> The importance of the presence of interested and attentive others is usually discussed in relation to emotional development and the formation of attachment bonds. It is suggested here that these social interactions are also crucial in providing a culturally shared context for experiencing the world and constructing the basic relations for dealing with reality. From this viewpoint, assessment of the environmental conditions for an infant must involve the environmental opportunities created by the activities of others.
>
> (p. 110)

My hope is that the preceding discussion of object manipulation begins to address the sociocultural concerns that Ina Užgiris so eloquently considered in her own work.

References

Adolph, K. (1997) "Learning in the Development of Infant Locomotion", *Monographs of the Society for Research in Child Development*, *62*: (3, serial no. 251).

— (2000) "Specificity of Learning: Why Infants Fall Over a Veritable Cliff", *Psychological Science*, *11*: 290–295.

Adolph, K., Eppler, M. A. and Gibson, E. J. (1993) "Crawling Versus Walking Infants' Perception of Affordances for Locomotion over Sloping Surfaces", *Child Development*, *64*: 1158–1174.

Bakeman, R. and Adamson, L. (1984) "Coordinating Attention to People and Objects in Mother–Infant and Peer–Infant Interactions", *Child Development*. *55*: 1278–1289.

Bayley, N. (1969) *Manual for the Bayley Scales of Infant Development*. New York: Psychological Corporation.

Belsky, J., Goode, M. K. and Most, M. K. (1980) "Maternal Stimulation and Infant Exploratory Competence: Cross-Sectional, Correlational, and Experimental Analyses", *Child Development*, *51*: 1168–1178.

Belsky, J. and Most, R. K. (1981) "From Exploration to Play: A Cross-Sectional Study of Infant Free Play Behavior", *Developmental Psychology*, *17*: 630–639.

Benson, J. B. (1993) "Season of Birth and Onset of Locomotion: Theoretical and Methodological Implications", *Infant Behavior and Development, 16*: 69–81.

Brand, R. J., Baldwin, D. A. and Ashburn, L. A. (2002) "Evidence for Motionese: Modifications in Mothers' Infant-Directed Action", *Developmental Sience, 5*: 72–83.

Bruner, J. S. (1983) *Child's Talk: Learning to Use Language.* New York: Norton.

Campos, J. J., Anderson, D. I., Barbu-Roth, M. A., Hubbard, E. M., Hertenstein, M. J. and Witherington, D. (2000) "Travel Broadens the Mind", *Infancy, 1*: 149–219.

Connolly, K. J. (1970) *Mechanisms of Motor Skill Development.* New York: Academic Press.

Fenson, L., Kagan, J., Kearsley, R. B. and Zelazo, P. (1976) "The Developmental Progression of Manipulative Play in the First Two Years", *Child Development, 47*: 232–236.

Gesell, A. and Amatruda, C. S. (1941) *Developmental Diagnosis: Normal and Abnormal Child Development.* New York: Hoeber.

Gibson, E. J. (1988) "Exploratory Behavior in the Development of Perceiving, Acting and the Acquiring of Knowledge", *Annual Review of Psychology, 39*: 1–41.

Gibson, E. J., Owsley, C. J., Walker, A. S. and Megaw-Nyce, J. (1979) "Development of the Perception of Invariants: Substance and Shape", *Perception, 8*: 609–619.

Gibson, E. J. and Pick, A. D. (2000) *An Ecological Approach to Perceptual Learning and Development.* New York: Oxford.

Gibson, J. J. (1979) *The Ecological Approach to Visual Perception.* Boston: Houghton Mifflin.

Gleitman, L. R., Newport, E. L. and Gleitman, H. (1984) "The Current Status of the Motherese Hypothesis", *Journal of Child Language, 11*: 43–79.

Hodapp, R. M., Goldfield, E. C. and Boyatzis, C. J. (1984) "The Use and Effectiveness of Maternal Scaffolding in Mother–Infant Games", *Child Development, 55*: 772–781.

Hofsten, C. von and Siddiqui, A. (1993) "Mother's Actions as a Reference for Object Exploration", *British Journal of Developmental Psychology, 11*: 61–74.

Kaye, K. (1982) *The Mental and Social Life of Babies.* Chicago: University of Chicago Press.

Lockman, J. J. (1984) "The Development of Detour Ability During Infancy", *Child Development, 55*: 482–491.

— (2000) "A Perception–Action Perspective on Tool Use Development", *Child Development, 71*: 137–144.

Lockman, J. J. and McHale, J. P. (1989) "Infant and Maternal Exploration of Objects: Developmental and Contextual Determinants" in Lockman, J. J. and Hazen, N. L. (eds.) *Action in Social Context.* New York: Plenum.

Meltzoff, A. N. (1988) "Infant Imitation and Memory: Nine-Month-Olds in Immediate and Deferred Tests", *Child Development, 59*: 217–285.

Moore, C. and Dunham, P. (1995) *Joint Attention: Its Origins and Role in Development.* Hillsdale, NJ: Lawrence Erlbaum Associates.

Palmer, C. F. (1989) "The Discriminating Nature of Infants' Exploratory Actions", *Developmental Psychology, 25*: 885–893.

Piaget, J. (1954) *The Origins of Intelligence in Children.* New York: Norton.

— (1954) *The Construction of Reality in the Child.* New York: Free Press.

Rogoff, B. (1990) *Apprenticeship in Thinking: Cognitive Development in Social Context.* New York: Oxford University Press.

Shatz, M. and Gelman, R. (1973) "The Development of Communication Skills: Modifications in the Speech of Young Children as a Function of Listener", *Monographs of the Society for Research in Child Development, 38* (serial no. 152).

Siegler, R. S. (1996) *Emerging Minds: The Process of Change in Children's Thinking.* New York: Oxford University Press.

Smitsman. A. W. (1997) "The Development of Tool Use: Changing Boundaries Between Organism and Environment" in Dent-Read, C. and Zukow-Goldring, P. (eds.) *Evolving Explanations of Development* (pp. 301–329). Washington, DC: American Psychological Association.

Tamis-LeMonda, C. S. and Bornstein, M. H. (1989) "Habituation and Maternal Encouragement of Attention in Infancy as Predictors of Toddler Language, Play, and Representational Competence", *Child Development, 60*: 738–751.

Thelen, E. and Smith, L. B. (1994) *A Dynamic Systems Approach to the Development of Cognition and Action.* Cambridge, MA: MIT Press.

Tomasello, M. (1999) "The Cultural Ecology of Young Children's Interactions with Objects and Artifacts" in Winograd, E., Fivush, R. and Hirst, W. (eds.) *Ecological Approaches to Cognition* (pp. 153–170). Mahwah, NJ: Lawrence Erlbaum Associates.

Užgiris, I. Č. (1977) "Plasticity and Structure: The Role of Experience in Infancy" in Užgiris, I. Č. and Weizmann, F. (eds.) *The Structuring of Experience* (pp. 89–113). New York: Plenum.

— (1981) "Two Functions of Imitation During Infancy", *International Journal of Behavioral Development, 4*: 1–12.

Užgiris, I. Č., Benson, J. B., Kruper, J. C. and Vasek, M. E. (1989) "Contextual Influences on Imitative Interactions Between Mothers and Infants" in Lockman, J. J. and Hazen, N. L. (eds.) *Action in Social Context* (pp. 103–127). New York: Plenum.

Užgiris, I. Č. and Hunt, J. McV. *Assessment in Infancy.* Urbana: University of Illinois Press, 1975.

Vygotsky, L. S. (1978) *Mind in Society.* Cambridge, MA: Harvard University Press.

Willatts, P. (1990) "Development of Problem-Solving Strategies in Infancy" in Bjorklund, D. F. (ed.) *Children's Strategies: Contemporary Views of Cognitive Development.* Hillsdale, NJ: Lawrence Erlbaum Associates.

Zukow, P. G. (1989) "Siblings as Effective Socializing Agents: Evidence from Central Mexico" in Zukow, P. G. (ed.) *Sibling Interactions Across Cultures: Theoretical and Methodological Issues* (pp. 79–105). New York: Springer-Verlag.

Zukow-Goldring, P. G. (1996) "Sensitive Caregivers Foster the Comprehension of Speech: When Gestures Speak Louder than Words", *Early Development and Parenting, 5*, (4): 195–211.

8 The social and cultural context of the development of future orientation

Janette B. Benson, Ayelet Talmi and Marshall M. Haith

Introduction

Children and adults spend a good deal of time preparing for events in both the near- and far-term future, yet as a topic of both theory and empirical investigation psychology has virtually ignored how people understand the future (Haith, Benson, Roberts and Pennington 1994). Even more surprising is that while we recognize the importance of future orientation for mature skills, such as planning and problem-solving (Benson 1997, Benson and Haith 1995, Fraisse 1963, S. Friedman and Scholnick 1997, Haith 1997, Nurmi 1991, Nuttin 1984, 1985, Scholnick and S. Friedman 1993, Zaleski 1994), we know little about the developmental origins of these future-oriented processes. Future-oriented processes include planning, goal-orientation, anticipation, expectation, preparation, set and intention (Haith 1993, Benson 1994) – all important cognitive processes that contribute to how individuals acquire an understanding of the future. As such, it is important to know when in development such processes emerge and the means that guide the developmental course they take through infancy and early childhood.

Temporal knowledge

An understanding of the future is more generally linked to children's temporal knowledge. Time is a dimension along which all human experience is organized, and it is inherent in every aspect of human life, from the unconscious rhythms of breathing to the pacing of social discourse, to how one organizes present actions in order to achieve a future goal (e.g. deciding what to wear in the morning for an important meeting in the afternoon or investing for retirement). Even before birth, infants experience the biological rhythms that appear to aid their ability to temporally organize the flow of experience (e.g. sleep–wake cycles and other natural circadian rhythms). Some have even argued that time is fundamental to human experience, yet so abstract that it must be given a priori as a subjective intuition because it could not be easily learned (e.g. time was one of Kant's categorical imperatives). Unlike other dimensions of physical reality, such as the properties of objects, time is neither tangible nor directly perceptible, yet life would be chaotic without the ability to order the sequence of events or to situate events in past, present or future time.

Infants may be born with some rudimentary, biologically based abilities to temporally organize experience along the dimensions of physical reality, but cultural time conventions are acquired through social interaction. Throughout time and civilization, different cultures have created different conventions for marking time. However, we focus our discussion on cultural conventions for marking time in contemporary culture. For example, the units of time that dictate our lives, such as minutes, hours, days, months and years are culturally agreed-upon conventions (Aveni 1989) that are enacted throughout the course of social interaction. The tools we use to track events in time (e.g. clocks and calendars) and the very words we use to reference time (e.g. adverbials such as "tomorrow," "yesterday" and "today") are further examples of such cultural and social time conventions. Infants and young children must decipher temporal conventions and learn to abide by their logic (e.g. "Wait until your father gets home!"). Thus, part of the socialization and acculturation tasks of childhood is to master these conventions of time in order to become a member of the very cultural group that created them.

Time as past, present and future

The traditional divisions of time initially appear straightforward, but each has special distinguishing features. Those events that have already been experienced and occurred in the past typically fall under the domain of human memory. Such experienced events may be subject to the creativity of reconstructive memory, and various systems of memory have been elaborated to describe how past events are organized and remembered (e.g. Schacter 2001, also see Tulving 2000 for prospective memory). With respect to the present, it is arguable as to whether it actually exists, for the fleeting present soon becomes the past. During the heydays of behaviorism, psychology conceptualized the present in terms of a stimulus–response coupling in which the response is a reaction in the here and now to an eliciting stimulus. The future has been ignored by psychology. Though dependent on both the past and present, the future brings with it some degree of uncertainty. The future has yet to be experienced, even though it is often related to familiar elements from the past. Everyday experience contains many regular activities that are repetitive (e.g. daily times for waking, sleeping, eating, the yearly cycle of holidays and seasons), but not all future events are mere recasts of the past projected forward in time. Instead, organizing one's thoughts and behavior around the future involves the ability to coordinate the regularity of past temporal patterns with the possibility of uncertainty, likelihood and novelty. Thus we can form cognitive expectations for future events that permit us to organize our behaviors in anticipation of a likely scenario (Haith 1993), but if a future expectation is violated, we must adjust our anticipatory behaviors to adapt to events as they unfold. An unanswered question remains: How do children come to acquire an understanding of the future?

Individual, social and cultural processes

The intersection between innate, biological timekeepers that exist early in infancy and understandings of the future that infants and young children construct in their social and cultural worlds is the primary focus of this chapter. Our view about the development of future orientation has its foundation in ideas initially expressed by others. First, as discussed by Ina Užgiris (1996: 20), we agree, in part, with Piaget's view that there is a basic "continuity between biological and psychological functioning" with intelligence viewed as the means for successful adaptation throughout development. In the case of temporal development and future orientation, we view infants as possessing inherent biological rhythms that serve as the initial mechanisms for "keeping time." Eventually, a cognitive understanding and mastery of basic temporal concepts, including the future, emerges and is crucial to the successful adaptation that must be made to the demands of an increasingly busy and time-constrained world (Gleick 1999).

A second important and related idea was also expressed by Ina Užgiris (1996: 17) which is that "human actions, especially early in development, encompass both physical and social dimensions." We suggest that the origins of future orientation emerge from inherent biological processes in each individual that are also shaped by early social experiences. When making the transition from the intrauterine to the extrauterine environment, parents and caregivers attempt to co-regulate newborn biological cycles with that of the immediate family and larger culture (e.g. most families, except those who live in extreme northern locations, sleep at night when it is dark and would like their newborn to as well). For example, parents may attempt to put their newborn on a schedule of feeding and sleeping routines that mirrors their own, or modify – within limits – the family's routines to meet the newborn's demands. Either way, it is clear that both individual and social factors are at play. With development, common routines for daily activities, such as waking, bathing, dressing, feeding and sleeping, expand from their early physical emphasis to take on added psychological functions. We will argue later that the psychological and physical functions of the everyday routines and rituals that exist in most families are initially "imposed" by parents and caregivers, but eventually are also shaped by the actions of infants and toddlers.

Third, we acknowledge the larger role of the cultural context, in which both the individual and her social partners reside, as exerting an influence on future orientation and temporal development. Even though little theorizing exists on the development of time knowledge and future orientation, it is especially noteworthy that social and cultural influences on its acquisition have generally been ignored. For example, the predominant theory of time development (Piaget 1969) has focused almost exclusively on the acquisition of physical time, as constructed by "the epistemic child," to the virtual exclusion of social experience. However, building on a growing view, informed by a wide variety of theorists who emphasize the roles of the larger social and cultural context (e.g. Cole 1998,

Nelson 1996, Rogoff 1990, Užgiris 1996, 2000 and Vygotsky 1978), we will suggest that the cultural practice of everyday family routines and rituals, and the nature of the linguistic and communicative exchange that takes place during these interactions, provide a context and framework from which infants and young children learn about time in general, and about the future more specifically. Culture exerts an influence on temporal conventions (Aveni 1989) and our knowledge of them in a myriad of ways, and we will discuss the relevant literature on the use of language to convey time and the degree to which future time reference is used in adult speech to young children.

Family routines and rituals: A possible mechanism for understanding time

Little attention has been paid to the temporal features of family life until recently. In an effort to develop a theory of family time, sociologist Kerry Daly provides some interesting insights into how the temporal organization of the family impacts children:

> Socializing children to be attentive to time is central to the formulation of both individual and family identity. Through the development of temporal awareness, children learn how to manage time in interaction by being attentive to the intricacies of sequencing, sharing, or ending an interactive episode.
>
> (1996: 64)

> Family rituals require coordinated action from family members each time they are performed (Reiss 1981). Simple rituals such as coming together for dinner serve to keep the life plans of individual family members in lockstep with one another. Furthermore, it is not simply the shared ritual itself that gives the sense of synchrony in each other's lives, but it is the planning and the punctuality associated with the ritual.
>
> (1996: 125)

We have also suggested (Benson 1994) that family routines and rituals may be especially important in the acquisition of future orientation. We also believe that exposure to stable repetitive routines and rituals provides children with a sense of the regular order of events that occur in sequence that lead to some future endpoint. For example, most common routines such as diaper changing, dressing or bathing occur in a highly regularized, repetitive sequence that provides young children with a framework for understanding that a series of events leads up to an eventual endpoint. In this way we suggest that common family routines and rituals provide infants and toddlers with a structure from which they begin to learn about how specific events are linked in time, sequenced, what events might happen next, and the eventual endpoint to a sequence of particular events. The repetitive nature of everyday routines and rituals highlights the regularity of events that eventually permit infants and toddlers to predict what comes next in the sequence and to coordinate their actions with those of a parent or caregiver (e.g. raising hands over head in the dressing routine to anticipate putting on a shirt). During these and other everyday situations adults provide communicative cues through their speech to forecast and forewarn infants and toddlers about events that will occur next and in the near-term future. Together, routines and adult speech communicate in both actions and words a structure from which infants and toddlers learn about the future and make predictions about near-term future events in their lives.

Overview

The study of the development of future orientation is an admittedly nascent arena. We begin with a very brief overview of the relevant existing laboratory and language studies that suggest limitations in what is known about young children's future orientation but also provide the foundation and guidance for the approach we have adopted. Next, we describe the empirical approaches we have pursued to document the existence of the gradual development of future orientation in early childhood and provide suggestions along the way as to possible mechanisms for its growth. Finally, we close with a discussion around the speculation that infants are initially *relatively passive* participants in parentally guided family routines and rituals. However, as young children begin to understand the temporal and sequential nature of routines and rituals from such experiences, they develop expectations about the future actions of others, leading them to engage others in familiar exchanges, to insert deviations from familiar routines, often to avoid an eventual endpoint (e.g. stalling tactics to avoid the eventual "lights out" at bedtime), and to plan a course of action that will lead to future goals.

Future orientation: brief review of relevant laboratory and language studies

Laboratory studies

The earliest roots of future-oriented processes are likely to be expectations that are formed in highly predictable situations. In a highly constrained laboratory paradigm, Haith and colleagues (Canfield and Haith 1991, Haith 1994, Haith, Hazan and Goodman 1988, Haith, Wentworth and Canfield 1993) explored the extent to which young infants can detect regularities in the sequence of very brief stimulus presentations (e.g. 700 to 1300 ms) and can use that experience, as manifest in anticipatory eye movements, to form visual expectations about future stimulus events. Infants as young as three months demonstrate visual expectations when they correctly move their eyes to a target location prior to stimulus onset. Infants reveal that they can detect and use spatial, temporal, content and even numeric regularities in the pattern of stimulus presentations to form visual expectations.

This research demonstrates that even very young infants form visual expectancies for constrained laboratory events that they can only observe, but not control. Although the stimulus events in this laboratory situation occur in a relatively short amount of time (i.e. sixty trials in less than two minutes), it is remarkable that infants can detect simple regularities and use that information to organize their behavior to anticipate a very near-term future event. While this demonstration suggests very limited future-oriented processes at a young age, it also prompts us to ask about what might be occurring in infants' everyday lives. We still know very little about early future-oriented behaviors as they occur outside the laboratory in more familiar situations in which young children can exert some control (for example, when a two-year-old runs to retrieve a favorite doll from her bedroom to take with her when she is told she will soon be leaving the house). This is an example of a common future-oriented behavior that occurs within the social context of everyday life, a context that is particularly rich in meaning, familiarity, and social support (Rogoff and Lave 1984). We might therefore expect that these factors would be especially important in encouraging the emergence and development of future-oriented processes in infancy and early childhood.

Language studies

Unfortunately, just as the development of children's time concepts is a woefully understudied issue, reports of future-oriented behaviors and their developmental course are even more scant. In part, this dearth of information motivated us to catalogue the types of behavior that parents recognize in their children which suggest they possess some degree of future orientation. However, before attempting to do so we discovered that the language development literature provided some information about when children might demonstrate their understanding or expression of temporal concepts.

While this related literature has value, we do caution that there are several problems with depending solely on children's linguistic skills to gain a window into their future orientation. First, the very structure of the language a child speaks can impact the expression and communication of time. For example, unlike the French language which has a clear future tense, English has no clear future tense that is marked by inflections; instead, we use modal auxiliaries (e.g. "may", "will", "must") to communicate about future events (Harner 1982). Therefore, even though a child may use past tense inflections (e.g. "-ed") prior to using modal auxiliaries, this pattern may reflect a constraint of the English language rather than a cognitive constraint, and we should not take this as evidence that children understand the past before they understand the future. A second caution is that young children do not always say what they mean or mean what they say. As young children are mastering linguistic conventions their conceptual understandings may not match their linguistic constructions. For example, it is difficult to infer what a child understands about past and future events when she utters, "Tomorrow I went to the zoo."

Language researchers have described examples of early future-oriented behavior as they occur in early everyday life; however, such examples have usually been described in passing, because the research focus was on some aspect of early language development not temporal development. Into this category we would put studies of children's acquisition of the past tense. While important to our understanding of grammatical development, studies of children's use of inflections or even modal auxiliaries alone do not provide sufficient information about the temporal concepts these language devices typically denote. While there are numerous studies that do provide some insight into children's temporal language development (for an interesting discussion, see Bates, Elman and Li 1994, Weist 1986, 1989), for our purposes they are not sufficient by themselves for studying children's temporal understanding. Many of the traditional language studies relevant to temporal development do not specifically emphasize the importance of the everyday conversational routines engaged in by children and adults that we believe are critical for encouraging the development of future orientation. We describe a few studies from the language development literature that are exceptions to these limitations.

Conversational routines

A few language studies, though not specifically focused on future orientation, have described examples of early future-oriented behavior as they occur in early everyday life that also highlight the important role of conversational routines. Nelson's (1989) analysis of the audiotaped pre-sleep monologues of the toddler known as Emily are particularly interesting. Many of Emily's pre-sleep monologues would begin after her conversations with a parent as part of her bedtime routine. Although any number of topics might be discussed, it was common to review Emily's day and even talk about events that would occur in the short-term future (i.e. after a nap or the following day). Nelson (1989a) specifically comments on how often issues pertaining to the future (e.g. what might happen after a nap or the next day) were likely to be carried over from these dialogues with parents to Emily's pre-sleep monologues more often than topics pertaining to memory talk, or the discussion of events that already occurred. One can speculate that Emily's monologues about future events were her attempt to create representations about things that would happen soon. The formation of such representations could then lead to expectations about such future events.

Basing her work on the analysis of this evidence and other language studies, Nelson (1996) developed an experiential theory of early intellectual development that addresses the reciprocal role of language and cognition in context. Her theory describes how participatory social interactions, such as dialogues and conversational routines between parents and children, serve as an important platform from which children acquire representational capacities, including those that permit them to place themselves in time generally, and more specifically, to form expectations about future events.

Similar to Nelson's analysis, Sachs (1983) argued that displaced reference, or the ability to use language to go beyond the here and now to talk about objects and events that are not immediately present, is likely to emerge from "conversational routines" between parents and children. Sachs presents data to show that such conversational routines typically focus on "talking about events and plans for the day."

The powerful role of conversational routines does not appear to be limited to human infants. Savage-Rumbaugh and colleagues (Savage-Rumbaugh 1990, Savage-Rumbaugh *et al.* 1993) reported research on symbol use and language acquisition in non-human primates who were raised by human caregivers. Savage-Rumbaugh (1990) argued that one motivation for acquiring language, even by non-human primates, is to understand and therefore gain control of events that might happen in the future. While data from these and other language studies suggest that caregivers frequently include references to the future in conversation to young children and even non-human primates, little research exists on the relative degree to which adults talk to their young about events in past, current and future time.

Each of these studies provides intriguing evidence that young children and non-human primates reference future events relatively early in the rich context of everyday life. However, these studies typically report data from only one research subject and were primarily concerned with language acquisition per se rather than the origins of children's understanding of future events. We also know from common observations of young children that prior to language acquisition, infants and toddlers engage in non-linguistic instrumental actions that are future-oriented, such as sequential actions that lead to a goal (e.g. dragging a chair across the room to stand on to reach the cookie jar that sits on the kitchen counter). While language clearly permits us to communicate and represent events in time, prior to language young children also demonstrate actions that are indicative of some knowledge of time-related events. Thus, there is a gap between identifying the development of future orientation as an important research topic and research techniques that permit the study of both language and non-language-behaviors indicative of future understanding.

Multiple methods: The development of future-oriented processes questionnaire and the analysis of adult speech

In an attempt to begin filling this gap, we adopted two research strategies. First, we designed studies to generate an empirical knowledge base about the development of future orientation in the first four years of life. Second, we explored the extent to which adult speech about events in time may be linked to the development of future orientation. Next, we present data from a questionnaire study that was developed to assess the existence of differentiated domains of future-oriented processes and their course of development in early development. Such evidence is crucial in our view because it documents the general developmental trajectory of early future-oriented processes that we believe provide a foundation for more mature future-orientation behaviors. These data show normative developmental trends in future orientation. We also present new findings from our examination of parent–child narratives in an attempt to document the degree to which adult speech consists of references to past, present, and future events.

The development of future-oriented processes questionnaire

We developed an instrument to chronicle early future-oriented processes that are representative of young children's everyday instrumental activities based on parental reports (Benson 1994, Benson, Haith, Bihun, Talmi and Hager, under revision). An initial questionnaire was developed based on a pilot interview study with the parents of young children. Based on the pilot interview study, questionnaire items were generated to investigate the facets and developmental progression of future orientation and the social, cultural, and familial factors that contribute to growth in children's understanding of the future. This was the first empirical effort to organize thinking about the development of future-oriented processes in the form of a measurement instrument and to describe the development of these processes in early childhood. The questionnaire also detailed normative, age-related trends in the development of a wide array of future-oriented processes that emerged from data collected from two different samples (see Benson 1994 for details about the initial questionnaire instrument). From this initial study the questionnaire was revised to include additional domains that were previously overlooked and to eliminate problematic items.

For the purposes of this chapter, we will provide a brief description of the revised domains of future orientation in a second study and recent findings demonstrating their developmental course over the first four years. These findings come from a large sample ($\underline{n}$ = 286) of parents with children between twelve and forty-two months of age. Also relevant are findings from the first version of the questionnaire (Benson 1994) that revealed interesting information about some contextual factors, such as parental beliefs and family practices, both suggestive of influences on the development of future-oriented processes.

The revised Development of Future-Oriented Processes questionnaire contains items organized into seven behavioral domains that assess a wide range of future-oriented behaviors. The original and revised domains are shown in Table 8.1 along with sample items. For each item within a domain, parents used a four-point rating to indicate how true the item was for their own child, ranging from "Very true" to "Not at all true."

Domains of future orientation

Items in the "Order" domain examine children's understanding of the ordering of temporal relations, including the notions of "before, after, and sequence." An understanding of these basic temporal relations is critical for the ability to partition time into past, present, and future (Harner 1982, Piaget 1969). The

Table 8.1 Sample items for future-oriented processes domains

Initial questionnaire Initial domains (Benson, 1994)	Revised questionnaire Revised domains	Sample item
Order	Order	My child wants some things done the same way every time.
Routines	Routines	My child can follow a routine that I begin.
Planning	Preparation	My child does things that show preparation for the future.
Expectation	Expectation	If I tell my child something unfamiliar will happen, my child is able to expect it.
Time	Time	My child can tell me about things he or she wants to do later.
Problem-solving	Problem-orientation	My child will try different ways to solve a problem when the first way doesn't work.
	Emotion/Compliance	My child pretends to be upset to get something s/he wants.

items in the "Routines" domain tap children's knowledge about familiar routines, including those initiated by either the child or the parent. The next domain, "Preparation," contains items that assess the extent to which children attempt to get ready for upcoming events. The "Expectation" domain included items that capture various types of expectations formed by young children on the basis of their experiences (Haith *et al.* 1993), along with their reactions when expectations are violated. The items in the "Time" domain assess children's understanding of different aspects of time, including duration, time units and societal conventions for keeping track of time (e.g. the use of clocks and calendars). An understanding of time concepts is important for many future-oriented behaviors, such as planning (Benson 1997, W. Friedman 1990). The items in the "Problem-orientation" domain tap the degree of persistence the child shows in goal achievement and the child's understanding that a social agent can be recruited to help obtain a goal. In the revised instrument (Benson *et al.* under revision), the "Emotion/Compliance" domain was added with items designed to examine the degree to which children understand emotional cues that relate to future consequences of their actions.

The final sample included responses from parents of 286 twelve- to forty-two-month-old children (146 male; 140 female), with at least forty-six participants in each of the six following age groups: twelve, eighteen, twenty-four, thirty, thirty-six, and forty-two months. The children were from predominantly Caucasian, middle-class, well-educated families living in and around the local Denver Metropolitan area. The majority of families had both parents living in the household (97.6%), and child care was provided by a parent in the home in over

half the sample. Despite our efforts to use US census-track information to recruit
culturally diverse families, the final sample of respondents who mailed back their
questionnaires was relatively homogenous.

An analysis of items in all domains showed similar levels of internal
consistency in the form of computed alphas as was found for the original
questionnaire (see Benson 1994 for details), suggesting the revised instrument
had reasonably sound and acceptable psychometric properties.

Age trends

Our primary interest was to determine whether parents would report systematic,
age-related changes in children's understanding within the various domains. In
particular, we were interested in whether the age function for all domains would
be similar or whether some domains would change more rapidly than others.
Fig. 8.1 shows the relation between each of the major domains and age. Trend
analyses revealed significant linear trends for each domain at $p < .001$. However,
as Fig. 8.1 reveals, the slope of the various trends differed. Ratings were relatively
high for the "Problem-orientation" and "Routines" domains across age with
performance leveling off by twenty-four months. On the other hand, reported
understanding for the "Time" and "Emotion/Compliance" domains was
relatively low across all ages, with gradual increases across age reaching only a
moderate level by forty-two months. The strongest trends were obtained for the
"Order, Preparation and Expectation" domains, respectively, with ratings low
at twelve months of age and high at forty-two months of age. All but the
"Preparation" and "Time" domains yielded significant nonlinear trends as
well.

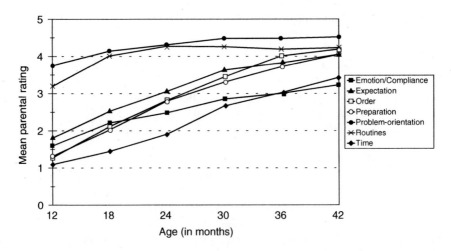

Figure 8.1 Reported levels of understanding for each domain by age

Age-related trends and developmental transitions

The patterns of parental responses revealed distinct age-related, normative developmental trends for the specific domains of future-oriented behaviors. These findings suggest that the domains of future-oriented behaviors do not emerge in an all-or-none, synchronous fashion. Instead, parents reported that their young children acquire different degrees of understanding across the domains and subdomains of future-oriented processes according to different timetables. For example, at one extreme, parents rated their child's understanding of items in the "Problem-orientation" and "Routines" domains as fairly high in each of the six age groups we studied, with only slight improvement from twelve to forty-two months of age. At the opposite extreme, parental ratings of child understanding of items in the "Time" and "Emotion/Compliance" domains indicated limited child understanding at twelve months, with only very gradual improvement by forty-two months. In fact, even by forty-two months of age, the average parent rating of child understanding for the "Time" and "Emotion/Compliance" domains was no greater than the midpoint of our rating scale. It may be that parents rate their children as high in understanding on the "Problem-orientation" and "Routines" items because many of these behaviors are well practiced and have relatively immediate consequences for children, even by twelve months. In contrast, items from the "Emotion/Compliance" and "Time" domains require more child experience. Some items from the "Emotion/Compliance" domain require that children learn to interpret the consequences of another's emotional signal, something that is gained over time through varied social experiences. Similarly, some items from the "Time" domain are relatively abstract and experienced-based in that the child must learn social conventions that are used to mark time (e.g. the use of clocks and calendars and specific words that denote time). Thus, the normative trends that we found converge with the empirical and theoretical literature on which they were based, as well as parents' observations of their children's behaviors.

Trend analyses of age-related patterns also revealed that the most rapid increases in child understanding occurred during the ages of eighteen to thirty-six months of age for items in the "Order", "Preparation" and "Expectation" domains. During the eighteen- to thirty-six-month age period several important cognitive achievements occur that contribute to a growing understanding of the future, that are not simply linked to either maturation (as indicated by chronological age) or progress in language development. Such achievements include growth in symbolic, representational and cognitive achievements that are likely to affect children's ability to sequence and order events and to entertain notions of possibility and uncertainty. These findings thus serve a primary goal of this research, because the questionnaire appears to provide reasonable guidelines for researchers to focus on the eighteen- to thirty-six-month age period to better understand developmental transitions in future orientation.

We were interested in determining what motivated the changes during the eighteen- to thirty-six-month period as a number of factors could explain the trends we found. First, we know that decalage exists in cognitive development so that children's cognitive abilities do not develop across all domains uniformly and simultaneously.

Second, based on preliminary interviews with mothers used to develop the questionnaire and responses to items assessing parental beliefs and family practices from the initial questionnaire (Benson 1994), there is some variation across families in the beliefs parents have about how their children come to learn about the future and the practices parents engage in that might facilitate its development. For example, we know that not all parents have the same beliefs about how their child acquires an understanding of the future. When asked to use a three-point scale to rate the importance (from "Not very" to "Very") of different parental beliefs about how children acquire an understanding of the future, parents gave the highest ratings to the following two items: "By having a regular routine" and "By my talking about things that are going to happen." The lowest importance ratings were given to the following two items: "Simply by getting older" and "Naturally, because my child is born with this ability." This pattern suggests that most, but not all, parents endorse parental belief statements that reflect an experience- or learning-based orientation to how their child acquires an understanding of the future, while statements that suggest little or no parental intervention received the lowest ratings but were endorsed by some parents nonetheless.

The pilot interview also revealed differences in the extent to which parents involve their children in planning for family events. The behaviors of the following two families – when it comes to taking a vacation – provides an illustration of the type of differences that may exist in how parents involve their children in preparing for a future event. In one family, children are informed of the vacation plans in advance, encouraged to select items they would like to bring along, and are generally prepared for what might happen during the vacation trip. In another family, the children are put in the backseat of the car while asleep, with no advance discussion about vacation plans, only to wake and learn that they are on vacation! We have only preliminary evidence at this point to support the role we attribute to parental beliefs and family practices. A future direction for our research is to collect more systematic evidence to determine the extent to which parental beliefs and family practices support the development of future orientation.

These examples about parental beliefs and family practices, along with the role of routines and rituals in family life, clearly suggest that social factors impact the early development of future orientation. An additional finding from the initial questionnaire study prompted us to explore the extent to which parents talk about future events to their children. In the initial questionnaire study parents reported that they regularly talked to their children as young as nine months about events that would occur in the future despite the fact that they also admitted that they believed their children did not entirely understand the future (Benson 1994). Thus the recognition that parents know they talk to their children about the future raised the question of whether parents are more likely to talk to their children about events in the past, the present or the future. We designed the next two studies to explore how much talking parents were doing to their children about past, present, and future events and to evaluate whether the reference time that parents were talking about might underlie the age-related trends revealed in the questionnaire data.

Adult speech to young children: exploration of CHILDES adult–child narratives

From our preliminary findings from the questionnaire study and language studies it is clear that the content of what parents say to their children during conversational routines has the potential to impact the development of future orientation. Because we do not pretend to be experts in language research, we were interested in accessing language data that were already collected to explore whether evidence might exist for the relative proportion of time parents were talking about events in the past, present and future. The Child Language Data Exchange System (CHILDES, MacWhinney 1995) provides access to language transcripts of conversations between parents and young children collected longitudinally. We developed a coding system to conduct an exploratory investigation of whether the content and temporal orientation of adult talk to infants and young children is equally emphasized among events located in past, current or future time, and whether parents change emphasis from one predominant time frame to another during early development. This coding system was developed from an analysis of transcribed adult utterances to young children obtained from CHILDES (MacWhinney 1995). All linguistic utterances made during dyadic interaction were transcribed according to the CHILDES "chat" convention (MacWhinney 1995). We selected adult–child narrative transcriptions from the CHILDES database that met our criteria of being longitudinal over ages, complementary to the developmental periods within the questionnaire study, and that provided narrative transcriptions that occurred in a semi-structured conversational setting with specific objects present.

Each adult utterance was analyzed for its discourse function by noting the event time of such "time talk." Event time took precedence over verb tense, was defined as the time frame of the subject or event of the utterance, and was coded as: a) *past*; b) *current*; or c) *future*. Utterances that did not fall into the category of "time talk" were termed "other talk" and consisted of three different categories. Other talk discourse was coded as: a) *naming* – the utterance was informational (e.g. "This is a duck"); b) *imperative* – the utterance was a command (e.g. "Put the chicken to bed"); or c) *ambiguous* – the function or event time was uncertain (see Table 8.2). Three raters coded each transcript until 100% agreement was reached.

Using the CHILDES database, we addressed three main hypotheses. First, based on previous research on adults' reports of their talk to infants and toddlers about events in the future (Benson 1994), we expected adult time talk would show a higher proportion of utterances about events in the future than in the past, particularly at ages before children were themselves speaking. Second, parents are known to adjust their behavior to the changing competence of their

Table 8.2 Sample adult utterance, coding category and rationale

Adult utterance	Coding category type	Rationale
	Time talk	
"We danced at ballet class yesterday."	Past	Past event, past tense
"I put that on chicken when I make some dishes."		Past event, current tense
"Now here we are."	Current	Current event, current tense
"You've got too much in it."		Current event, current tense
"We need to write it down."	Future	Future event, future tense
"Let me see if I can do that myself."		Future event, future tense
	Other talk	
"This is a duck."	Naming	Naming an object
"Elmo is playing soccer."		Naming an action
"Put the chicken to bed."	Imperative	Command statement
"Let me see your finger."		
"What?"	Ambiguous	Unsure of the reference of the utterance
"Hmmm."		

children (Dix and Grusec 1985). As children acquired language skills that allowed them to join in the conversation and talk about past events and parents recognized these skills as changes in the level of child understanding, we expected that the proportion of adult talk about past events would increase relative to talk about future events. Third, as child language skills and temporal knowledge grew, we expected that the proportion of adult time talk utterances would increase relative to other utterances.

Study 1

We analyzed CHILDES transcripts from thirty-six child–parent dyads in the NEW ENGLAND database (Snow 1989). The dyads were part of a large longitudinal study observed at fourteen, twenty and thirty-two months of age.

The children were healthy, English-speaking and of lower-middle and upper-middle socioeconomic status. The parent was generally the mother. Parent–child dyads were videotaped in a laboratory while interacting in a series of semi-structured activities for a total of twenty to twenty-five minutes. The activities included five minutes each of a free-play warm-up and the presence of an object children could not touch, followed by the presentation of four successive boxes containing, in order, a ball, a cloth for peekaboo, paper and crayons, and a book. Only one box could be open at a time. At the thirty-two-month observation, only the four boxes were presented and age-appropriate objects, such as hand puppets and a toy house, replaced the ball and cloth respectively.

Regarding our first hypothesis about whether adults talk to young children more about events in the past or future we found that, averaged over all observations (see the left side of Table 8.3), adults talked more to young children about *future events* ($M = 13.93\%$) than *past events* ($M = 2.0\%$). Although most adult time talk centered on *current events* ($M = 30.43\%$), we focus primarily on the comparison between past and future events. Our second research question addressed developmental changes in adult speech to children. Contrary to expectation as shown in Fig. 8.2, adult time talk about past events remained constant over the fourteen-months ($M = 1.6\%$), twenty-months ($M = 2.1\%$) and thirty-two-months ($M = 2.3\%$) observations ($F_{(2,68)} = 1.753$, $p > .05$). However, adult time talk about future events monotonically increased over the fourteen-months ($M = 10.9\%$), twenty-months ($M = 15.3\%$) and thirty-two-months ($M = 15.6\%$) observations, yielding a statistically significant longitudinal trend ($F_{(2,68)} = 13.875$, $p < .0001$).

We were also interested in the proportion of adult utterances to young children concerning time talk compared to other talk. As shown in Fig. 8.3, the proportion of adult time talk utterances increased from 35.8% at fourteen months to 57.5% at thirty-two months. The relative proportion of adult other talk utterances decreased from 64.2% at fourteen months to 42.5% at thirty-two months.

Study 2

The results from the NEW ENGLAND database were interesting, but we were concerned that the age range was not sufficient to capture children's growing language skills, which would likely influence their parents' speech. Thus, we were interested in extending the age range of our sample beyond thirty-two months to continue our exploration of adult time talk to children. By extending the age range beyond thirty-two months we would also parallel the age range sampled in

Table 8.3 Mean percent of total utterances by age and totals for utterance categories

	Study 1 (N = 36)			Study 2 (N = 10)		
	Age in months					
	14	20	32	36	39	42
Utterance categories						
Percent time talk	35.8	46.4	57.5	50.4	48.1	51.7
Current	23.1	28.8	39.4	22.9	28.7	24.6
Future	10.9	15.3	15.6	20.7	14.3	20.3
Past	01.6	02.1	02.3	06.7	05.2	06.8
Percent other talk	64.2	53.6	42.5	49.6	51.9	48.4
Imperative	19.7	16.1	07.5	15.9	20.0	16.0
Naming	06.7	09.5	05.3	06.0	01.8	06.7
Ambiguous	37.6	27.9	29.5	33.2	30.2	31.7

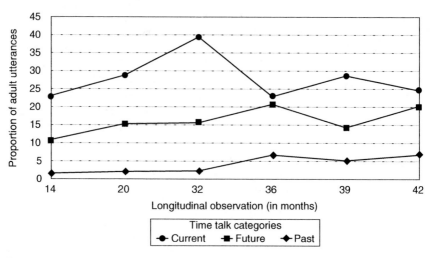

Figure 8.2 Age trends for time talk categories (combined New England and Wells databases)

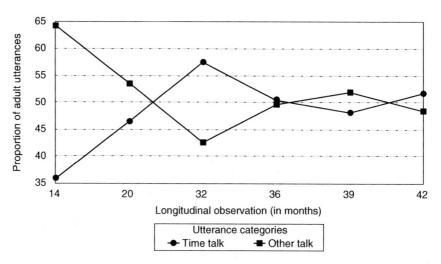

Figure 8.3 Age trends for adult utterance categories (combined New England and Wells databases)

the revised questionnaire study. Using the WELLS database (Wells 1981) from CHILDES, we selected ten adult–child dyads from whom thirty-six-, thirty-nine- and forty-two-month data existed.

The children were healthy, English-speaking, and British. Researchers recorded spontaneous conversations between adults and children for ninety seconds at approximately twenty-minute intervals throughout the day. Parents and observers recalled details of the day to provide a context for the recorded conversations.

Regarding our first hypothesis about whether adults talk to young children more about events in the past or future we found that, averaged over all observations (see the right side of Table 8.3), adults talked more to young children about *future events* ($M = 18.4\%$) than *past events* ($M = 6.2\%$), but as in Study 1 most adult time talk centered on *current events* ($M = 25.4\%$). However, the percentage of time talk for all categories was lower than in Study 1. Our second research question addressed developmental changes in adult speech to children. Contrary to expectation, adult time talk about past events remained constant over the thirty-six- ($M = 6.7\%$), thirty-nine- ($M = 5.2\%$) and forty-two-months ($M = 6.8\%$) observations ($F_{(2,18)} = 0.18$, $p > .05$). Similarly, as shown in Fig. 8.2, adult time talk about future events remained constant and at a higher level than past event talk over the thirty-six- ($M = 20.7\%$), thirty-nine- ($M = 14.3\%$) and forty-two-months ($M = 20.3\%$) observations ($F_{(2,18)} = 1.56$, $p > .05$).

As in Study 1, we were interested in the proportion of adult utterances to young children concerning time talk compared to other talk. As shown in Fig. 8.3, the proportion of adult-time talk utterances remained constant over the thirty-six- ($M = 50.4\%$), thirty-nine- ($M = 48.1\%$) and forty-two-months ($M = 51.7\%$) observations ($F_{(2,18)} = 0.30$, $p > .05$) as did the relative proportion of adult other talk utterances, thirty-six- ($M = 49.6\%$), thirty-nine- ($M = 51.9\%$) and forty-two-months ($M = 48.4\%$) observations ($F_{(2,18)} = 0.30$, $p > .05$).

Taken together, the findings from these studies suggest that adult speech to infants and toddlers focused primarily on events in current time. However, between the ages of fourteen and thirty-two months, adult speech about events in the past remained constant while speech about future events increased. Across these same ages there were increases in adult speech about events in time and reductions in speech about other non-time events (see Fig. 8.3). Interestingly, between thirty-six and forty-two months of age, the relative proportions of future and past talk increased slightly but the trend observed at younger ages continued with significantly more talk about the future than the past. During this period, current talk decreased and the relative proportions of time talk and other talk were approximately equal. Thus, whereas parental time talk increased over the fourteen- to thirty-two-month period, it decreased relative to other talk from thirty-six to forty-two-months.

Discussion and conclusions

The findings from both the questionnaire and adult speech studies suggest that future orientation plays a central role in mental life, and as such, it is important to understand its various facets and how this understanding develops in its own right, especially in the context of early social interactions. More generally, future thinking is pivotal to cognitive organization and functioning, so our understanding of cognitive development would be enriched by knowing the role future thinking plays.

The revised Development of Future-Oriented Processes questionnaire is a reasonable parental self-report instrument that adequately captures a variety of domains of future-oriented behaviors readily observable in young children. The pattern of parental responses suggests that the domains of future-oriented processes, initially based on the existing empirical and theoretical child development literature, are also discernible, age-appropriate future-oriented behaviors that were easily recognized by parents of twelve- to forty-two-month-old children. Analysis of parental responses suggests that adults had little difficulty evaluating the various questionnaire items as examples of common future-oriented behaviors that were or were not present in their child's everyday behaviors. Although parents often informally acknowledged that they had not previously thought about their young child's understanding of the future without our prompting them to do so, the behaviors described in the questionnaire items provoked their thinking about their child's understanding and orientation to the future.

The analysis of coded adult–child narrative transcripts revealed that adult talk to infants and toddlers is oriented more to the future than the past, which would suggest one possible mechanism by which very young children are able to form expectations for future events. The findings are consistent with previous findings, based on self-report data, that parents talk to their children about future events despite also recognizing that their children have a limited knowledge of the future (Benson 1994). These findings also demonstrate that parents talk more to their young children about future events than they do about past events, providing additional support to claims about the existence and importance of future orientation in early development (e.g. Benson 1994, Haith *et al.* 1994). It is also important to consider that our findings are likely to be very conservative estimates of the amount of future talk because we excluded utterances coded as imperatives from the time talk category, which some language researchers consider to be references to the immediate future. In addition, the longitudinal nature of the data might have inflated the amount of talk about the past because the repetition of a situation should have drawn parents to talk about events in the past (e.g. "Remember the last time we were here to talk?") more so than they would spontaneously. Thus, the difference between parent talk about the future and parent talk about the past may be even greater than suggested by our present findings.

In Study 1 we found no support for the hypothesis that the proportion of adult time talk about past events would increase with development and as children's language skills improved. Surprisingly, analyses of two different CHILDES databases provide convergent evidence that parent talk about the past does not increase across early childhood. The fact that this trend was repeated across the analysis of two different CHILDES databases is compelling. Therefore, a more likely possibility is that parents place a greater emphasis on talking to their children about events in the future, rather than events in the past.

Why do parents talk more about the future than the past to their young children? In general, as a construct, the future is more difficult to understand than the past. The future is abstract, amorphous, intangible and not directly perceptible, in part, because it has not yet been experienced. In contrast, the past is known, experienced, and can be recollected using memory. Further, while the past is clearly marked in the English language by past tense verbs, the future is not as clearly demarcated by linguistic conventions. To express the future, we must use modal auxiliaries such as "would" and "may." Thus, parents face several challenges when attempting to convey information about the future to their young children. Our findings suggest that during social interactions with their children, parents use conversations about the short-term future to facilitate the development of future orientation in much the same way that they scaffold and engage in guided participation to promote other areas of development. For example, parents have told us that they will refer to the duration of an upcoming event by using time units that fit with their children's experience, such as "The cookies will be ready after two *Sesame Streets*." Thus, parental talk about the future seems to fit with the general orientation parents have to behave in ways that help promote their children's development.

Limitations

It is important to note a number of limitations to the approaches we have taken. First, the language samples we examined from CHILDES were obtained from a longitudinal study of child–parent interaction in structured activities. This constraint limits conclusions about the generality of our findings to adult speech to young children in more naturalistic situations, such as everyday family routines and rituals. The reported percentages of adult time talk utterances should be taken only as conservative estimates. Second, the language data spanned two separate samples. As such, these findings do not represent developmental trajectories from one group of children, but rather, we have interpolated developmental trends across different children from studies in different situations. The decrease in current talk observed between thirty-two and thirty-six-months could be a function of sampling differences or a true decline in the extent to which parents talk about events in current time. This trend might also be a function of children's increasing role as conversational partners. That is, as children approach the age of three they may be more likely to talk about what is in their immediate environment than about the past or future. If children are talking more about the present, parents may yield the lead to their children and talk about present events to a lesser extent.

Importantly, the issue of children as conversational partners may help explain some additional findings during the thirty-six- to forty-two-month period. In contrast to the fourteen- to thirty-two-month period during which time talk increased, from thirty-six- to forty-two-months time talk and other talk occurred about equally in their frequency. Conceivably, older children may refer to the current, past, and future themselves, thereby reducing the necessity for their parents to attempt to engage their child in time talk.

At least one direction for future research involves the examination of what young children are saying as conversational partners with respect to time and other talk. In very cursory examinations of the thirty-six- to forty-two-month data, it is clear that children increasingly contribute to the conversations and, in fact, often lead the discussions. The bi-directional and reciprocal relation between language and cognition (Nelson 1996) suggest this may be a fruitful area to examine with respect to the development of future oriented processes.

We know that young children often do not mean what they say or say what they mean. Therefore, we need to develop multi-method approaches to help us analyze the interactions among parents' speech, children's speech, and children's cognitive development regarding the future. Such methods include studies to identify *what* both children and adults express and the *manner* in which they express themselves while engaged in family routines and rituals, along with the creation of laboratory tasks that permit us to systematically explore factors relating to children's understanding of temporal concepts, specifically concepts about the future.

Finally, we need a better understanding of the extent to which family routines and rituals function to foster children's development of the future. As we speculated at the start of this chapter, it is entirely possible that children initially need the repetitive, multi-step structure of everyday routines that lead to a known endpoint, that are accompanied by adult commentary, to understand what will happen in the near-term future. Once children become familiar with such routines, deviations from them disrupt their ability to predict what will happen next. Evidence for this claim comes from anyone who has tried to skip a few pages while reading a favorite book to a young child or who hears "Again! Again!" after reading that favorite book for the tenth time! As children gain mastery over understanding that a sequence of events leads to a predictable outcome, it should soon follow that the child might attempt deviations from the typical routine to further her own goals. There are several common examples of the deviations young children begin to insert into common routines, such as asking for a drink of water, one more book, or saying good night to every stuffed animal in the room to avoid the eventual endpoint of lights out in the bedtime routine. These deviations, once documented, should provide at least one additional piece of evidence that children are exerting mastery over understanding the consequences of sequenced events to the extent that they are attempting to impact the behaviors of others to achieve their own future goals. These speculations, however, await additional study before they can be confirmed.

Studying the development of future-oriented processes is a rich and exciting area that highlights both biological and psychological development and transcends the individual, social and cultural contexts of human life. The recognition of the continuum between biological and psychological development and the reminder to view behavior as it emerges across the individual, social, and cultural contexts are important lessons that live on from Ina Užgiris' legacy. In the next several years we hope that our multi-method research effort will continue to further that legacy as we inform and develop our understanding of how children acquire a basic understanding of the future.

References

Aveni, A. F. (1989) *Empires of Time: Calendars, Clocks and Cultures.* NY: Kodansha International.

Bates, E., Elman, J. and Li, P. (1994) "Language in, on and About Time" in Haith, M. M., Benson, J. B., Roberts, R. J. and Pennington B. F. (eds.) *The Development of Future-Oriented Processes* (pp. 375–407). Chicago, IL: University of Chicago Press.

Benson, J. B. (1994) "The Origins of Future Orientation in the Everyday Lives of 9- to 36-month-old Infants" in Haith, M. M., Benson, J. B., Roberts, R. J. and Pennington, B. F. (eds.) *The Development of Future-Oriented Processes* (pp. 375–407). Chicago, IL: University of Chicago Press.

— (1997) "The Development of Planning: It's About Time" in Friedman, S. L. and Scholnick, E. K. (eds.) *The Developmental Psychology of Planning* (pp. 43–75). Mahwah, NJ: Erlbaum.

Benson, J. B. and Haith, M. M. (1995) "Future-Oriented Processes: A Foundation for Planning Behavior in Infants and Toddlers", *Infancia y Aprendizaje*: 69–70, 127–140.

Benson, J. B., Haith, M. M., Bihun, J. T., Talmi, A. and Hager, L. (under revision) "The Development of Future-Oriented Processes: A Parental Report Instrument", manuscript submitted for publication.

Canfield, R. L. and Haith, M. M. (1991) "Active Expectations in 2- and 3-month-old Infants: Complex Event Sequences", *Developmental Psychology, 27*: 198–208.

Cole, M. (1999) "Culture in Development" in Bornstein, M. H. and Lamb, M. E. (eds.) *Developmental Psychology: An Advanced Textbook* (4th ed.). Mahwah, NJ: Erlbaum.

Daly, K. J. (1996) *Families and Time: Keeping Pace in a Hurried World.* Thousand Oaks, CA: Sage.

Dix, T. and Grusec, J. E. (1985) "Parent Attribution Process in the Socialization of Children" in Sigel, I. E. (ed.) *Parental Belief Systems* (pp. 201–233). Hillsdale, NJ: Erlbaurm.

Friedman, W., (1990) *About Time.* Cambridge, MA: A Bradford Book, MIT Press.

Fraisse, P. (1963) *The Psychology of Time.* NY: Harper & Row.

Friedman, S. L. and Scholnick, E. K. (1997) *The Developmental Psychology of Planning.* Mahwah, NJ: Erlbaum.

Gleick, J. (1999) *Faster: The Acceleration of Just About Everything.* NY: Pantheon Books.

Harner, L. (1980) "Comprehension of Past and Future Reference Revisited", *Journal of Experimental Child Psychology, 29*: 170–182.

— (1982) "Talking About Past and Future" in Friedman, W. J. (ed.) *The Developmental Psychology of Time* (pp. 141–169) NY: Academic Press.

Haith, M. M. (1997) "The Development of Future Thinking as Essential for the Emergence of Skill in Planning" in Friedman, S. L. and Scholnick, E. K. (eds.) *The Developmental Psychology of Planning* (pp. 25–42). Mahwah, NJ: Erlbaum.

Haith, M. M, Benson, J. B., Roberts, R. J. and Pennington, B. F. (1994) Introduction in Haith, M. M., Benson, J. B., Roberts, R. J. and Pennington, B. F. (eds.) *The Development of Future-Oriented Processes* (pp. 1–7). Chicago, IL: University of Chicago Press.

Haith, M. M., Hazan, C. and Goodman, G. G. (1988) "Expectation and Anticipation of Dynamic Visual Events by 3.5-month-old Babies", *Child Development, 59*: 467–479.

Haith, M. M., Wentworth, N. and Canfield, R. L. (1993) "The Formation of Visual Expectations in Early Infancy" in Rovee-Collier, C. and Lipsitt, L. (eds.) *Advances in Infancy Research* (pp. 251–297). Norwood, NJ: Ablex.

MacWhinney, B. (1995) *The CHILDES Project: Tools for Analyzing Talk*. Hillsdale, NJ: Erlbaum.

Nelson, K. (1989) "Monologue as Representation of Real-Life Experience" in Nelson, K. (ed.) *Narratives from the Crib* (pp. 27–72). Cambridge, MA: Harvard University Press.

Nelson, K. E. (1996) *Language in Cognitive Development*. Cambridge, England: Cambridge University Press.

Nuttin, J. (1984) *Motivation, Planning, and Action: A Relational Theory of Behavior Dynamics*. Leuven & Hillsdale, NJ: Leuven University Press & Erlbaum.

Nurmi, J.-E. (1991) "How Do Adolescents See Their Future? A Review of the Development of Future Orientation and Planning", *Developmental Review, 11*: 1–59.

Piaget, J. (1969) *The Child's Conception of Time* (Pomeras, A. J., trans.). NY: Basic Books. (Original work published 1946.)

Reiss, D. (1981) *The Family's Construction of Reality*. Cambridge, MA: Harvard University Press.

Rogoff, B. and Lave, J. (1984) *Everyday Cognition: Its Development in Social Context*. Cambridge, MA: Harvard University Press.

Schacter, D. L. (2001) *The Seven Sins of Memory: How the Mind Forgets and Remembers*. Boston: Houghton Mifflin.

Sachs, J. (1983) "Talking about There and Then: The Emergence of Displaced Reference in Parent–Child Discourse" in Nelson, K. E. (ed.) *Children's Language* (vol. 4, pp. 1–28). Hillsdale, NJ: Erlbaum.

Savage-Rumbaugh, E. S. (1990) "Language as a Cause-Effect Communication System", *Philosophical Psychology, 3*: 55–76.

Savage-Rumbaugh, E. S., Murphy, J., Sevcik, R. A., Brakke, K. E., Williams, S. L. and Rumbaugh, D. M. (1993) "Language Comprehension in Ape and Child", *Monographs of the Society for Research in Child Development, 58*.

Siegler, R. S. (1998) *Children's Thinking*. Upper Saddle River, NJ: Prentice Hall.

Scholnick, E. K. and Friedman, S. L. (1993) "Planning in Context: Developmental and Situational Considerations", *International Journal of Behavioral Development, 16*: 145–167.

Tulving, E. (2000) *Memory, Consciousness, and the Brain*. Philadelphia, PA: Psychology Press.

Užgiris, I. Č. (1996) "Together and Apart: The Enactment of Values in Infancy" in Reed, E. S., Turiel, E. and Brown, T. (eds.) *Values and Knowledge*. Mahwah, NJ: Erlbaum.

— (2000) "Words Don't Tell All: Some Thoughts on Early Communication Development" in Budwig, N., Užgiris, I. Č. and Wertsch, J. V. (eds.) *Communication: An Arena of Development*. Stamford, CT: Ablex.

Vygotsky, L. S. (1978) *Mind in Society: The Development of Higher Psychological Processes* (Cole, M., John-Steiner, V., Scribner, S. and Souberman, E. (eds. and trans.). Cambridge, MA: Harvard University Press.

Weist, R. A. (1986) "Tense and Aspect: Temporal Systems in Child Language" in Fletcher, P. and Garman, M. (eds.) *Language Acquisition*. Cambridge: Cambridge University Press.

— (1989) "Time Concepts in Language and Thought: Filling the Piagetian Void from Two to Five Years" in Levin, I. and Zakay, D. (eds.) *Time and Human Cognition*. Amsterdam: North-Holland.

Zaleski, Z. (1994) *Psychology of Future Orientation*. Lublin, Poland: Towarzystwo Naukowe KUL.

9 *Level this, Level that*

The place of culture in the construction of the self

Michael J. Chandler and Bryan W. Sokol

> "... Order is cheap and the variety of possible orders the mind can suggest indefinite."
>
> (A. Edel, *Integrative Levels*, 1988)

The organizing intuition that frames the account to follow is that, somewhere buried deep within the avalanche of contemporary smart talk about hierarchy theory and the design–computation–hardware distinction (a form of Newspeak about *level this* and *level that* practiced primarily by the friends of computer simulation and homuncular modularity), is the germ of a newer, silicon-free way of talking about different levels of psychological explanation. The start of a glossary for this alternative language is, we will argue, to be found in Ina Užgiris' recent and posthumously published writings (e.g. Užgiris 1999) – an interrupted work-in-progress that this chapter is meant to help extend.

The generic page that we mean to lift from Užgiris' work is that characteristic one on which it is written that, by focusing attention upon "activities" and "actions," rather than concentrating (as psychologists are sometimes inclined to do) only on particular, decontextualized "acts," new prospects arise for our otherwise lost hopes of ever repairing the chronic individual–society antinomy that has regularly cut psychology off from cultural life. Speaking against this tendency to become lost in the details, and from within the context of her own work on imitation, Užgiris regularly argued that the costs of doing otherwise (that is, the costs of perseveratively attending only to the narrow particulars of immediately observable behaviors) need to be counted in the coinage of lost opportunities to see the interpersonal and social relevance of still broader imitative "actions," and to understand their significance in terms of the systems of cultural values within which such activities are naturally embedded. Drawing on the work of Piaget (1968), as well as that of Vygotsky (1978) and Leontev and his followers (see Wertsch 1981), she regularly promoted the competing idea that human conduct in general, and imitation in particular, "has to be analyzed at different *levels*, with activity [as opposed to mere movement] being taken as the highest among these levels" (Užgiris 1999: 188). Such "activities" (e.g. the broad enterprise of learning through exploration), she worked to show, are not only key to understanding Piaget's account of individual "operations" but are necessarily "linked" to larger social structures and are defined in terms of common motives that remain in force over long periods of time. Something of the same thing is true of her next "level," which is said to be made up of "actions" (e.g. throwing a ball) that, because they occur in different manners depending on the specific social context in which they are carried out, are, if anything, even more reliant upon the details of the child's culturally structured world. Finally, there are, in her own way of parsing things up, particular case-specific "acts" – mere "movements," if you will – that, while conveniently susceptible to being measured in detail, are emptied of much of their human meaning unless or until they are also understood as particular ways of instrumenting the culturally embedded actions and activities of which they are only one expression. High on the list of gains to be had by this practice of keeping three sets of books (i.e. of multiply describing the same psychological event at different levels of analysis) is, then, according to Užgiris, that it opens a promising window onto the possibility of viewing culture as integral to human conduct as opposed to something to be tacked on only after the fact.

As it is, Užgiris' early intuition that the best route around the classical antinomy between individuals and their society lies along a path sculptured and terraced by different levels of description or explanation is an insight that others (ourselves included) have increasingly come to share (e.g. Chandler 2000, 2001, Chandler, Lalonde and Sokol 2000). The problem, however, as the whole of this chapter is meant to show, is that, while talk of ordered levels of explanation may well be the new talk of the town, "order," as Edel (1988: 66) reminds us, "is cheap and the variety of possible orders that the mind can suggest is indefinite."

Not surprisingly, at such bargain-basement prices, just about everyone is into their own version of the levels game. For some, the particular sort of levels that are had in mind, if not exactly lightly held, are taken to belong more properly to the realm of epistemology than to metaphysics. For others, the levels being counted out are earnestly taken to be substantive and ontologically real. Some are "top-down" theorists, whose highest levels are thought to be nearest to the real heart of the matter. Others are of a more "bottom-up" persuasion, and assume that anything that doesn't have a nucleus, or that exists beyond the grass-roots level of concrete experience, amounts to little more than a mere shadow on the cave walls of our minds. And then there is the matter of counting. Just how many levels do we really need to get the job of explaining mental life done? Historically, "two" has been taken as the right answer – particularly for those intent on preserving the independence of a psychological level of description by driving a wedge between minds and their physical embodiments. Of late, "three" would appear to be the more popular number. For others – "homuncular functionalists" as they rather oddly choose to refer to themselves (Sterelny 1990) – every level is naturally seen to presuppose still another. Even fleas, as they would have it, have lesser fleas upon their backs to bite them, and on and on and on it goes, and so ad infinitum.

Even assuming – as it would obviously be dangerous to do – that we were already clear enough about just how many such levels we ought to be making provision for, and what such levels are actually meant to be levels of, and (more than that) supposing still further that we already knew for certain whether we ought to be counting "up from the bottom" or "down from the top" – even then, we would still need to work out the nature of the possible relations assumed to obtain *between* such levels. Are the things at the top the causes of, or boundary conditions for, what falls below, or is it, rather, just the opposite, such that everything at the "macro" level is necessarily or always constrained (or supervened upon) by matters on the "micro," or base, level (Salthe 1988)? If not relations of cause and effect, are we instead dealing with whole-part or type-token relations? Are our "higher" levels really more like roles and our "lower"-level behaviors merely their immediate occupants? Are these ordered relations more like one of those "command hierarchies" (Griffiths 1997) which ensure that generals are never mistaken for their own subordinates, or are they instead more similar to those "authority relations" (Zylstra 1992) whose "control structures" work, for example, by turning the furnace off and on, thereby causally determining the temperature? Are the different levels we have in mind somehow recursive, embedding one another after the fashion of nested "Chinese" boxes, or are they mere typologies, or aggregations, or "just another boring way of arranging things" (Grene 1988: 9)? Are we all simply babbling?

Once again, it would seem, we are left to our own devices. Abandoned to this fate, but still guided by the intuition that the task Užgiris set out to accomplish with her working distinction between "activities" and "actions" and "acts" remains a job still very much worth doing, our plan is to move out onto this thin ice in three cautious steps. In Part 1 of what follows, we hope to say something clarifying about what we will allege boils down to two distinctive and irreducible approaches to the generic problem of stratifying the stuff out of which any adequate account of psychological life has to be built. Here, our point will be to convince you that, for some (call them the "essentialists"), the different levels of description and explanation required are metaphysical in nature and necessarily refer to different ontologically real things – things that occupy different levels in some subsumptive chain of *causes and effects*. For others (call them the "narrativists"), the problem of levels is best understood as an epistemological problem, and all open questions about the merits and demerits of any candidate system for stratifying you, or hierarchicalizing me, turn on the "epistemic gain" to be had by choosing to put things in this, as opposed to some other, particular way (Putnam 1999: 138). The good news – as we will attempt to make clear – is that you are not obliged to choose between these alternative accounts, but, rather, are as free as anyone else to treat both as resources to be called upon in a pinch.

In Part 2, we mean to go on to make the case that there is a natural predisposition for those who traffic in what have been characterized as ontologically real control hierarchies, and who count deeper levels as "causes" and more superficial levels as simply "effects," to also promote what we have called an "essentialist" view of self or personhood. By contrast, those who regard the explanatory details of selves, and other such, as best understood as meaning-bearing aspects of some larger epistemic whole (e.g. Bruner 1986, 1990, Holland 1997, Rorty 1973) tend instead to understand the conditions of their own and others' personal persistence or self-continuity in altogether more "narrative" terms.

Finally, in Part 3, we will go on to illustrate these competing ways of stratifying psychological matters, in general, and conceptions of selfhood, in particular, by pointing to important differences in the ways that Canada's culturally mainstream[1] and aboriginal (or First Nations) youth differently draw upon narrative and essentialist forms of self-understanding in their efforts to find persistent diachronic meaning in their own and others' changing and temporally vectored ways of being. In doing all of this, we hope to come full circle by demonstrating – as Užgiris promised we could – that, by making full use of *both* of these competing approaches to the study of psychological explanation, it is possible to go some important distance toward repairing the individual–society antinomy that has cost psychology proper access to the study of cultural life.

Part 1: Analysis versus subsumption

The promiscuity of order

Talk of different levels of theorizing, or explanation, or description is obviously neither new nor the exclusive province of psychology. Rather, levels analyses of varying sorts are everywhere in evidence, including, for example, in Aristotle's classic distinction between form and function, in Linneaus' *scala naturae*, in the Hegelian march of the Spirit through different *epoche*, and in the Marxian presentation of successive social systems (Edel 1988). Rather closer to home, philosophers and psychologists of mind, particularly those of an early functionalist stripe, such as Putnam and Lewis (see Griffiths 1997) have, along with Marr, Dennett, Newell, Millikan, Pylyshyn and others, all defended the proposition that a comprehensive account of mental life necessarily requires descriptions couched at different levels of analysis (Sterelny 1990).

While all of these distinctive efforts to impose some order on the scale and scope of psychologically relevant matters involve counting on the same fingers (i.e. Level One, Level Two, etc.), the similarities often end there. For some, the specification hierarchies they create are intended to be only aggregational, or taxonomic (Mayr 1982). Others are meant to describe epistemic rather than substantive relations (Edel 1988). For still others, the different levels that are envisioned are thought to be ontologically real, and to involve different levels of command or control between the entities that are described (Sterelny 1990). What we as consumers are left with, in the wake of all of this diversity, is a further series of unanswered questions. What are all of these levels being proposed actually levels of, and just how many of them are there? Will concrete versus abstract, or hardware versus procedural levels be enough? Is what we ordinarily have in mind in talking about such levels best modeled on the familiar Aristotelian distinction between availability and accessibility (Lefebvre-Pinard and Pinard 1985), or are these differences more like differences between capacity and its use (Goodnow and Cashmore 1985), or some other variation upon the classical competence–performance distinction (Overton 1991a)? Or is it rather that what we are dealing with here is more like the connections that link roles with their occupants, or wholes to their parts? Is there no more to choosing between these alternatives than blind liking?

The broad claim that we mean to detail in what follows is that, despite appearances to the contrary, whenever and wherever there is talk about different levels of psychological explanation, then really only one or the other of just two vernaculars is likely being spoken (Cummins 1983). *One* of these, which we have characterized as essentialist or entity-based, standardly employs an ontological language of cause and effects, and seeks to "ground" our understanding of mental events by locating their place within the causal structure of the world (Putnam 1999: 138). For some, these diverse levels, and the causal–subsumptive relations that obtain between them, are understood to be bottom-up in character, with events at the base level supervening upon higher-order levels of organization. Others, no less committed to authority relations of cause and effect, take a more top-down approach by assuming that events which belong to the lower, or more subordinate, of these levels of description are merely the consequences of otherwise deeper and more generic boundary conditions that exercise downward and often hidden causal constraints upon the concrete, contingent details of our changing psychological lives (Olson 1978). Because, according to either of these antecedent-consequent accounts, effects necessarily follow rather than proceed their causes (Lycan 1981), the actual occupants of the different descriptive or explanatory levels being proposed are automatically seen to reference different and "numerically distinct" things (Brand 1970). Things which, in order to avoid awkward confusions, are typically thought of as best kept in separate rooms of our mind (Taylor 1985). Scientific progress, in this account, requires being understood either as a) an instance of receding atomism in which entities at higher levels give way to progressively smaller entities which are understood as the true seat of causality or b) made up of our cumulative successes in reductively subsuming concrete particulars under some such smaller subset of rather more heady and abstract "covering laws" – laws that work by relegating everything belonging to the mundane and situated level of our actual moment-to-moment behaviors to the status of a kind of shadow of the real machine. On such an account we are, for example, typically understood to behave as we do simply "because" (i.e. b[y]–cause of the fact that) we have one sort of orchestrating personality structure or another.

According to what we mean to hold up as a *second* and fundamentally different way of talking about such distinctive strata of psychological description or explanation – the one which, for lack of a better alternative, we have labeled here as Relational or Narratively based – the structures, or steps or levels that are had in mind are not taken to be something literally "discovered" in the objective relations connecting actual events in the "real" world, but are rather seen to be products of human construction and so largely "internal" to some "epistemic corpus" (Putnam 1999: 138) or organized body of knowledge or belief. As such, any and all of the levels that are distinguishable through such "analysis" are seen to involve details that are best understood as alternative ways of describing what amounts to the same thing. On this more patterned conception we do not behave as we do *because* of some overweening personality structure. Rather, what it means to be fairly described as an instance of this as opposed to that sort of person is just to be someone who routinely acts in ways that lend themselves to such a re-description. On this view, then, all straightforwardly causal accounts of supposedly different levels of functioning tend to be dismissed as "technologists" (Habermas 1979), or "objectivistic" (Smedslund 1977), or "automation" models (Flavell and Wohlwill 1969) which condemn those who use them to endlessly pawing through the debris of visible effects in search of invisible causes – an enterprise which, as Broughton (1981) points out, is not unlike trying to catch sight of the dark by switching on the lights suddenly.

On the prospect that something like this second epistemological based vision is at least a live possibility – that is, on the assumption that the various levels that make up our more and less abstract accounts of ourselves need not necessarily be understood as playing cause to other effects – then, "What is it...", we need to ask, along with Dilthey (1961), "which, in the contemplation of one's life links the parts to the whole?" His answer, along with that of Užgiris and others who adopt the relational or narrative stance under discussion, is that "it is the fact that the connectedness of life can only be understood through meaning" (as cited in Cohler 1988: 552). That is, on this second and less familiar reading, the function of what passes for higher levels of analysis or explanation is to elucidate, rather than casually account for, events at other descriptive or explanatory levels. Such more abstract levels of analysis do not, then, "do or produce anything in the sense that a 'cause' is usually thought of as producing an effect... Instead they are principles that make the object or event intelligible or understandable" (Overton 1991b: 278). They accomplish this, it is argued, by providing a more formal description of whatever rules or patterns are brought into evidence through an examination of the details of those concrete actions whose common meanings they are intended to help explicate by gracing them with some new level of coherence, intelligibility or understanding (Bernstein 1983). We come to appreciate such patterns or designs, it is argued, by a process of abduction (von Glasersfeld and Kelley 1982) that involves imaginatively sifting through various concrete behavioral actions and reconstructing them by means of a process of "thick description" (Nelson 1978) that aims to situate various behavioral particulars within some larger, rationally constructed set of concepts or rules or schemata within which they are thought to operate (Olson 1978). The patterned relations between various levels of description generated in this fashion are, then, understood to be relations of identification or correspondence rather than empirical connections of cause and effect and are meant to specify the kinds of concrete behaviors that are consistent or compatible with them (Chandler 1991), or might be reasonably expected from anyone characterized by attributes of the more general type already had in mind. Because such more general and more particular descriptions are seen to constitute different vocabularies for describing one and the same thing, it is always at least potentially possible to map identity– relations between such different levels, and to do so in just the way that Užgiris, for example, envisioned particular "acts" as constituting (without being reducible to) some particular "action" or "activity" writ small.

What we mean to have brought out by rehearsing certain of the important points of difference usually said to divide causal–subsumptive from other more patterned approaches to the stratification of psychological life is that, while theorists of every stripe naturally engage in efforts to distinguish more or less abstract aspects of their subject matter, not everyone goes about doing so in the same way. Quite to the contrary, some – call them essentialists – commonly imagine that in brushing aside the more particular levels of psychological description they also somehow succeed in working their way closer towards the true, causal bedrock of mental life – that foundational place from which all of the concrete details of mundane experience can be, if not dismissed, at least regarded as the mere phenotypic expressions of other more commanding or authoritative genotypic causes. By contrast, others – referred to here as narrativists – routinely imagine a quite different sort of unity binding together the different levels of what are, for them, different orders of meaning. On this account the thick details that make up the particulars of your and our psychological experience need not be sacrificed on the altar of some more generic cause but instead require being understood as different renderings of what, at different viewing distances, can be alternatively described as analogous to the plot or genre or narrative structure of one and the same story.

In the end, we mean to suggest two things. One of these is that essentialist and narrativist solutions to the problem of psychological explanation deserve to be seen as occupying different but no less legitimate footings. That is, there are circumstances that sometimes favor one or the other of these available interpretive resources. The second is that while both can sometimes be made to work, and while many opportunistically rely on either in a pinch, individuals, and perhaps whole communities, appear to be marked by a preference for putting the bulk of their explanatory weight on either narrativist or essentialist interpretive frameworks. This, however, is not the place to begin. Rather, it first needs to be acknowledged that, at least for those of us who, by accident of birth, just happen to belong to the Judeo-Graeco-Roman-Christian-Renaissance-Enlightment-Romanticist intellectual tradition that, as Rorty (1987: 57) points out, pervades Euro-American culture, essentialism often seems to be, if not the only game in town, at least the only kind of explanation worth having. That is, for just about everyone belonging to this intellectual tradition, most complex things – including people – are automatically thought to require being understood as hierarchically organized systems whose deepest and most subterranean levels naturally contain all of the essential stuff that is required to work out the details of what happens next. Nor is this essentialist bias only to be found in the vernacular. Whether by cause, or as an effect, contemporary evolutionary biologists, computer scientists, and "machine functionalists" of just about every stripe also tend to equate explanation with causal accounting, and to suppose that something critical has been left out unless or until everything finds its proper place in the causal nexus. Consequently, those readers concerned with meaty matters involving the organizational structure of plants and animals, along with those steeped in the ways of silicon chips and the computer sciences would all be well within their rights to assume that, wholes and parts not withstanding, nothing is really explained until we know what brought it about.

What is obviously left out of all such antecedent-consequent scenarios is the competing, but underdeveloped, possibility that the unity that binds together the different levels of our internal organization need not be exclusively of that cause-and-effect variety so dear to the hearts of contemporary cognitive scientists but can, just as well, be found in other interpretive systems of a more narrative sort – systems that, for example, bind together the fragments of stories or situate them within different genres of the literary canon. Although we mean to come to this second possibility, and to illustrate it with evidence suggesting that persons reared apart from our own Euro-American culture do commonly understand the diachronic unity of themselves and other persons through just such narratively based interpretive schemes, this is also not the place to begin. Rather, what needs to be done first is to say something short and synoptic about those different and better-worked-out ways of explaining how plants and animals, and perhaps computer systems, are ordinarily broken down into their respective and usually causally related levels.

Machine functionalism and other approaches to double-entry bookkeeping

Psychologists are hardly the first or fastest out of the functionalism gate. Among contemporary biologists, for example, talk of functional systems whose existence and structure is said to have a *design,* and so a teleological explanation, is so commonplace as to be hardly worthy of comment (see, for instance, Greenberg and Tobach 1988). Evolved organisms, while arguably not the result of conscious design, just are, by virtue of their evolutionary history, more or less universally appreciated to have been naturally selected in such a way as to accomplish various tasks, and no one, or at least no one lately, is in the least embarrassed to say so (Sterelny 1990). Similarly, computer scientists are required, as a condition of their employment, to not only describe matters of layout and circuitry and otherwise detail the operating systems that govern the flow of information through their machines, but must, on risk of otherwise inadvertently building something else entirely, continually rehearse what it is that their devices are actually meant to do. By contrast, students of mental kinds and mental properties, lacking either a market niche or anything quite as bulletproof as natural selection within which to take refuge, have been generally slower to risk the charge of vitalism by frankly identifying psychological mechanisms by what they do, or what they are for. At least that is how it used to be. Of late, however, as no one will have failed to notice, the recent "mind meld" between neuroscientists, computational psychologists and certain philosophers of mind has given birth to a new breed of machine functionalists for whom easy talk about the hierarchical nature of the relations between "design features," "computational algorithms" and the "hardware" of physical implementation has become the common parlance. Charter members of this new language community include early functionalists such as Putnam (1967), whose intention was to demystify reductionism, and whose efforts consisted primarily of an attempt to preserve the integrity of intentional descriptions by driving a wedge between the computational structures of psychology and their physical, wet-lab realizations (Griffiths 1997). Still, whatever the original intent, these early attempts at double description have typically come to a bad end, promoting, for example (see Neimark 1985), the unhelpful idea that Chomsky and Piaget were pure "competence theorists," supposedly disinterested in the particular mundane behaviors of those concrete subjects presumably dear to the hearts of so-called "performance theorists" (Overton 1991a).

Tiring of such either-or approaches, a number of different theorists, employing diverse terminologies, have subsequently gone on to argue that there are in fact not *two*, but *three* distinctive domains of psychological explanation (Sterenly 1990: 43). High on any early list of those who have advocated just such a tripartite accounting strategy is David Marr (1982), whose seminal book *Vision* has become a classic (perhaps *the* classic) example of machine functionalism at work. In this much-cited text

> Marr proposed that an adequate approach to psychology must make use of three levels of description. The highest level describes the task which the psychological system accomplished ... the intermediate level describes how the system computes information in order to accomplish this task [and] the lowest level describes how the computational processes are implemented in the brain.
>
> (Griffiths 1997: 107)

More or less explicitly contained within this and other like-minded essentialist accounts is the idea that the highest of the three levels is automatically ceded to various evolutionary theorists (e.g. Cosmides and Tooby 1992), who take as their task the job of detailing the problems that certain mental mechanisms must solve. Neuroscientists are assigned the task of describing the physical mechanisms or hardware involved in implementation or "realization," while the intermediate or computational level is taken to be the natural province of psychology. Somewhat disappointingly, then, when the dust has finally settled around all of this supposedly cutting-edge conceptual machinery, everyone is revealed to be back at work in her or his original place, pretty much doing what they have always done. Without wishing to cost anyone their job, one could be forgiven for having held out hope for a bit more novelty from what is regularly billed as a new holistically regulated, hierarchical system of explanation (Overton 1991b).

All such understandable disappointments notwithstanding, it would nevertheless be a mistake to under-appreciate the significance of a collective enterprise that has gone as far as this one has in recognizing and perhaps legitimizing the importance of making a proper conceptual place for those idealized, abstract, formal or even mathematical design features that serve to specify the adaptational problems that various psychological systems are obliged to solve.

As Wertsch (1985) points out, Western approaches to cognitive psychology have traditionally kept their noses so close to the computational and hardware levels of description that they have often lost sight of the broader adaptational problems that particular cognitive systems are designed to solve. Rather more recently, however, just about everyone appears to be getting into the levels game. Millikan (1990), for example, talks of the importance of "remote functional descriptions," Pylyshyn (1984) stresses the significance of a "semantic" level of analysis, Dennett (1987) advocates attending to what he calls higher-order "fictional notational systems," Newell (1982) insists on the importance of a "knowledge level" of description, Griffiths (1997) refers to the importance of higher-order "task description," and Sterelny (1990) militates for something that Marr (1982) infelicitously called the "computational level" and which he prefers to describe as the "ecological level" of analysis.

In what follows, we mean to take all of these admonitions seriously, and to quickly agree that any accounting system that aims to provide an adequate description of psychological life must – in addition to working out certain necessary hardware and computational details – also concern itself with those recurrent functional problems that each of us, as exemplars of our own natural kind, are necessarily designed to grapple with. That much, at least, we happily stipulate to. What is not so obligatory, or so universally required, we mean to argue, is the arbitrary presumption that choosing to attend to matters of design (as well as the other more procedural levels of any functional system) also necessarily commits us to some variant of "machine functionalism" and its unwavering allegiance to a causal–subsumptive interpretation of the relations that obtain between the resulting levels of analysis. Neurons, as Marr (1982) suggests, may very well globally supervene upon the computational mechanisms of perception, and the broad functional design requirements of object perception may well set boundary conditions, or exercise a form of downward causation (Campbell 1970) upon the possible mechanisms of vision. None of this requires, however, that the relation, for example, between Užgiris' levels of "activity," "action" and "acts" also need to be understood as similarly constituting links in some causal chain. "Actions," on her account, neither cause nor are caused by the particular "acts" that instrument them, nor do the design features of "activities" somehow bring "actions" about. Activities, actions and acts are not different things in the way that causes are necessarily antecedent to, and so different from, their effects. Acts are actions reduced to the smallest common denominator, whereas activities are patterned relations among, and not the causal antecedents of, actions and acts. Rather, the three differ from one another in grain or scope but not in kind, and, instead of being similar descriptions of different things, constitute different descriptions of the same thing. In short, the causal–subsumptive relations thought to obtain between the putatively real entities proposed by Marr and other machine functionalists, and the various analytic or epistemologic relations said to hold between the several levels of description proposed by Užgiris are similar in their openness to functional analysis but differ in their assumed ontological status. Marr and others like him are what we will go on to describe as entity-based theorists or essentialists, whereas Užgiris advocates a form of connectedness between levels that we will characterize as more relational (Overton 1991b), or narrative-like.

Having hopefully raised the serious possibility that not all attempts to characterize the functional relations that hold between various levels of psychological explanation need be of a common piece, and that there is adequate room in the conceptual place that we keep such interpretive tools to accommodate both narrative-based and entity or essentialist forms of explanation, we mean to go on to raise a number of little-explored prospects, including the possibilities that: a) not only speculative philosophers and psychological theorists but also the rank and file, including young persons, can and do invoke *both* essentialist and narrative explanations in attempting to make sense of their own and others' psychological lives; b) certain cultural–historical factors work to "prime" or "privilege" one or the other of these explanatory modes, according it something like "the right of first refusal" in any attempt to negotiate a sense of personal coherence; c) either or both of these organizational schemes are approached differently by persons at differing junctures in the course of their own ontogenetic development; and d) anyone who fails to effect one or the other of these modes of self-interpretation risks falling into incoherence and losing any workable sense of connection to their own past or commitment to their own future. Before attempting to come to any of these more real-world possibilities, however, an important hurdle remains. The problem is that, if you are anything like a standard-issue instance of your own time and place, then, while talk of essentialism is likely to have about it the real ring of truth, the different things that are typically said about narrative schemes of organization risk being dismissed as just so much hand-waving. That is, no one – or at least no one born and bred to mainstream Euro-American culture – is likely to have any difficulty imagining that the particulars of their moment-to-moment behavior are merely the tail-like effects of the wagging of some bigger and more causal dog. Rather, such essentialist rhetoric is likely to seem as familiar and comfortable as an old shoe. By contrast, seemingly slippery talk about "narrative this" and "narrative that" initially comes across as decidedly foreign and is often recognized as already our own only with prompting. The section to follow aims to help level the playing field by reassuring you that while, given your likely history, essentialism may at first seem the only way to go, in actual point of fact our culture (perhaps any culture) also makes provision for a different and more narrative means of falling off the same log.

Part 2: Essentialists are from Mars, Narrativists are from Venus

Proposing, as we have already begun to do here, that it is reasonable to parse the great variety of available ways of stratifying psychological life into either narrativist or essentialist alternatives is obviously a dangerous business, best undertaken by falling in behind others who have preceded us out onto this thin ice. As it is, such potential stalking horses are hardly in short supply. It is possible, for example, to take refuge behind William James, who argued that "to say that all human thinking is essentially of two kinds, [essentialist] reasoning on the one hand, and narrative, descriptive, contemplative thinking on the other, is to say only what every reader's experience will corroborate" (as cited in Bruner 1986, first epigraph). Bruner's own "dual landscape" account amounts to much the same thing, and divides things (in roughly the ways we have divided them) into accounts that are primarily "propositional" and "paradigmatic," on the one hand, and different and more "narrative"-based approaches on the other. Mandler (1984) invoked much the same dichotomy between so-called "taxonomic" and "schematic" thought; as do Nisbett and his colleagues (Choi, Nisbett and Norenzayan 1999, Ross and Nisbett 1991), who distinguish between "analytic" and "holistic" schematic strategies.

The fact that we are not alone in playing the dangerous game of attempting to divide up whole intellectual traditions does nothing, however, to change the fact that more than two thousand years of Western intellectual history have especially prepared those of us who are its heirs to initially cast our lots with Plato and "the philosophers," and against Narratology and the practitioners of "mere" rhetoric (Ring 1987). As a result, our default strategy works to favor everything that is formal, and logical, and deductive (Hermans 1996) at the expense of anything that is abductive, relational, dialogical or multi-voiced. As a result we are led to collectively imagine that understanding matters as we might understand a story is just a way of whiling away our time before getting down to the really serious business of assigning each thing its proper place in the causal nexus. The alternative possibility – the possibility that, by focusing on objects instead of subjects, or by caring more about being rather than becoming (Berzonsky 1993), or by attending more to the a-chronology of models than to the chronology of sequence (Ricoeur 1985), we may have missed some or all of the real point – hardly occurs to us, and, if it does, it is rarely our first, or what we would judge to be our best, thought on the matter. Summing up such essentialist views, Schwartz (1979: 13) speaks for most of us in saying that:

> It seems to me that people observing the developmental stages in animals, or the changes in form of, say, water, would naturally be led to assume the existence of some underlying trait that makes some stuff or thing to be of a kind. It seems to me that there must be such an essence or my world view is radically false.

Of course, if that were all there were to it, if we were, after all, really ready to stand pat on our first intuition about essences and their authority over all of life's concrete details, then there would be no problem, and no need for this chapter. As it really is, however, doubts are often right around the corner, ready to creep in. In fact, in many cases, and especially in the case of ourselves, "creep in" will hardly cover it, and doubts – wholesale doubts – thunder about with a vengeance. What if, we ask ourselves, "being was not given once and for all, complete and perfect in an ultimate system of essences" (Schlesinger 1977: 271)? What if our familiar "container/substance view" of things is frankly mistaken, or even only sometimes mistaken (Holland 1997)? What if the real prospects of finding some enduring metaphysical something "standing behind the passing states of consciousness and our always shifting ways of being" really are as slim as William James (1891: 196) originally imagined? If any or all of these doubts are doubts worth having, "What is it then," we would need to ask again, "which links the parts to the whole?" An answer, and often our answer, it that "It is the fact that the connectedness of life can only be understood through meaning" (Dilthey 1961, as cited in Cohler 1988: 552) – meaning that can only be conferred by linking up the otherwise disparate parts of our understanding into some overarching narrative structure (Bruner 1986, Fraisse 1963, Nicolopoulou 1997).

Our point in naming names is not proselytory, or at least not to the point that we mean you to deny your faith in essentialism. Rather, we hope only to give assurances that, by professing some commitment to what we allege is more or less everyone's already present conviction that narrativity counts as a legitimate alternative means of giving unity and continuity to our experiences, you would not be entering into a pact with some postmodern devil. In fact, the prospect that narrativity also needs to be counted among the ways that we naturally order events can, as Peacock and Holland (1993: 368) point out, "be traced through many fields, from the cultural–historical school of psychology and related approaches (Volosinov 1986, Vygotsky 1987), to literary criticism (Bakhtin 1981, Lukács 1914) ... and to anthropological debates about the real versus constructed emphasis in self." If more reassurances are needed, it is also apparent that contemporary psychologists and philosophers of mind quick to applaud narrativity are themselves everywhere thick on the ground (e.g. Bruner 1990, Cohler and Cole 1996, Hermans, Kempen and Van Loon 1992, Kerby 1991, MacIntyre 1984, McAdams 1997, Polkinghorne 1998). While these names may or may not belong to your particular reference group, they do help to make the case that narrativity is not only the passion of the other and the obscure. In fact some (e.g. Miller 1996: 13) are prepared to argue that such narrative accounts have always been present in all societies, and were merely driven out of awareness, at least professional awareness, by certain "probabilistic modes of reasoning unique to only a handful of 'modern' cultures".

Be all this as it may, our point is not, as some would have it, either to win the argument that essentialist-based accounts have no legitimate standing as a way of ordering psychological experience, or to convince you that they can or should be entirely set aside in favor of other more narratively based alternatives. Any such new-lamps-for-old exchange would, we believe, have the unwanted effect of turning a blind eye, not only to roughly half of our potential explanatory resources, but to what it is that people ordinarily do when they go out in search of ways of making interpretive sense out of their psychological lives. Still, we don't wish to be seen as entirely even-handed, or as other than convinced that real gains are to be had by making room for interpretive schemes that include the possibility of narratively based order. Some of these interpretive advantages derive from the fact that narrative viewpoints open up a whole range of otherwise unfamiliar analytic strategies of the sort introduced into literary and historical scholarship by theorists such as Bakhtin (1986), Frye (1957), Propp *et al.* (1968), Rorty (1973), and White (1978), and recently put to especially good use by numerous psychologists (e.g. Bruner 1986, 1990, Lightfoot 1994, 1997, Nicolopoulou 1997, Sutton-Smith 1986), including Užgiris (1999). Similarly, because they have intended audiences, narratives often succeed, where essentialists' accounts fail, in being inherently more dialogical (Hermans 1996, Lewis and Ferrari, in press, Sarbin 1986, 1993). For much the same reasons, essentialist accounts fail by being situationally impermeable (Shweder and Bourne 1984), narrative frameworks of understanding are also more or less automatically open to the possibility that persons from different cultures might make use of different interpretive frameworks, discourses, practices, concepts, means and modalities for organizing experience (Holland 1997). As such, narrative accounts open a window onto the possibility of productive cultural comparisons that – as Užgiris pointed out – is characteristically closed to essentialist approaches which set themselves contrastively against any and all social and historical backgrounds by working to locate the real heart of any psychological matter in an abstract place as remote as possible from the inherently messy concrete details of cultural life.

To the degree that we have succeeded in our purpose, we will, by now, have brought you along with us to a point where you are at least willing to entertain the possibilities that what we have come to call essentialist and narrative approaches to the ordering of experience a) both count as viable alternative interpretive resources, b) are both likely present in some degree in the explanatory repertoires of professionals and laypersons alike and c) are potentially accessible to different degrees as a consequence of the operation of various cultural or historical factors that predispose some but not others to choose between them in their own efforts to order their experience. What follows in the third and final section of this chapter is an attempt to put some of these ideas to the test by exploring how young persons from Canada's cultural mainstream and from various aboriginal, or First Nations, communities differently undertake to interpret questions about their own self-continuity or personal persistence in time.

Part 3: Narrative and Essentialist conceptions of personal persistence: A cross-cultural comparison

If not the "self," then something very much like it, was doubtlessly on the minds of those responsible of getting the whole enterprise of articulating different "levels of explanation" under way in the first place. Like their counterparts concerned with other such complex systems, those in the business of describing matters of selfhood have traditionally tended to run off in opposite directions, with some imagining that what is "essential" about one self is equally true of them all, while others see only diversity, utter and absolute. What is clearly no longer in doubt is that the world's cultures do actually realize or instantiate selves in radically different ways (Holland 1997). This is, of course, music to the ears of your average dyed-in-the-wool relativist, for whom such evidence is seen as proof positive that there is not now, nor has there ever been, anything remotely like a necessary or constitutive design feature common to selves of every stripe. Rather, on this account, our certain knowledge about the clear and distinct ways that selves are differently manifested in other times and other places effectively gives the lie to all remnant claims about presumptively "universal" features of selfhood, unmasking them as just so many residual bits of lingering Eurocentric, phallio-tropic, neocolonialist thought.

In sharp contrast, others – including well-travelled others with their own otherwise winning ethnographic ways – wholly reject this "free to be you and me" rhetoric, and argue instead that, in order to be recognized as an instance of the category, selves must necessarily and always display certain universal design features that are taken to be constitutive of what selfhood must necessarily amount to in any understandable social world.

In the face of such starkly incommensurable prospects several possibilities present themselves, including the harsh alternatives that there either is, or there is not, something (anything) that is true of one self because it is true of them all. The better alternative, or so we will argue, is that when selves are envisioned as complex and multilayered systems, then it is entirely possible that, while, at one level of description, there are aspects of selfhood that require being understood as legitimately universal, there are other procedural or hardware levels of description or explanation on which some or all of what needs to be said requires to be said in the particular, leaving little that could aspire to be taken as common to all comers. That, at least, is the premise that has guided the ongoing program of research that we mean to briefly characterize as a way of ending this chapter – a cross-cultural study aimed at detailing what is common and what is not about the ways that culturally mainstream and aboriginal adolescents undertake to explain their own and others' self-continuity in the face of inevitable personal and cultural change.

Our purpose in rehearsing certain early aspects of these continuing empirical efforts is, we take it, something like the same purpose that guided Užgiris' attempts to explore the divisible places of activities, actions and acts in arriving at a broader understanding of imitation. That is, the aim of our colleagues and ourselves has been, and continues to be, to find a conceptual means of arbitrating between the competing universalistic and relativistic, or context-dependent, claims that continue to be made on the behalf of (in our case) selves – an analytic scheme that promises to go some distance toward repairing the chronic individual–society antinomy that has regularly cut psychology off from cultural life.

Again, like Užgiris, we mean to go about this task in three parts, by considering not only the particular responses of our young subjects to specific challenges to their own and others' personal persistence, but also by attempting to understand how these concrete "acts" instrument more generalized and culture-bearing procedures or mechanisms of self-understanding, which, for their own part, constitute different algorithmic (or "computational") means of realizing still more generic "social existence themes" (Shweder 1982: 46) or – dare we say it? – "universal" design features (Marr 1982) of the self. In what follows, then, we intend to say something about each of these distinctive levels of analysis. We begin by starting at the top.

Level I: Generic design features of the self

Notwithstanding the obvious fact that the great bulk of what has been written about selves focuses on how they are different one from another, there is, as it turns out, a perhaps surprisingly strong concert of opinion about the sorts of jobs that selves are evidently obligated to accomplish, including, for example, the widely agreed-to claims that they serve as the essential seat of human agency, and supply the synchronic coherence necessary for leading a unified life (James 1891). Of course, not every task analysis invariably leads to the same results, and, not surprisingly, there are always those who are prepared to write off agentiveness as a remnant of vitalism or who view claims about unity as an unwelcome legacy of the Enlightenment, wholly out of place in a postmodern world (Chandler 1997). What is, perhaps, surprising is that no one – or at least no one hesitant about riding unbridled relativism over the edge of some deconstructionist cliff – seems similarly prepared to doubt that continuity is a necessary, constitutive and therefore universal design feature of selves of any description. This is widely held to be the case for the reason that any account of selves that did not make adequate provision for counting each of us as somehow "timelessly" self-same across the various phases of our temporal existence would simply strike us as nonsensical (Luckman 1979) and fail to qualify as an adequate description of what selves are standardly taken to be (Cassirer 1923). This is seen to follow, not only because those aspects of formal logic having to do with such identity relations would otherwise be left in tatters, but because personal persistence appears to be a necessary prerequisite for any recognizably decent human social world. That is, without a workable means of understanding one another as somehow continuous in time the concept of moral duty would be emptied of meaning (Rorty 1973), grounds would no longer exist for allocating legal or political or moral responsibility (Whittaker 1992), and all prospects of looking forward to our own just desserts would no longer have meaning (Unger 1975). As such, the fundamental logic of identity is said to necessarily understand persons to be self-identical (Haber 1994) and as having whatever sort of temporal structure is necessary to allow them to be reidentified as one and the same person through time (Strawson 1959). For such reasons, it is perhaps not surprising that, what Flanagan (1996) calls the "one self to a customer rule" is generally endorsed and elaborated by a still longer list of contemporary philosophers (e.g. Hirsch 1976, MacIntyre 1977, Parfit 1971, Perry 1976, Taylor 1991, Wiggins 1980) and by a similar complement of touchstone psychological theorists (e.g. Piaget 1968, Erikson 1968). What is perhaps more unexpected is the extent to which continuity is also regarded as a non-elective design feature of the self by a host of otherwise committed cultural relativists (e.g., Geertz 1973, Hallowell 1976,

Shweder and Bourne 1984), all of whom agree that a sense of personal persistence is an immanent province at work in the whole of human affairs (Shotter 1984), a "universal in the human experience" (Levine and White 1986: 38), and so "ubiquitous to all of human kind" (Harré 1980: 397). Surprised or not, you are at least meant to be impressed that, in a world where even the best of friends rarely agree, this much concert of otherwise scattered opinion is uncommon at best, and goes some distance toward justifying the claim that continuity is an arguably universal design feature common to the whole of humankind.

Although scholarly consensus about the constitutive place of continuity in the design of selves clearly counts for something, it is, by itself, hardly enough to make the case. What is minimally needed, in addition, is some good empirical reason to believe that, in the regular conduct of their affairs, "ordinary" people also ordinarily struggle to defend the proposition that all of the different time-slices that together form their own careers necessarily represent different manifestations of one and the same continuous person. That is, it will hardly do to insist – for whatever heady philosophical reasons – that continuity is a constitutive condition of selfhood unless it can also be shown that more or less all of us proceed as though this were true. As it turns out, the data we and our colleagues are hard at work collecting (e.g. Chandler 2000, 2001, Chandler, Lalonde and Sokol 2000) goes some important distance toward making just this case.

Although this is not the place to go into elaborate detail about the particular procedures that have led to our being able to say so, as things have turned out, just about all of the nearly four hundred young persons that we have so far interviewed on the subject have gone to considerable lengths to convince us that, certain appearances to the contrary, they and others arguably persist as one and the same continuous individual despite often radical personal change. We say "just about all" advisedly because, to date, only some eighteen of our long list of respondents have utterly failed to come up with any, to them convincing, way of warranting the conclusion that they remain persistently themselves despite evident personal change. Interestingly (or so we mean to argue) all of these outlier adolescents were actively suicidal at the time of our testing (Ball and Chandler 1989, Chandler and Ball 1990), and had, through the various attempts they had made to end their own lives, already demonstrated a failed hope for any future filled with their own just desserts. Evidently, then, as our data strongly suggest, the conviction that continuity is a necessary design feature of any self worth having is not confined to a closeted group of academics, but is equally alive and well among rank-and-file adolescents.

The list of unanswered questions that the evidence so far cited still leaves open is obviously exceedingly large. If young people are as unanimous as we claim them to be in their first-order convictions that continuity is a non-elective design feature of selves, then: a) what are the second-order algorithms or procedural strategies by means of which they undertake to defend this common conviction; and b) how are these several potentially different ways of "computing" their own and others' self-continuity actually realized or instantiated in the particular concrete things they choose to say about their own and others, temporal persistence? More than all of that, how is it, in particular, that we have gone about putting such heady questions to a long train of usually closed-mouthed adolescents, and what is it, exactly, that they say in response? What, in short, do our data actually look like?

In undertaking to answer these various questions it seems best to break ranks with our own ordering system by continuing, not with an account of the broad Level II heuristics or procedural strategies employed by young people in warranting their own claims about self-continuity but rather by telling you first about the more concrete Level III responses of our various respondents, and the ways we went about soliciting them.

Level III: Concrete realizations of personal persistence

Because spontaneous remarks about continuities in one's self and others tend to be quite thin on the ground, our research group (e.g. Ball and Chandler 1989, Boyes and Chandler 1992, Chandler 2000, 2001, Chandler and Ball 1992, Chandler, Lalonde and Sokol 2000) has worked to invent methods and procedural ways of better insuring that the topic does regularly arise. We have gone about doing this in two ways. With specific reference to the self, we have standardly begun by asking the young people we have interviewed to describe themselves, both now and at an earlier point five-years in the past. We then hold up the discrepancies that normally characterize these two accounts, and ask our subjects to explain how it is that such different characterizations could possibly qualify as alternative descriptions of one and the same temporally continuous individual. In addition, and as a way of promoting discussion about continuities in the lives of others, we also regularly present these same respondents with standardized story materials about various fictional characters whose lives are marked by radical personal change. In particular, we have presented all of our adolescent subjects with either "Classic Comic Book" or heavily edited filmed versions of Victor Hugo's *Les Miserables* and Dickens's *A Christmas Carol*, and asked them to comment on the changing lives of Jean Valjean and Ebenezer Scrooge. Because some of our samples were drawn from different First Nations communities, we have also gone on to supplement these obviously culturally saturated bildungsromans with other versions of similar-story characters that were drawn from the local canon of aboriginal folk tales. After being exposed to some systematically varied subset of these testing materials, participants were routinely asked to describe these fictional characters at the beginning and at the end of their stories, and to offer reasons as to why these protagonists either were or were not the same person throughout. Whether being asked to focus on their own life, or on the lives of these story characters, subjects were regularly pressed to detail their reasons for concluding that the disparate time-slices in question are in fact different moments from the life of one and the same continuous person.

Not surprisingly, no two of our respondents ever "realized" the connections thought to obtain between different junctures in their own and others' lives in precisely the same way. That is, at this third level, comparable to Užgiris' specific "acts," individual differences are pervasive. There are, nevertheless, many fewer wholly unique ways of going about this task than there are individuals in our various samples of Native and non-Native youth. It is these evident similarities and differences that have informed our efforts to distinguish remarkably different algorithms, computational heuristics, or genre in the Level II self-continuity warranting strategies practiced by the culturally diverse targets of our research.

Although, depending upon how fine a grid one aims to draw, it is possible to distinguish between two and roughly ten different ways of categorizing the alternative self-continuity warranting practices that we have observed, our data do strongly support drawing a primary distinction between what we have characterized earlier as essentialist and narrativist approaches – this time to the problem of personal persistence.

Essentialist and narratively based self-continuity warranting strategies

Imagine yourself as a participant in our research. Imagine that you are either one of the one hundred and twenty adolescents that we have so far interviewed in two more or less remote First Nations communities, or, alternatively, one of their non-aboriginal age-mates living in a major metropolitan area. Suppose further that it had just been brought home to you that there are glaring discrepancies between the way that you currently describe yourself, and the ways you view yourself as having been some five-years earlier. Your task, on having this evidence of personal change rudely held up to you, is to explain why anyone should, nevertheless, take your present and former selves as understandably continuous or numerically identical instances of one and the same person. How would you proceed?

Well, if you are anything like the young participants in our several studies (or at least like all of those who were not actively trying to kill themselves at the time), then you would automatically take it as a given that all of the various episodes in your life are in fact episodes in the life of one and the same person. Your puzzle would be to make understandable to yourself and others how this could possibly be so. In the process, our data tell us, you would, in all likelihood, start down one or the other of two irreducibly different paths. Having started down one of these routes – the essentialist alternative – you would insist that, in spite of incontrovertible evidence of change, there is, nevertheless, still something about you, some more or less central or causally generic something (perhaps even your featureless and attributeless, God-given soul) that has stood sufficiently apart from the ravages of time to successfully vouchsafe your claims of personal persistence by itself stubbornly refusing to change. "My name, or my fingerprints, or my personality," you would say, "didn't change." Alternatively, you might regard any attempt to ferret out some essential something immune to the workings of time as a fool's errand, and opt instead to follow a more narrative path. On this account, what makes you persistently yourself is not the existence of some timeless entity but rather the fact that, when taken as a whole, your life amounts to a followable story of which you are the perennial hero. Like others, you might say, "I just grew up." Or, better still, you might say that you have "found a thread" tying together the various chapters of your life. In short, you would, if you were like one of our subjects, approach the problem of warranting your own self-continuity either by understanding your varied life as a container which houses some timeless causal essence, or as a narrative structure whose form and plot successfully weaves the various chapters in your life into a single coherent story.

Of course, neither essentialists nor narrativists are born into the world fully fledged, and so you might, if you were young in the ways of essentialism, think it enough to have identified almost anything at all about yourself (e.g. your "DNA" or your "street address") that stayed relentlessly the same while everything else was left free to vary. Or you might, as do still older essentialists in our sample, even suppose that the real you is some sort of productive genotype capable of generating endless phenotypic expressions of what is essentially you. "I was always a competitive guy," you might say. Alternatively, if you happen to be only a fledgling narrativist, you might, as do many of our less mature respondents, imagine that the story of your life is less like the elaborate plot of a classic bildungsroman or story of character development and more like the stripped-down chronologies of still simpler medieval romances or picaresque novels – stories in which the various time-slices of a life are only juxtaposed with one another or merely strung together like so many beads on a string. "First I did [this], and later went on to do that," you might claim. In fact, our own research (Chandler 2000, 2001, Chandler, Lalonde and Sokol 2000) suggest that it is possible to distinguish as many as four or five increasingly complex and age-graded ways of unwinding either essentialist or narrativist approaches to the problem of warranting personal sameness. That, however, is a different story.

This story is one of cultural variation. As it turns out, if you happen to be part of the Canadian cultural mainstream – that is, if, by accident of birth, you were born into that Judeo-Graeco-Roman-Christian-Renaissance-Enlightenment-Romanticist intellectual tradition which pervades Euro-American culture (Rorty 1987: 57) – then the chances are better than eight out of ten that you will also attempt to solve the problem of your own self-continuity by supposing that there is some more or less abstract essential part of you that has successfully stood outside of time and that accounts for your own personal persistence. If, on the other hand, you happen to be a young First Nations person whose ancient storytelling tradition dominates your cultural life, then, like some two thirds of your cohort, your default strategy will be to understand yourself in relational terms by arguing that there is an underpinning plot of narrative structure evident in your life that is responsible for ensuring that all of the chapters in your life are chapters in one and the same autobiography.

Summary and conclusion

In the context of her own work on imitation, Ina Užgiris argued persuasively that the logjam in our thinking – the one that consigns culture to the status of an afterthought cobbled onto the rest of our theorizing about cognitive and identity development only at the last minute – can only be broken by submitting our explanatory efforts to a kind of levels analysis that distinguishes the potentially universal design features of any operative system from the procedural heuristics and hardware realizations of its applications. She reasoned that without doing so we would remain the victims of the classical individual–society antinomy that has so consistently cut psychology off from cultural life.

In our own effort to better understand the dialectic between sameness and change that allows individuals to see themselves as continuous in the face of inevitable growth or decline, we have borrowed from this important page of Užgiris' work by undertaking to show that, while personal persistence needs to be counted as a universal design feature of every workable conception of selfhood, culture does not wait in the wings to dictate how our efforts to solve the problem of self-continuity are realized or instantiated at only the hardware level. Rather, as our own ongoing research clearly shows, culture reaches directly into the heart of those procedural or algorithmic or computational heuristics that allow us to solve the same design problem in radically different and culturally specific ways.

Note

1 The term "culture" is one of those deeply contested notions that has come to be so emptied of shared meaning that many contemporary anthropologists now judiciously avoid its use altogether (Holland 1997). As employed in this chapter, talk of this as opposed to that culture is meant only as a summarial gesture useful in pointing to the naked fact that, until scarcely more than a century ago, the First Nations of Western Canada lived lives separate and apart from traditions common to those European immigrants who subsequently colonized their land.

Acknowledgements

This research was supported by a Social Sciences and Humanities Research Council of Canada Standard Research Grant to the first author.

References

Bakhtin, M. M. (1981) *The Dialogic Imagination: Four Essays* (Holquist, M. (ed.), Emerson, C. and Holquist, M. (trans.)). Austin, TX: University of Texas Press.

Ball, L. and Chandler, M. J. (1989) "Identity Formation in Suicidal and Nonsuicidal Youth: The Role of Self-Continuity", *Development and Psychopathology*, *1*(3): 257–275.

Bernstein, R. (1983) *Beyond Objectivism and Relativism*. Philadelphia, PA: University of Pennsylvania Press.

Berzonsky, M. (1993) "A Constructivist View of Identity Development: People as Postpositivist Self-Theorists" in Kroger, J. (ed.) *Discussions on Ego Identity* (pp. 169–203) Hillsdale, NJ: Lawrence Erlbaum Associates.

Boyes, M. C. and Chandler, M. J. (1992) "Cognitive Development, Epistemic Doubt, and Identity Formation in Adolescence". *Journal of Youth and Adolescence, 21*(3): 277–304.

Brand, M. (1970) *The Nature of Human Action*. Glenview, IL: Scott, Foresman.

Broughton, J. (1981) "Piaget's Structural Development Psychology: II. Logic and Psychology", *Human Development, 24*(3): 195–224.

Bruner, J. S. (1986) *Actual Minds, Possible Worlds*. Cambridge, MA: Harvard University Press.

Bruner, J. S. (1990) *Acts of Meaning*. Cambridge, MA: Harvard University Press.

Campbell, K. (1970) *Body and Mind*. London: Macmillan.

Cassirer, E. (1923) *Substance and Function*. Chicago: Open Court.

Chandler, M. J. (1991) "Alternative Readings of the Competence-Performance Relation" in Chandler, M. and Chapman, M. (eds.) *Criteria for Competence: Controversies in the Conceptualization and Assessment of Children's Abilities* (pp. 5–18). Hillsdale, NJ: Lawrence Erlbaum Associates.

— (1997) "Stumping for Progress in a Post-Modern World" in Renninger, K. A. and Amsel, E. (eds.) *Change and Development: Issues of Theory, Method, and Application* (pp. 1–26). Mahwah, NJ: Lawrence Erlbaum Associates.

— (2000) "Surviving Time: The Persistence of Identity in This Culture and That", *Culture and Psychology, 6*: 209–231.

— (2001) "The Time of our Lives: Self-Continuity in Native and Non-Native Youth" in Reese, H. W. (ed.) *Advances in Child Development and Behavior (28*, pp. 175–221). New York: Academic Press.

Chandler, M. J. and Ball, L. (1990) "Continuity and Commitment: A Developmental Analysis of the Identity Formation Process in Suicidal and Non-Suicidal Youth" in Bosma, H. and Jackson, S. (eds.) *Coping and Self-Concept in Adolescence* (pp. 149–166). New York: Springer-Verlag.

Chandler, M. J., Lalonde, C. E. and Sokol, B. (2000) **"**Continuities of Selfhood in the Face of Radical Developmental and Cultural Change" in Nucci, L., Saxe, G. and Turiel, E. (eds.) *Culture, Thought, and Development* (pp. 65–84). Mahwah, NJ: Lawrence Erlbaum Associates.

Choi, I., Nisbett, R. E. and Norenzayan, A. (1999) "Causal Attribution Across Cultures: Variation and Universality", *Psychological Bulletin, 125*(1): 47–63.

Cohler, B. J. (1988) "The Human Studies and the Life History: The Social Service Review Lecture", *Social Service Review, 62*(4): 552–575.

Cohler, B. J. and Cole, T. (1996) "Studying Older Lives: Reciprocal Acts of Telling and Listening" in Birren, J. E. and Kenyon, G. M. (eds.) *Aging and Biography: Explorations in Adult Development* (pp. 61–76). New York: Springer.

Cosmides, L. and Tooby, J. (1992) "Cognitive Adaptations for Social Change" in Barkhow, J. H. and Cosmides, L. (eds.) *The Adapted Mind: Evolutionary Psychology and the Generation of Culture* (pp. 163–228). New York: Oxford University Press.

Cummins, R. (1983) *The Nature of Psychological Explanation*. Cambridge, MA: The MIT Press.

Dennett, D. C. (1987) *The Intentional Stance*. Cambridge, MA: MIT Press.

Dilthey, W. (1961) *Pattern and Meaning in History: Thoughts on History and Society*. New York: Harper.

Edel, A. (1988) "Integrative Levels: Some Reflections on a Philosophical Dimension" in Greenberg, G. and Tobach, E. (eds.) *Evolution of Social Behavior and Integrative Levels* (pp. 65–74). Hillsdale, NJ: Lawrence Erlbaum Associates.

Erikson, E. H. (1968) *Identity: Youth and Crisis*. New York: W. W. Norton and Associates.

Flanagan, O. (1996) *Self Expressions: Mind, Morals and the Meaning of Life*. New York: Oxford University Press.

Flavell, J. H. and Wohlwill, J. F. (1969) "Formal and Functional Aspects of Cognitive Development" in Elkind, D. and Flavell, J. H. (eds.) *Studies in Cognitive Development: Essays in Honor of Jean Piaget* (pp. 67–120). New York: Oxford University Press.

Fraisse, P. (1963) *The Psychology of Time*. New York: Harper & Row.

Frye, N. (1957) *Anatomy of Criticism: Four Essays*. Princeton, NJ: Princeton University Press.

Geertz, C. (1973) *The Interpretation of Cultures: Selected Essays*. New York: Basic Books.

von Glasersfeld, E. and Kelley, M. F. (1982) "On the Concept of Period, Phase, Stage, and Level", *Human Development, 25*: 152–160.

Goodnow, J. J. and Cashmore, J. (1985) "Some Reflections on Competence and Performance" in Neimark, E. D., DeLisi, R. and Newman, J. L. (eds.) *Moderators of Competence* (pp. 77–98). Hillsdale, NJ: Lawrence Erlbaum Associates.

Greenberg, G. and Tobach, E. (eds.) (1988) *Evolution of Social Behavior and Integrative Levels*. Hillsdale, NJ: Lawrence Erlbaum Associates.

Grene, M. (1988) "Hierarchies and Behavior" in Greenberg, G. and Tobach, E. (eds.) *Evolution of Social Behavior and Integrative Levels* (pp. 3–17). Hillsdale, NJ: Lawrence Erlbaum Associates.

Griffiths, P. E. (1997) *What Emotions Really Are: The Problem of Psychological Categories*. Chicago: University of Chicago Press.

Haber, H. F. (1994) *Beyond Postmodern Politics*. New York: Routledge.

Habermas (1979) *Communication and the Evolution of Society*. Boston: Beacon Press.

Hallowell, A. I. (1976) *Contributions to Anthropology: Selected Papers of A. Irving Hallowell*. Chicago: University of Chicago Press.

Harré, R. (1980) *Social being: A Theory for Social Psychology*. Lanham, NJ: Littlefield Adams.

Hermans, H. J. (1996) "Voicing the Self: From Information Processing to Dialogical Interchange", *Psychological Bulletin, 119*(1): 31–50.

Hermans, H. J., Kempen, H. J. and Van Loon, R. J. (1992) "The Dialogical Self: Beyond Individualism and Rationalism", *American Psychologist, 47*(1): 23–33.

Hirsch, E. (1976) *The Persistence of Objects*. Philadelphia: University City Science Center.

Holland, D. (1997) "Selves as Cultured: As Told by an Anthropologist Who Lacks a Soul" in Ashmore, R. D. and Jussin, L. J. (eds.) *Self and Identity: Fundamental Issues* (pp. 160–190). New York: Oxford University Press.

James, W. (1891) *The Principles of Psychology*. London: Macmillan and Company.

Kerby, A. P. (1991) *Narrative and the Self*. Bloomington, IN: Indiana University Press.

Lefebvre-Pinard, M. and Pinard, A. (1985) "Taking Charge of One's Cognitive Activity: A Moderator of Competence" in Neimark, E. D., DeLisi, R. and Newman, J. L. (eds.) *Moderators of Competence* (pp. 77–98). Hillsdale, NJ: Lawrence Erlbaum Associates.

Levine, R. A. and White, M. I. (1986) *Human Conditions: The Cultural Basis of Educational Development*. New York: Routledge and Kegan Paul.

Lewis, M. and Ferrari, M. (in press) "Cognitive-Emotional Self-Organization in Personality Development and Personal Identity" in Bosma, H. A. and Kunnen, E. S. (eds.) *Identity and Emotions: A Self-Organizational Perspective*. Cambridge, England: Cambridge University Press.

Lifton, R. J. (1970) *Boundaries: Psychological Man in Revolution*. New York: Random House.

Lightfoot, C. (1994, June) *Literary Forms of the Hero, and Adolescents' Narratives of Risk-Taking*. Paper presented at the 24th Annual Meeting of the Jean Piaget Society, Chicago, IL.

— (1997) *The Culture of Adolescent Risk-Taking*. New York: Guilford Publications.

Luckman, T. (1979) "Personal Identity as an Evolutionary and Historical Problem" in von Cranach, M. (ed.) *Human Ethology: Claims and Limits of a New Discipline* (pp. 56–74). New York: Cambridge University Press.

Lukács, G. (1914) Zur sociologie des modernen dramas. *Archiv für Sozial wissenschaft und Sozialpolitik, 38*: 303–345.

Lycan, W. G. (1981) "'Is' and 'Ought' in Cognitive Science", *The Behavioral and Brain Sciences, 4*: 344–345.

MacIntyre, A. (1977) "Epistemological Crises, Dramatic Narrative and the Philosophy of Science", *The Monist, 60*: 453–472.

—— (1984) *After Virtue: A Study in Moral Theory.* Notre Dame, IL: University of Notre Dame Press.

Mandler, J. M. (1984) *Stories, Scripts, and Scenes: Aspects of Schema Theory.* Hillsdale, NJ: Lawrence Erlbaum Associates.

Marr, D. (1982) *Vision.* New York: W. H. Freeman.

Mayr, E. (1982) *The Growth of Biological Thought.* Cambridge, MA: Harvard University Press.

McAdams, D. P. (1997) "The Case for Unity in the (Post)modern Self: A Modest Proposal" in Ashmore, R. D. and Jussim, L. J., *Self and Identity: Fundamental Issues* (pp. 46–78). New York: Oxford University Press.

Miller, J. G. (1996) "Theoretical Issues in Cultural Psychology" in Berry, J. W., Poortinga, Y. H. and Pandley, J. (eds.) *Handbook of Cross-Cultural Psychology: vol. 1. Theory and Method* (pp. 85–128). Boston: Allyn and Bacon.

Millikan, R. G. (1990) "Truth Rules, Hoverflies, and the Kripke-Wittgenstein Paradox", *Philosophical Review, 99*(3): 323–353.

Neimark, E. D. (1985) "Moderators of Competence: Challenges to the Universality of Piagetian Theory" in Neimark, E. D., DeLisi, R. and Newman, J. L. (eds.) *Moderators of Competence* (pp. 1–14). Hillsdale, NJ: Lawrence Erlbaum Associates.

Nelson, K. (1978) "Structural and Developmental Explanations: Stages in Theoretic Development", *The Behavioral and Brain Sciences, 1*(2): 196–197.

Newell, A. (1982) "The Knowledge Level", *Artificial Intelligence, 18*: 87–127.

Nicolopoulou, A. (1997) "Worldmaking and Identity Formation in Children's Narrative Play-Acting" in Cox, B. D. and Lightfoot, C. (eds.) *Sociogenetic Perspectives on Internalization* (pp. 157–187). Mahwah, NJ: Lawrence Erlbaum Associates.

Olson (1978) "A Structuralist's View of Explanation: A Critique of Brainerd", *The Behavioral and Brain Sciences, 1*: 197–198.

Overton, W. F. (1991a) "Competence, Procedures, and Hardware: Conceptual and Empirical Considerations" in Chandler, M. and Chapman, M. (eds.) *Criteria for Competence: Controversies in the Conceptualization and Assessment of Children's Abilities* (pp. 19–42). Hillsdale, NJ: Lawrence Erlbaum Associates.

—— (1991b) "Historical and Contemporary Perspectives on Developmental Theory and Research Strategies" in Downs, R. M., Liben, L. S. and Palermo, D. S. (eds.) *Visions of Aesthetics, the Environment and Development: The Legacy of Joachim F. Wohlwill* (pp. 263–311). Hillsdale, NJ: Lawrence Erlbaum Associates.

Parfit, D. (1971) "Personal Identity", *Philosophical Review, 80*(1): 3–27.

Peacock, J. L. and Holland, D. C. (1993) "The Natural Self: Life Stories in Process", *Ethos, 21*(4): 367–383.

Perry, J. (1976) "The Importance of Being Identical" in Rorty, A. O. (ed.) *The Identities of Persons* (pp. 67–90). Berkeley, CA: University of California Press.

Piaget, J. (1968) *On the Development of Memory and Identity* (Duckworth, E., trans.). Barre, MA: Clark University Press/Barre Publishers.

Polkinghorne, D. (1988) *Narrative Knowing and the Human Sciences.* Albany, NY: SUNY Press.

Propp, V., Wagner, L. A., Scott, L. and Dundes, A. (1968) *Morphology of the Folktale.* Austin: University of Texas Press.

Putnam, H. (1967) "Psychological Predicates" in Capitan, W. H. and Merrill, D. D. (eds.) *Art, Mind, and Religion: Proceedings of the 1965 Oberlin Colloquium in Philosophy* (pp. 37–48). Pittsburgh, PA: University of Pittsburgh Press.

— (1999) *The Threefold Cord: Mind, Body, and World.* New York: Columbia University Press.

Pylyshyn, Z. (1984) *Computation and Cognition.* Cambridge, MA: MIT Press.

Ricoeur, P. (1985) "History as Narrative and Practice", *Philosophy Today, 29*: 213–222.

Ring, M. (1987) *Beginning with the Pre-Socratics.* Mountain View, CA: Mayfield Publishing.

Rorty, A. O. (1973) "The Transformations of Persons", *Philosophy, 48*: 261–275.

— (1987) "Persons as Rhetorical Categories", *Social Research, 54*(1): 55–72.

Ross, L. and Nisbett, R. E. (1991) *The Person and the Situation: Essential Contributions of Social Psychology.* New York: McGraw-Hill.

Salthe, S. N. (1988) "Notes Toward a Formal History of the Levels Concept" in Greenberg, G. and Tobach, E. (eds.) *Evolution of Social Behavior and Integrative Levels* (pp. 53–64). Hillsdale, NJ: Lawrence Erlbaum Associates.

Sarbin, T. R. (1986) "The Narrative as a Root Metaphor for Psychology" in Sarbin, T. R. (ed.) *Narrative Psychology: The Storied Nature of Human Conduct* (pp. 3–21). New York: Praeger.

— (1993) "The Narrative as the Root Metaphor for Contextualism" in Hayes, S. C. and Hayes, L. J. (eds.) *Varieties of Scientific Contextualism* (pp. 51–65). Reno, NV: Context Press.

Schlesinger, A. (1977) "The Modern Consciousness and the Winged Chariot" in Gorman, B. and Wessman, A. (eds.) *The Personal Experience of Time* (pp. 268–288). New York: Plenum Publishing.

Schwartz, S. P. (1979) "Natural Kind Terms", *Cognition, 7*: 301–315.

Shotter, J. (1984) *Social Accountability and Selfhood.* Oxford: Basil Blackwell.

Shweder, R. A. (1982) "Beyond Self-Constructed Knowledge: The Study of Culture and Morality", *Merrill-Palmer Quarterly, 28*(1): 41–69.

Shweder, R. A. and Bourne, L. (1984) "Does the Concept of the Person Vary Cross-Culturally?" in Shweder, R. A. and Levine, R. A. (eds.) *Culture Theory: Essays on Mind, Self, and Emotion* (pp. 158–199). Cambridge, England: Cambridge University Press.

Smedslund, J. (1977) "Piaget's Psychology in Practice", *British Journal of Educational Psychology, 47*: 1–6.

Sterelny, K. (1990) *The Representational Theory of Mind: An Introduction.* Cambridge, MA: Blackwell.

Strawson, P. F. (1959) *Individuals.* New York: Routledge.

Sutton-Smith, B. (1986) "Children's Fiction Making" in Sarbin, T. R. (ed.) *Narrative Psychology: the Storied Nature of Human Conduct* (pp. 67–90). New York: Praeger.

Taylor, C. (1985) *Philosophical Papers: vol. 1. Human Agency and Language.* New York: Cambridge University Press.

— (1991) *The Malaise of Modernity.* Concord, Canada: House of Anansi Press.

Unger, R. M. (1975) *Knowledge and Politics.* New York: The Free Press.

Užgiris, I. Č. (1999) "Imitation as Activity: Developmental Aspects" in Nadel, J. and Butterworth, G. (eds.) *Imitation in Infancy* (pp. 186–206). New York: Cambridge University Press.

Volosinov, V. N. (1986) *Marxism and the Philosophy of Language.* Cambridge, MA: Harvard University Press.

Vygotsky, L. S. (1987) *The Complete Works of L. S. Vygotsky: vol. 1. Problems of General Psychology* (Rieber, R. W. and Carton, A. S. eds.) New York: Plenum Press.

Vygotsky, L. S., Cole, M., John-Steiner, V., Scribner, S. and Souberman, E. (1978) *Mind in Society: The Development of Higher Psychological Processes.* Cambridge, MA: Harvard University Press.

Wertsch, J. V. (1981) "The Concept of Activity in Soviet Psychology: An Introduction" in Wertsch, J. V. (ed.) *The Concept of Activity in Soviet Psychology* (pp. 3–36). Armonk, NY: M. E. Sharpe.

— (1985) *Vygotsky and the Social Formation of Mind*. Cambridge, MA: Harvard University Press.

White, H. (1978) *Topics of Discourse*. Baltimore, MD: Johns Hopkins University Press.

Whittaker, E. (1992) "The Birth of the Anthropological Self and its Career", *Ethos, 20*(2): 191–219.

Wiggins, D. (1980) *Sameness and Substance*. Cambridge, MA: Harvard University Press.

Zylstra, U. (1992) "Living Things as Hierarchically Organized Structures", *Synthese, 91*: 111–133.

Part III

Some final thoughts

Infancy as the foundation for intersecting individual, social, and cultural processes

10 Lessons from our infancy

Relationships to self, other, and nature

Alan Fogel

What is the developmental legacy of the sensorimotor period? In some accounts this period of life before language is treated as merely a stepping stone to later social and cognitive competence, necessary but something to be transcended and forgotten. Others place more value on this period as the basis for motor skills, such as how to reach and manipulate, navigate in the world, and find hidden objects. These are obviously important skills that remain and continue to grow as new motor skills are added: everything from athletics to complex tool use.

I shall argue that the sensorimotor period constitutes the foundation for the embodiment of the self, which encompasses all aspects of the adult psyche. During the sensorimotor period, the individual acquires ways of relating, of being-in-the-world, that are foundational to every later experience of relationship. During the sensorimotor period, for example, we acquire some of the following patterns of relational connection which will be reviewed in more detail in the remainder of this chapter.

- People establish a connection with themselves, with their physical bodies, senses and feelings including emotions.
- People establish a connection with the important other people in their lives.
- People establish a connection with the natural world.

Each of these relationships is embedded in a culture that educates and regulates the types of connections that are possible. Užgiris saw that sensorimotor development was as much a sociocultural process as the acquisition of language and cognition. She wrote: "It is my hope that researchers in the future will systematically examine nonverbal systems across cultures much as language socialization researchers have begun examining verbal routines as powerful sites of socialization" (Užgiris 2000: 139). Cultural traditions – familial, community and society – pattern the way we relate to ourselves, to other people and to nature, patterns which may last a lifetime and be communicated to successive generations.

A relational perspective

All living systems are networks of relationships both within the organism and between the organism and its surround. For Piaget (1952, 1954), schemes are conceptualized as a relationship between child and environment. Schemes are relational procedures such that the meaning of an event to the individual is the scheme: that is, the way in which the child engages with the environment through action. An object is not taken by the infant as separate from the self but rather in relation to the self. Objects are suckable, graspable, or viewable (Lockman, Chapter 7). The same is true of adults. Objects are always perceived and conceived in terms of sensorimotor and/or sociocultural schemes which concretely link action and intention (movement, thought, feeling) to the world.

In a systems perspective, relationships are primary and the "entities" are characterized by their part in the relationship (Fogel 1993). The distinction between discrete and systems views is similar to the constructive versus essentialist distinction made by Chandler and Sokol in the previous chapter. Systems views of relationship can be found in the concept of negotiated meaning proposed by Budwig (Chapter 5), and the idea of fluid dynamics in relationships proposed by Valsiner (Chapter 1).

An elementary example is the relationship between plants and animals in the biosphere. Plants have receptors for carbon dioxide. They are waiting to be completed by an animal's exhalations. Animals expect and need the oxygen given off by plants. In the discrete view, you can say that essentially distinct animals communicate with essentially distinct plants by an exchange of gases. In the systems view, you would say that animals cannot be complete as living beings without oxygen. They would die, but it is not that trivial. Animals have a blank spot, an incompleteness, that must merge with something from our planetary companions. By becoming complete the animals can breathe, and that makes the plants complete. When the plant–animal system moves toward completion, plants and animals have the opportunity to take on specific forms and characters in relation to each other. Flowers and bees, grazing animals and grasslands: these are relationships whose inherent processes (large herds allow only grasses to survive and grasses sustain the herd size) define the evolution of individuals through time.

A human relationship is an historically developing communication system encompassing action, physiological processes and the psychological meaning of those processes to each individual. When we use the word "relationship", therefore, we are talking about a living, developing system. To say that people are inherently relational means that they are inherently incomplete and indeterminate (Fogel, Lyra and Valsiner 1997, Valsiner, Chapter 1). It means that people must find themselves in the Other, become who they are through the Other intersubjectively (Toma and Wertsch, Chapter 6). The baby requires milk, love, toys, and touch to flesh out the possibilities of sensorimotor experience. The child requires teachers to realize fully the dimensions of the cultural self (Raeff, Chapter 2).

Many of the authors in this book recognize that the possibilities for the self are connected to other people and to the culture. Different people emerge out of living in an essentialist compared to a narrativist culture (Chandler and Sokol), in a chaotic compared to an organized one (Wachs and Çorapçi), in a culture that values parent–child symmetry as opposed to asymmetry (Ramirez), or in a social world dominated by one's own compared to another's perspective (Budwig).

Constructivist perspectives on development may or may not be relational. If essentially separate entities are being constructed via their discourse with each other, mediated by cultural forms of communication, this is not relational in my sense. If "the other" comes into being at the same time that I do, and if the self-other system forms a cultural character in the process, that is relational (Buber 1958, Fogel 1993, Levinas 1969). It is relational if constructivism means something like "a system in the process of coalescing into recognizable or describable characteristics," or "forms emerging out of an ongoing oneness which itself and at the same time is taking form and informing the emerging forms within it."

Hinde's (1985) analysis of animal conflict, for example, suggests that the initial postures and threat displays of rival animals do not exactly specify their internal states. The animals may not be entirely certain of their intentions at the time of the displays. Hinde writes: "Such signals are thus to be seen as involving negotiation with the rival as well as an expression of internal state. The term negotiation does not necessarily imply manipulation but emphasizes the continuous interaction between the two individuals involved" (1985: 111).

This observation suggests that under some conditions, information – in the form of each individual's experience of the partner – is the *result*, and not the cause, of communication. The communication process, therefore, is a dynamic system in which the whole is more than the sum of its parts, in which order emerges as constituents self-organize, and in which meaning–information is created in the process (Fogel 1993).

An alternative view of relationships, called the discrete perspective, is that relationships are linkages of separate entities. Virtually all theories of communication and human development – with the exception of Piaget, Vygotsky, and dynamic systems theory – rest on this Cartesian dualistic assumption. There are senders and receivers who exchange signals. There are innate and acquired characteristics. There are mothers and children who have endowments to reach out toward the other. In this perspective, the entities are primary and the relationships are an afterthought, a way of connecting these lonely parts.

Discrete or essentialist approaches differ from relational approaches in their conceptualization of change. In the discrete approach, separate entities come to "know" each other, to "share" states of consciousness intersubjectively. This is believed to occur via a learning process in which repeated signals from the "other" are decoded and interpreted from the "individual's" perspective and then coded into signals for sending to the "other." Change in this view is an incremental building-up of associations between each "individual's" "internal" state and particular communication signals (gestures or symbols).

The words enclosed in quotes in the previous paragraph refer to conceptual entities that are bounded and complete. These entities know themselves and what they mean to communicate to other such bounded entities. The interpersonal relationship is a collection of entities engaged in coding and decoding messages from "outside themselves." Growth is the incremental mapping of codes to already known feelings or thoughts.

Piaget (1952) described the limitations of essentialist thinking when used as an explanation of development. Associations were not sufficient to capture development because there was no reason for the individual to care about which associations were more or less interesting. Piaget saw that the motive for change was a perceived incompleteness, what he called disequilibration. Essentialist entities are by definition complete (or else they would not be entire, total, bounded, self-known). And, if they were incomplete they would be in need of something from "outside themselves." But to need something from "outside" as an essential component of one's being must mean that the "outside" is part of the individual after all (because the "outside" is needed to constitute and complete the individual).

Piaget's concept of assimilation is at the heart of his relational perspective. Individuals are inherently incomplete and need to take in and digest in order to move toward completion or equilibration. But the individual can never be fully complete. The constant assimilation process gives an inherent motive to change because the individual requires particular forms of nourishment creating intentions to seek them out. Since no form of nourishment is itself complete, the individual must accommodate to accept it, changing the form of the nourishment in the same process of self change.

Levinas (1969) described the Greek essentialism that is the foundation of Western culture as totalizing. Each person is complete in itself and could be fully described and known if enough time and effort were expended to exhaust its list of characteristics. The alternative view is infinitizing. There is no way to know all the characteristics of the other because the other is incomplete, waiting to be defined by communication, communication that never completely exhausts the possibilities (see also Ganguly 1976, Whitehead 1978). The act of communication changes the other and the self in the process. The person one began to get to know is not the same person later.

In my research, I have found that some interpersonal processes have the character of totalizing. The other is seen as an essential object, treated stereotypically or with contempt, leaving no room for the other to open to new possibilities. These types of communication feel strained, alienating or coercive. This is what Buber (1958) called an "I–It" relationship.

When one approaches the other with an acceptance of their own and the other's incompleteness, both people change. There is an opening toward each other, a mutual assimilation and accommodation that I call symmetrical co-regulation (Fogel and Lyra 1997). Each person allows the other to enter into the spaces of their own incompleteness, to take them in and to change in the process, what Buber called the "I–Thou" relationship.

All such communications are inherently creative. People make discoveries about themselves and about the other person, and even about the cultural media by which they communicate. Change occurs by a spontaneous process of creativity or emergence that needs no further explanation. Call it equilibration, or creativity, or emergence, or discovery: something new arises when people approach each other with acceptance and a willingness to be affected. The alter ego is the person with whom we allow ourselves to be altered.

In the remainder of this chapter, I will describe the types of relationship that are being formed during the sensorimotor period: with self, with other, and with nature. I conclude with a discussion of the importance of this period for later life.

Relationship to self

Because people are inherently incomplete and indeterminate, people spend a lifetime getting to know themselves. People are not always aware of their thoughts, feelings or sensations. During the sensorimotor period, people establish a connection with themselves, with their physical bodies, senses, and feelings including emotions. Primary and secondary circular reactions are discoveries about how one part of the self is or is not connected to another part, as when babies visually inspect their moving hands. This is the period in life when all the basic emotions are developed. Babies also acquire an awareness of the ability to make competent intentional actions and feel a sense of accomplishment or despair.

Infants in the first six months are able to tell the differences between the movements of their own bodies and the movements of other people and objects. At five months, infants perceive the hand as a visual entity that "belongs" to the self by comparing the limits of the hand's trajectory with that of the environmental background while at the same time feeling the hand proprioceptively with respect to intentional movements. The infant's psychological experience of the hand's proprioceptive and tactile perspective is in a dialogical relationship with the infant's psychological experience of viewing the hand, from the proprioceptive and visual perspective of the eyes and head (Fogel, de Koeyer, Bellagamba and Bell 2002).

The research currently being done in my laboratory shows that from the first days of life, the infant's intrapersonal self-dialogues are embedded in interpersonal dialogues, leading some to reject the notion of an "autistic" or "individual" sense of self in early infancy (cf. Stern 1985, for a discussion of these views and their alternatives). Young infants experience "primary intersubjectivity," in which the self emerges as part of a mutually regulated exchange between infant and adult (Trevarthen and Hubley 1978).

In the following example, from our research (Fogel *et al.* 2002), nine-month-old Susan is pounding a table as her mother participates. Susan was one of ten infants videotaped weekly in the first year and biweekly in the second year of life during free play with their mothers.

Susan sits in the high chair with mother opposite her. As mother taps the table, Susan turns her head to watch mother's hands. Mother says, "Show mama how you pound." Susan looks straight into mother's eyes. Mother repeats the same sentence in a rhythmic fashion, as if she is pounding. The infant starts to pound the table with a faint smile on her face. Mother exclaims, "YEAH! That's a good girl!" and starts smiling too. Susan starts to alternate between looking at her own and at mother's pounding hand. She starts hitting the table more and more vigorously while looking intently at her hands. Again, she alternates between looking at mother's hand and her own hand. Then, she grabs mother's hand and watches it closely. She looks at its palm, turns it upside down, puts it palm-down on the table and turns it back up. Then, she drops it. She lifts up both arms, hits them forcefully on the table and shouts, "Ah!" Mother smiles while she softly repeats the infant's "Ah." Susan rests her hands and head on the side of the chair.

(Fogel *et al.* 2002: 198)

Susan clearly compares her own experience of herself with that of the mother. The mother seems to amplify Susan's self-awareness by imitating the infant's actions and rhythm with her hand and her voice. In this manner, Susan establishes a new relationship with herself: she comes to experience her own hand in a novel way by comparing it to mother's hand. Susan's emotions are linked to her emerging self-awareness in relation to the creative expansion of those emotions by the mother's emotional responses.

One legacy of the interpersonal process in which relationships to self are embedded is the ability – or lack of it – to accept, feel, recognize, and be open to one's own and other's actions, thoughts, sensations and emotions. In the previous example, Susan and her mother engage in an open, infinitizing process in which there is ample opportunity for creative expansion of self and other awareness. In the following example from our data, a more totalizing one, Susan at fifteen months and her mother engage in a battle of wills. Susan wants to climb up the slope of the slide. Her mother wants her to climb up from the steps. This pattern repeats several times without many variations, over several months of observation.

Susan and her mother are playing with the slide. Susan attempts to climb up the slope. Mother resolutely intervenes, "No, Susan, no! Don't climb up the slide like that!" Susan looks at her mother and continues her behavior. Mother catches Susan by the arm and says, "Come on, walk around!" Susan appears to understand mother's prohibition but she continues to climb up from the same side. Mother raises her voice saying, "No, no, no!" as she holds Susan, bringing her forcefully to the opposite side of the slide. Susan starts screaming and wriggling. She arches her body, shakes her head to say "no" and throws herself on the floor. Mother stops holding her and Susan walks right back to the slope. Before climbing, Susan turns around and stares at her mother's face, as if to see her reaction. Mother, in anger, says again, "No, don't!" Susan persists in attempting to climb the slope.

(Fogel *et al.* 2002: 201)

Mother's prohibitions appear to strengthen Susan's tendency to do it her own way. Because this battle of wills is repeated more or less without change over several months, this is a dialogue without creativity and spontaneity, in which each partner is totalizing the other and there is little room for change.

Susan appears to be a normally developing infant who has primarily creative (infinitizing, I–Thou) patterns of communication with her mother, as illustrated in the example of pounding the table. Susan and her mother also engage in rigid (totalizing, I–It) patterns such as the example of the slide. In some cases – when there is need for safety, protection, or establishing limits on behavior – totalizing patterns are necessary in relation to the background of primarily infinitizing communication. In this way, children may learn the physical and cultural limitations of their action. Standing apart from the parent may also allow the child to develop emotional resources for dealing with difficult situations.

Other infants in our sample have a relationship to mother that is primarily totalizing, with relatively little opportunity for creativity. Our observations show that under these conditions, the infant loses touch with his or her own body, sensations, and emotions. One mother did not like her infant son to suck on his hand. Even when he was as young as three months of age, she used strong prohibitions and pulled his hand out of his mouth. Similar patterns arose later as this mother continued to limit or prohibit the infant's initiative and intentional actions. By five months, this baby showed severely restricted and tense facial expressions. His smiles were strained and brief, lacking evidence of joy and spontaneity. His infrequent attempts to resist were subdued and barely visible, very unlike the ready availability of Susan's active defiance. His affect was flat and his behavior often seemed aimless, as if this child was not aware of having his own intentions.

It is impossible to ascertain whether these developmentally emerging patterns of communication – toward more infinitizing or totalizing processes – are due to the mother or to the child. Attribution of cause or blame comes from an essentialist paradigm. All we can say is that the mother–infant relationships tend to evolve or grow into a number of recognizable patterns, some of which lead the infant into a fuller and more creative relationship with the self and others of which lead to a more constrained and apparently painful relationship with the self.

Relationship to other people

Relationships to the self are embedded within interpersonal relationships. The process by which early relational patterns become transformed into later ones is as yet unknown but it is clear that the sociocultural management of infant self-exploratory dialogues in infancy may form predispositions toward particular forms of relational communication, with self and with others, in later life (Fogel, in press, Freud 1926, Lewis 1995, Stern 1985, Winnicott 1971).

The prevailing view of how early relational patterns are preserved later is Bowlby's internal working model of attachment. In this perspective, the relational patterns experienced by the infant become internalized and reconstituted when that person enters into other intimate relationships that evoke strong needs for proximity maintenance. This view, however, tends to suggest that each individual carries an essentialist trait-like ability to evoke certain kinds of communication patterns with another person.

Maintaining a relational perspective, on the other hand, it may be speculated that the developmental continuity is carried in the self–self relationship. A primarily infinitizing and creative relationship to oneself, as opposed to a primarily totalizing and self-limiting relationship, is likely to be a relational seed that is implanted into all later interpersonal relationships. This seed can propagate itself, even reproduce itself, because self–self relationships are from birth commingled with interpersonal relationships. There is no need, in this view, to locate the "carrier" of attachment patterns inside the individual because the self–self relationship is inherently relational with respect to other people.

One source of evidence for this perspective is that attachment patterns during the first two years of life are not remembered in the form of explicit memory; they cannot be "located" inside the self. Recent research shows that, contrary to earlier views of infantile amnesia, older children and adults appear to retain memories of infancy experiences that are embodied in action and emotion in relational contexts (Fogel, in press). Some of these memories are implicit while others are what I call participatory memories because they are enacted and felt in the self–self relationship rather than thought about, such as a sudden fearful feeling of falling, or a feeling of safety when curled up in a fetal position.

Explicit memory – also called autobiographical memory – begins in the third year of life. It is linked to a rational system that is analytical, with conscious appraisal processes, and encoded in symbols. There is no evidence that people have explicit memories from earlier than three years of age (Rubin 2000). Implicit memory is part of an experiential system that is primarily emotional, concrete, and mediated by "vibes" from past experiences rather than by explicit judgements and appraisals (Epstein 1991). This is similar to William James's distinction between knowledge by description (explicit) and knowledge by acquaintance (implicit).

Implicit memories have been used to explain skill learning, such as driving a car or playing a musical instrument. Implicit memories are specific to the context (sitting behind a steering wheel or at a piano keyboard) and are sensorimotor. These are not memories "about" driving an automobile or performing music. Rather, the memory is constituted relationally in the performance itself, not separate from it. Implicit memories are from the past but may not correspond to a specific source event, time or location (Schacter 1996). According to Siegal (2001: 74),

Although we may never recall 'explicitly' what happened to us as infants, the experiences we had with our caregivers have a powerful and lasting impact on our implicit processes. These experiences ... involve our emotions, our behaviors, our perceptions, and our mental models of the work of others and of ourselves. Implicit memories encode our earliest forms of learning about the world. Implicit memories directly shape our here-and-now experiences without clues to their origins from past events.

Because implicit memory is relational, a salient organizing factor of the psychological and neurological structures underlying infant implicit memory is the infant's history of communication and emotion with significant others (Schore 2001). Recently, attachment theorists have re-conceptualized internal working models of attachment in terms of "implicit relational knowing" (Beebe 1998, Lyons-Ruth 1998, Siegel 2001). This implicit memory is acquired through experience with separation, reunion, and mutual availability issues in relation to attachment figures from infancy and early childhood. Infants learn, via such social experiences, to view the social world as fundamentally threatening or fundamentally friendly (Panksepp 2001).

Recent evidence suggests that we also may have participatory memories of interpersonal experiences in infancy. Participatory memories are lived reenactments of personally significant experiences in contexts similar to those in which they were first acquired. Participatory memories are emotionally experienced as a being with or a re-living of past experiences (Bråten 1998, Fogel 1993, Fogel 2001a, in press, Heshusius 1994).

Some attachment-related behavior having its origins in infancy may be constituted in children and adults by participatory in addition to implicit memory. Children and adults with insecure attachment histories, for example, are more vigilant for signs of abandonment, gaining approval and avoiding rejection (Goodman and Quas 1997, Main 1999), manifested in body postures of holding back, withdrawing and in lived emotional experiences of shame and anxiety. Anxious styles of attachment are seen in clinging, reaching, and a hunger for body contact, while avoidance is seen as pushing away and aversion to interpersonal closeness. These are participatory memories that are most likely to be reenacted with close friends, parent figures, romantic and sexual partners but not necessarily with other people, that is, in emotional and postural situations (e.g. lying down, close holding) in which the original experiences may have occurred (Lisa Diamond, personal communication).

Long-term retention of infancy experiences have been investigated in children who had a traumatic injury that brought them to the hospital emergency room some time during their first three years of life (Peterson 1999, Peterson and Bell 1996, Peterson and Rideout 1998) and in children who were under the age of five years at the time they were exposed to documented traumas such as sexual abuse, physical injuries, witnessing the death of a family member, or accidents (Terr 1988). If the trauma occurred after the age of two years, most children had explicit, verbal, autobiographical memories of the event. If the trauma occurred before two years, on the other hand, children showed participatory memories but no explicit autobiographical memories of the event. In one play therapy session, for example, a child poked at her abdomen and talked about spears pointed at her during an imagined visit to Disneyland. The spot she touched was exactly the place where videotapes of her sexual abuse at the age of twelve months (made by the perpetrators) revealed a man's erect penis jabbing her and not, as might be presumed, in her genital area.

It is difficult to document these kinds of memory from early infancy, especially for non-traumatic events. When children and adults are placed in contexts that reenact the conditions of infancy, however, such memories are more likely to be revealed (cf. Fogel, in press for a review). I have conducted studies in which college students are asked to lie on a carpeted floor in semi-dark rooms and reenact infant-like behaviors, alone and with companions. Students report sensations, movements, and emotions that are very similar to what infants are likely to experience under similar conditions. In some cases, students were able to get confirmation from their parents that their experiences were in fact memories from infancy. All the students who reported having feelings of discomfort or anxiety when doing an exercise reenacting sucking behavior later found out from their parents that they had mild or severe feeding problems as a baby. None of these students had an explicit memory of these problems and they were not told about them by their parents, who may have thought they were too minor to transmit as part of the family lore (Fogel 2001a, in press).

During the sensorimotor period, with the help of experience–dependent brain development, we learn how to experience and regulate our most basic needs such as sleeping, eating, eliminating, and feeling our emotions in relation to the cultural management or mismanagement of these processes. We also acquire an open or closed body orientation toward others that includes the senses, the genitals, the arms and legs, and the emotions; ways of exposing or hiding the self from others that persist for years to come. These processes, and the ways in which our bodies remember them at the sensorimotor (and primarily nonverbal level) within the self–self relationship, have important implications for research and clinical practice (Fogel 2001a, in press).

Relationship to the natural world

Infants explore the possibilities in their cultural milieu for connections with the physical environment. There is a lot of research documenting how infants do this with respect to the physical and cultural objects in their surround (Lockman, Chapter 7, Piaget 1952). Wachs and Çorapçi (Chapter 3) show how order and chaos in the physical environment have profound effects irrespective of culture.

But there is much more to the physical environment: there is the entirety of the natural world including objects, plants, and animals. There is relatively little research on how infants embrace the smells, sounds, feels, and sights of the natural world or are cut off from them. Spending early infancy in direct contact with nature – smelling the earth and feeling the sun on one's body or in a primarily manufactured indoor environment – can lead to a lifelong pattern of relationship of connection to or of disconnection from the earth (Fogel 2001b, Friedrich-Cofer 1986).

The importance of our connection with the natural world is revealed by Janette B. Benson in Chapter 8 and in her research on season of birth in relation to developmental outcomes. Recent research has shown that one's relationship to diurnal cycles (whether one is an evening person or a night person) is established during the prenatal and early infancy periods and has sociocultural consequences that last a lifetime (e.g. how one fits in at school and work) (Cofer *et al.* 1999). These are not traits of the individual but rather types of relationship.

Just as the self–self relationship is embedded within interpersonal cultural relationships, so too is our relationship with nature embedded within the self and social relationships. Our connection to the morning sun in early life most likely creates a way of relating to self (one feels happy, warm, comforted in the sunlight and perhaps more frightened at night) that has a tendency to self-preserve over long periods of time. This tendency for preservation of self–self relationship patterns is an observation from research, not a theoretical speculation. A relational theory explains that observation in the following way. As that relational pattern (by connecting to the morning sun I feel more connected to my self) becomes embedded within sociocultural relationships, they have the potential to enhance or to disrupt the connection to the self and to the natural world.

Humans descended from hunter-gatherers who first appeared in Africa during the Pleistocene epoch, between 1.6 million years ago and 10,000 years ago. *Homo sapiens* hunter-gatherer societies originated about 100,000 years ago. About 10,000 years ago, humans gradually abandoned nomadic patterns and began to occupy permanent settlements and to develop agriculture. Between 35,000 and 10,000 years ago, human groups were small bands of about twenty-five, who would roam less than twenty miles (thirty kilometers) rarely encountering another group (Wenke 1990). Bowlby (1969) considered the human ecology during the Pleistocene as the "environment of evolutionary adaptedness." To provide protection from predators and other dangers, infants were carried in a sling or pouch at all times, never left alone, and the caregiver responded immediately to fussiness in order not to attract the attention of predators. As a consequence, humans evolved a mother–infant relationship with continuous skin-to-skin contact and frequent breastfeeding (Barr 1990).

For a hundred thousand years people lived close to the earth, in caves and other natural shelters. They were aware of the earth's climate and seasons. The elements of earth, air, fire and water had both practical and spiritual meaning. People did not distinguish themselves as essentially separate from their ecology. They believed themselves to be no more important than the basic elements, the plants, and animals (Abram 1996, Eisler 1987, Shepard 1998).

Prehistorical infancy was a sensual experience. Infants were aware of other human bodies from which they obtained nourishment, constant touch, affection, warmth and support. They had the benefit of an extended family of group members. Once they began crawling and walking, infants became familiar with the feel and smell of raw earth and of plants. Living primarily outdoors and in earthen shelters, they became sensitized to changes in light and temperature, to the cycles and rhythms of the earth and its climate.

Infancy in the First World today is no less sensual but infants develop their first relationships with primarily manufactured and indoor environments rather than directly with the earth. The growing fields of evolutionary medicine and evolutionary psychology have set their agendas to ask about the consequences of these differences in infancy experience. This writer wonders whether the systematic destruction of our natural world in favor of a human-made world is a consequence of the lack of an early relational foundation with the earth for infants reared primarily indoors. Impervious to the changes in climate and the gradations of sunlight and darkness, infants may unwittingly indulge in a relational pattern of control rather than creativity, of totalizing the earth rather than seeing its infinite possibilities. It should be relatively easy to study individual differences in people's relationships to themselves and to others as a consequence of variations in exposure to, playing with, and appreciation of the outdoors during early life.

Conclusions

Beginning about 35,000 years ago, humans developed what has been called *mythic culture* with symbols, representations, language, and storytelling. Myths worldwide tell us that the natural world, and all its creatures including humans, is sacred. Myths in prehistory and ancient history integrated and explained the various facets of life and death, which were accepted and never questioned (Donald 1991). Symbolic culture, when it first arose as myth, served to highlight and enhance our direct connection with nature and our common planetary past and future.

In Western societies today, those symbolic tools often serve to distance us from "lower order" direct experience. The elevation of symbols as the primary means of communication has had the effect of lessening the importance of our pre-symbolic early infancy and our pre-symbolic human ancestral history of close to 100,000 years. If we cannot think about infancy, if we are unable to recall it explicitly, then we assume it does not exist as a living part of us.

Our developmental science and our society are in need of rebalancing mind and body, preverbal and verbal, direct with mediated experience. Is the education of the cognitive mind and its ability to manipulate symbols and technologies more important than the cultivation of the rich possibilities of taste, touch, hearing, sight and smell? By rebalancing we can break down these dichotomies to reveal relational partnerships. There is no access to symbols and technologies in the absence of a highly developed sensorimotor system able to perceive subtle differences in visual and auditory patterns that constitute differences between written and spoken words.

But when the senses are used only or primarily to read or watch a computer display, balance is lost. Using the senses to process symbols must be in a balanced relationship to the enrichment of the senses purely for their own sake, just as we did when we were babies. We can rebalance in the appreciation of and participation in art, music and athletics. We can rebalance by eating well, bathing in a lake or ocean, watching the sunrise or sunset, meditating, touching and being touched. Developmental science has not put a premium on the study of these aspects of human life. Many children growing up today – and many adults – have lost touch with these infantile pleasures and, as a consequence, with themselves.

Acknowledgements

This work was supported by a grant to the author from the National Institute of Mental Health (MH57669).

References

Abram, D. (1997) *The Spell of the Sensuous*. New York: Vintage Books.

Barr, R. G. (1990) "The Early Crying Paradox: A Modest Proposal", *Human Nature, 1*: 355–389.

Beebe, B. (1998) "A Procedural Theory of Therapeutic Action: Commentary of the Symposium, 'Interventions that effect change in psychotherapy'", *Infant Mental Health Journal, 19*, (3): 333–340.

Bowlby, J. (1969) *Attachment and Loss: vol. 1. Attachment*. New York: Basic Books.

Bråten, S. (1998) "Infant Learning by Altercentric Participation: The Reverse of Egocentric Observation in Autism" in Bråten, S. (ed.) *Intersubjective Communication and Emotion in Early Ontogeny. Studies in Emotion and Social Interaction, 2nd series*. (pp. 105–124). New York, NY: Cambridge University Press.

Buber, M. (1958*) I and Thou*. 2nd ed. (Smith, R. G., trans.). New York: Scribner.

Cofer, L. F., Grice, J. W., Sethre-Hofstad, L., Radi, C. J., Zimmerman, L. K., Palmer-Seal, D. *et al*. (1999) "Developmental Perspectives on Morningness-Eveningness and Social Interactions", *Human Development, 42*: 169–198.

Donald, M. (1991) *Origins of the Modern Mind: Three Stages in the Evolution of Culture and Cognition*. Cambridge, MA: Harvard University Press.

Eisler, R. (1987) *The Chalice and the Blade: Our History, Our Future*. San Francisco: HarperCollins.

Epstein, S. (1991) "Cognitive-Experiential Self Theory: Implications for Developmental Psychology" in Gunnar, M. R. and Sroufe, L. A. (eds.) *Minnesota Symposia on Child Psychology: vol. 23. Self Processes and Development* (pp. 79–123). Hillsdale NJ: Erlbaum.

Fogel, A. (1993) *Developing Through Relationships*. Chicago, IL: University of Chicago Press.

— (2001a) *Infancy: Infant, Family and Society* (4th ed.). Belmont, CA: Wadsworth.

— (2001b) "The History (and Future) of Infancy" in Bremner, G. and Fogel, A. (eds.) *Handbook of Infant Development*. Cambridge: Blackwell Publishers Ltd.

— (in press) "Remembering Infancy: Accessing Our Earliest Experiences" in Bremner, G. and Slater, A. (eds.) *Theories of Infant Development*. Blackwell Publishers.

Fogel, A. and Lyra, M. (1997) "Dynamics of Development in Relationships" in Masterpasqua, F. and Perna, P. (eds.) *The Psychological Meaning of Chaos: Self-Organization in Human Development and Psychotherapy* (pp. 75–94). Washington, DC: American Psychological Association.

Fogel, A., Lyra, M. and Valsiner, J. (eds.) (1997) *Dynamics and Indeterminism in Developmental and Social Processes*. Hillsdale, NJ: Erlbaum.

Fogel, A., deKoeyer, I., Bellegamba, F. and Bell, H. (2002) "The Dialogical Self in the First Two Years of Life", *Theory and Psychology*, *12*, (2): 191–205.

Freud, S. (1926/1953) [*Inhibitions, symptoms and anxiety.*] In Strachey, J. (ed. and trans.) The Standard Edition of the Complete Works of Sigmund Freud (Vol. 20). London: Hogarth Press. (Originally published 1926.)

Friedrich-Cofer, L. K. (1986) "Body, Mind, and Morals in the Framing of Social Policy" in Friedrich-Cofer, L. K. (ed.) *Human Nature of Public Policy: Scientific Views of Women, Children and Families* (pp. 97–173). New York, NY: Praeger.

Ganguly, S. N. (1976) "Communication, Identity, and Human Development", *Communication*, *2*: 221–244.

Goodman, G. and Quas, J. (1997) "Trauma and Memory: Individual Differences in Children's Recounting of a Stressful Experience" in Stein, N., Ornstein, P., Tversky, B. and Brainerd, C. (eds.) *Memory for Everyday and Emotional Events* (pp. 267–294). New Jersey: Lawrence Erlbaum.

Heshusius, L. (1994) "Freeing Ourselves from Objectivity: Managing Subjectivity or Turning Toward a Participatory Mode of Consciousness?", *Educational Researcher*, *23*, (3): 15–22.

Hinde, R. A. (1985) Expression and negotiation. In G. Zivin (ed.) *The Development of Expressive Behavior: Biology–Environment Interactions* (pp. 103–116). NY: Academic Press.

Levinas, E. (1969) *Totality and infinity: An essay on exteriority.* Lingos, A. (trans.) Pittsburgh: Duquesne University Press.

Lewis, M. (1995) "Cognition–Emotion Feedback and the Self-Organization of Developmental Paths", *Human Development*, *38*: 71–102.

Lyons-Ruth, K. (1998) "Implicit Relational Knowing: Its Role in Development and Psychoanalytic Treatment", *Infant Mental Health Journal*, *19*, (3): 282–289.

Main, M. (1999) "Attachment Theory: Eighteen Points with Suggestions for Future Studies" in Cassidy, J. and Shaver, P. (eds.) *Handbook of Attachment: Theory, Research and Clinical Applications* (pp. 845–887). New York: Guilford Press.

Panksepp, J. (2001) "The Long-Term Psychobiological Consequences of Infant Emotions: Prescriptions for the Twenty-First Century", *Infant Mental Health Journal*, *22*, (1–2): 132–173.

Peterson, C. (1999) "Children's Memory for Medical Emergencies: Two Years Later", *Developmental Psychology*, *35*, (6): 1493–1506.

Peterson, C. and Bell, M. (1996) "Children's Memory for Traumatic Injury", *Child Development*, *67*: 3045–3070.

Peterson, C. and Rideout, R. (1998) "Memory for Medical Emergencies Experienced by 1- and 2-Year-Olds", *Developmental Psychology*, *34*, (5): 1059–1072.

Piaget, J. (1952) *The Origins of Intelligence in Children*. New York: International Universities Press.

— (1954) *The Construction of Reality in the Child*. New York: Ballantine Books.

Rubin, D. (2000) "The Distribution of Early Childhood Memories", *Memory*, *8*: 265–269.

Schacter, D. (1996) *Searching for Memory: The Brain, the Mind, and the Past*. New York: Basic Books.

Schore, A. (2001) "Effects of a Secure Attachment on Right Brain Development, Affect Regulation, and Infant Mental Health", *Infant Mental Health Journal*, *22*, (1–2): 7–66.

Shepard, P. (1998) *Coming Home to Pleistocene*. Covelo, CA: Island Press.

Siegel, D. (2001) "Toward an Interpersonal Neurobiology of the Developing Mind: Attachment Relationship, 'Mindsight,' and Neural Integration", *Infant Mental Health Journal*, 22, (1–2): 67–94.

Stern, D. N. (1985) *The Interpersonal World of the Infant: A View from Psychoanalysis and Developmental Psychology.* New York, NY: Basic Books.

Terr, L. (1988) "What Happens to Early Memories of Trauma? A Study of Twenty Children Under the Age of Five at the Time of Documented Traumatic Events", *Journal of the American Academy of Child and Adolescent Psychiatry*, 27, (1): 96–104.

Trevarthen, C. and Hubley, P. (1978) "Secondary Intersubjectivity: Confidence, Confiding and Acts of Meaning in the First Year" in Lock, A. (ed.) *Action, Gesture and Symbol: The Emergence of Language* (pp. 183–227). NY: Academic Press.

Užgiris, I. Č. (2000) "Words Don't Tell All: Some Thoughts on Early Communication and Development" in Budwig, N., Užgiris, I. Č. and Wertsch, J. V. (eds.) *Communication: An Arena of Development* (pp. 131–141). Stamford, CT: Ablex Publishing.

Wenke, R. J. (1990) *Patterns in Prehistory: Humankind's First Three Million Years.* New York: Oxford University Press.

Whitehead, A. N. (1978) *Process and Reality, an Essay in Cosmology.* New York: The Free Press.

Winnicott, D. (1971) *Playing and Reality.* New York: Basic Books.

Index

Page numbers in **bold** refer to Figures and Tables.